blue
rider
press

An imprint of Penguin Random House LLC
375 Hudson Street
New York, New York 10014

ISBN 9780735218192

Printed in the United States of America
10 9 8 7 6 5 4 3 2 1

BOOK DESIGN BY SHUBHANI SARKAR, SARKARDESIGNSTUDIO.COM

Craig McDean, photographer
Jess Rotter, photo staging, illustration, and cover typography
Diego Montoya, mirror mask
Lee Kyle, photographer of Rob Roth's "Craig"
Cardboard chair designed by Chairigami
Styling and wardrobe, Leana Zuniga of Electric Feathers

*Penguin is committed to publishing works of quality and integrity.
In that spirit, we are proud to offer this book to our readers;
however, the story, the experiences, and the words
are the author's alone.*

You're on an Airplane

A SELF-MYTHOLOGIZING MEMOIR

Parker Posey

BLUE RIDER PRESS

New York

You're on an Airplane

Contents

Part I
You're on an Airplane

Part II
As the World Turns

Part III
Lost in Space

Part I
You're on an Airplane

Hi, I have the window seat. How very kind, thank you; chivalry is *not* dead but I'll just squeeze by. That's okay, I'll just smush them both under the seat and once we're in the air I'll take one out and use it as an ottoman. I sit cross-legged so Gracie can be on my lap once we're off, but thank you. She is, actually. My boyfriend at the time, Ryan, his grandmother had just died and they'd watch the Burns and Allen show together when he was a kid. I wanted a name that could evoke a quality because I knew I'd be repeating it. I didn't want to name her Snickers or something. "Something! Come here!"

I sat next to a dog and its owner at the Union Square dog run once, and the dog had on a collar that spelled "BOW WOW" in separated silver lettering that slid and turned and the "bow" part was under the dog's neck. I said to the owner, "I can't believe you named your dog 'Mom,'" and he was like, "It spells 'bow wow.'" I told him that I was joking and then it got awkward, because he seemed to be sad or depressed. These are strange times; maybe naming your dog "Mom" isn't so odd. It seems like everyone is feeling lonely, in some way—left out.

I'm working on a book, actually. It's about me. It's okay, Gracie. She's on a doggie downer. She'll be okay once the plane takes off and the slamming doors stop. They bang no matter how you close them, like they were made to slam. Yeah, I like those movies, too. *Best in Show*'s a classic. You'll hear more about it. Yes, she's an emotional support dog, so she can be in my lap. I have the papers in the seat flap in front of me, if you need me to reach down there to get them. Seltzer with ice, please. No, I'm good, no lime; don't bother.

It used to be so different, flying.

Yes, a book! I realized it was time. There were stories to share that my friends were entertained by, so I thought, you know, tell them. There's also a literary agent who lives in my neighborhood, whose partner art-directed *Party Girl*. I started feeling guilty when I'd see him, because he'd say, "I know there's a book in you." So I went into a sort of labor and produced a sort of baby, where instead of being human it's a bound object made of paper called "pages" with words on it. You bring it to life and make it talk. Just don't leave it alone for too long or it will start crying.

Can you hear Gracie snoring? Her little body vibrates when she does. I use my Southern accent when I talk to Gracie because she's just too sweet. Being number one on the tarmac is so winning and such an honor, so thrilling. I got interested in acting because I was born into it—born into turbulence. It's kind of simple: I'm a character actor because I come from a family of characters. When people ask if anyone in my family is an actor, I say all of them. They're performative people. They'll star somewhat in this, in the way Mother and Father star in our lives, constantly—as constant as the northern star—but I'll take the lead.

When my dad and I fought, he'd send me to my room to write him a letter. He wasn't good at expressing his feelings when he was angry, he was better at letter writing, and since he was an adult and I was just a child, he won. He was passionate and knew how to pull heartstrings. We'd joke in our family that he was the puppeteer and he'd splay his hand wide, moving it slowly from side to side, controlling the strings.

We'll be in the air soon and closer to the real stars, which make the constellations, which branched the first stories from the heavens.

My book is called *You're on an Airplane*. It's a memoir pronounced with the emphasis on "me."

Flying can be nice, once you're in the air. Don't you wish we could be here forever and never have to land?

1

To Perform

Taxi! I mean, flight attendant! Hi, can I have a scotch, neat?

Norma Desmond, the fading silent-film star who bemoaned the advent of "talkies," was portrayed by the inimitable Gloria Swanson, first clotheshorse and woman of indomitable spirit. You've seen it? So you know that she wore a turban in the film and said things like "I am big. It's the pictures that got small." Now look how small the pictures have gotten on these freaking iPhone screens. The tiny screens have gotten into people's hands, and there's all this swiping going on, all this shoo-fly bullshit. In the nineties, we had big screens in the cinema and big TVs in our homes. It boggles the mind that people can walk around with small televisions in their pockets and use them as telephones. I saw a baby in a stroller on an iPhone just the other day, on the sidewalks of Manhattan. Now, tell me: Who was that baby texting?

Are you on Facebook? It's wonderful that people have their Facebook friends but I don't have Facebook "friends" because I'm not on it. I want to read people's faces in present-time reality—and how could they be a book? It's presumptuous and absurd. I went on some-one's Facebook once (now, that just sounds crude) and what I really wanted was proof that these are real people, but there is no proof because I wasn't there. I wasn't on the vacation, at the graduation, at the spring break party. I wasn't there for the birth of the baby or for all those salads. It should be called "Scrapbookface," that's more ap-ropos. There was a movie made about that guy who invented it? Mark Zuckerberg, right, thank you. I never saw it but I did go to the premiere to mingle in the lobby of the theater and to social-network.

Anyway, my Instagram followers say not to join because it's a rabbit hole, and I trust them. Is this how I grow old? Saying things like "my followers," like a cult leader, and going on about turbans? Looks like it!

Headwear feels right, especially after you reach your mid-forties and start to see the older person you'll become. Would you like a brush? Eye drops? Oh my God, that feels good. Care to slather your face with moisturizer? You have pretty hair, young lady. Don't fall asleep; I want you to listen. Turbans apply to the men out there as well, who will become older ladies as they soften with age.

It's kind of fun getting older and giving advice, calling young people "dear," and talking to myself in public, not caring who hears me. Uttering sentences that come out as extraneous sounds and feel-ing no need to explain myself in words because a facial expression will do. It's "Perimenopausal Time," which to me sounds like an adorable puppet troupe—maybe not.

Here, let me put a turban on you; I travel with scarves, wraps, and throws. Press your finger on the fabric at the top of your forehead, where your hairline starts, and hold. I'll wrap you up.

It feels good to have something on your head that makes you feel like a witch or a genie, doesn't it? Let's get some magic back. Do you have a lover? You don't have to tell me if you do or don't, but if you do, they'll dig this. After you get out of the bath together and make breakfast, like dry toast with a poached egg and a side of cantaloupe. "Come here so I can look you in the eyes," you'll hear. "We're all multidimensional beings, babe, because everyone is a time traveler, if only for a moment. . . ." And then, maybe, "Are you upset about something? Do you need any help with anything?" Who knows what'll happen after that. One thing's for certain: your hair will dry and you'll go to work, where you can get wrapped up again, caught up in the picture of the vacation you weren't invited to join, and maybe you'll text that little baby back. You can shoo-fly your phone till the cows come home.

Don't you feel better now that you know your head won't fly off your body? Give me a headdress and a magic carpet, please. Why this diminishing of the feminine? Why is it still happening? I know it's been like this for a long while now—since we stopped worshipping the sun and the moon—but it feels like we should be beyond that. Sun and moon: good and evil—blah, blah, blah. It's All One. Will you press right here? Right between my thumb and forefinger? Yes, that's where my headache is. Did you know that the Hollywood system of storytelling quadruples, for men, as they age? I read that somewhere. I guess it's because the men are rarely home in those movies because the women don't want machine guns or aliens in the house.

I must've dozed off when you were pressing my hand like that. I had a dream I was running a marathon and staying in Matt Damon's home in the wilderness. He lived there whenever there was a marathon. No, wait, I wasn't running, I was on the side of the road walking to Matt Damon's. We shared some eroticism and I noticed glitter all over his bedsheets. He said he'd gotten divorced and I wondered why because I'd heard his wife was so lovely. Then I saw a little movie, like a commercial, in my mind: Strange Christmas decorations appeared and dissolved—an icicle plaque with "The Damons" written on it, and then a fire poker with children's names on it. Dinner was being served and the clang of silverware turned to Christmas. I don't like Christmas; it's too much of a production and I've already done too many. I do love Jesus, though.

I'll have the Chicken à la King.

I was staying in Hollywood, at Chris Kattan's house, and I was crying. This was not a dream; this was real. Chris is like a brother to me. I was sitting outside, on the stone steps Danny DeVito brought back from Big Sur or somewhere—Danny and Rhea Perlman owned the house before Chris bought it. Rhea had her dance studio in the bedroom where I slept. Anyway, I was on the phone with my manager at the time, and I was freaking out that I didn't have a job. To encourage me, he said, "Look at Jeremy Renner," who he also represented. "He didn't start getting work until his forties." And I said, "I know, but he's a man. I'm not a man."

There was a lull in the conversation, because I had a real point. I could hear my manager sense that I'd become too aware to be handled and coerced into delusion. Actors actually pay their agents and managers not only to negotiate contracts but also to encourage fantasies and help conjure them, which is what I think delusion is. It's why I still love every agent I've ever had. Look how cozy that salad is in its little bowl.

Well, my manager knew I wasn't having it anymore, and that I'd had it. It's possible that, somewhere in there, I'd remembered "not being available" to meet for one of those early action films with Matt Damon. It could've been the beginning of *The Bourne Identity*. I simply wasn't prepared to be scared in a car for a few months, even with Matt's daemon.

There was an *Anaconda* movie, too, that I turned down because I didn't want to wrestle with snakes or be in wet clothes while at work.

Whenever I get to the point of exasperation, I like to say, "I feel like my head has flown off of my body," or, "Where is the man who would want to put his hands on my head?" I will say that Jeremy Winner is a wonderful hugger because we were at Sundance and he gave me a really nice hug. I didn't get to the point of having him place his hands on my head, but I'm almost certain he would've if I'd asked.

I've maintained a career and I love to act, but I think every job is my last. And when I start the job, I forget that I know how to do it and by the time I find out that I do, I'm done. I'm always thinking of other jobs I could do instead, but maybe those are just characters I want to play. I'm not great at being a movie star; it's either too boring or too much work. I've had too much therapy, I think.

My career took shape organically (farm to table), when the culture supported independent films and I didn't have to feel like a movie star if I didn't want to. The independent film world in the early nineties had a real independence from the Hollywood system, much like in the seventies. It reminded me of my early silent-film work with auteurs like Cecil B. DeMille. And then, *Time* called me the queen of independent cinema and that's when my career in independent cinema virtually ended. Oh my God, this cough!

I don't like games. I wasn't, and I'm still not, good at them. They make me uncomfortable, even board games, and especially charades. I do like puzzles and an intimate in-house karaoke party. Singing is not a game. I do love *The Voice*. I make a really good cup of coffee.

Life is good.

When I was a little girl, my dad would recite Emily Dickinson's "I'm nobody! Who are you? / Are you nobody, too? / Then there's a pair of us—don't tell! / They'd banish us, you know." He's an entertainer and fighter by nature: a star in his own life. My mother comes to life through the lens of my father but holds her own, naturally. I obviously came to life from my mother. They were movie stars in my eyes—fabulous Southern characters. So my own character, what could be a fragmentation of selves, finds a wholeness in performing many different parts and finds recognition in others of similar makeup. The arts and show business are full of these people.

I had a "movie mother" in the late, great Nora Ephron. She sent me an email a few months before she left the planet that I've memorized and kept close to my heart: "Dear Parker, I love watching your life from the middle distance. No one has a career like yours, and although I understand it makes for moments that have to feel less than secure, it also means you have so many things you would never have done if your life were more conventional. Love, your mother." She'd tell me that there wasn't a conventional bone in my body.

A couple years back I wasn't sure I could handle how financially motivated and conventional showbiz had become. Even in the theater, which was surprising and devastating. I originated a role (to a great review in the *New York Times*, thank you), only to be replaced with an actress who was more "bankable," more of a "name," when the play went to Broadway. Then I had a real nervous breakdown and ended up in the ER. After that, I had a giant and delicious slice of pizza with fried eggplant and mushrooms— a few blocks from Beth Israel at three in the morning—and walked home with my friends Jenn Ruff and Michael Panes. I had a wonderfully deep sleep from the Xanax.

After a few days with curtains drawn, I'd somewhat accepted that the rules had changed and that things weren't going to go my way. I even accepted my nervous breakdown as something I needed to go through and come out of. I got my curiosity and dignity back, enough to go out and hobnob. Ironically, I did that at the premiere party for the second season of *Girls*. Judd Appetite was there, in the distance, with no appetite for me. I saw a friend involved with that play that had sent me over the edge—someone who'd stayed at my house before. So I asked about the play, naturally. "What happened?" I said. "What went down?" And he said, "Do you want to talk about it here?" and I said, "Sure, why not?" Then someone pulled my focus for a second (the party was huge) and when I turned around, he had disappeared. Being real in showbiz gets you nowhere, kid.

I met a really adorable Canadian fellow, around your age; a manager, with hopes of becoming a producer. He confided in me a recent epiphany: "I lie a little bit, all day long, over and over again . . ." He was dazed by the revelation and shook his head, perplexed. "I lie to people . . . on the phone, all day, that's my work. I lie . . ." He knew the truth of what was ahead and was not going to quit. Yeah, showbiz can be dark.

I did a little indie movie with Demi Moore and vividly remember her saying, "Sometimes you gotta pay the devil." She was walking backward and shrugging with swagger, like a star in a Western film, her hotel keycard in her hand, ready to open the door. We played Celebrity at her house that year, with other celebrities like Ashton Kutcher and Bruce Willis. I didn't play because I don't like games but I love watching people play them.

After that breakdown, I called my reps asking if they could look into pitching me as a weather girl on the *Today* show. They thought that was funny but I thought it was a good idea. Weather is something you can count on—whether the weather's inside or whether the weather is outside. The turban suits you.

2

How I Got My Name

I was born fighting for my life. That's how the story begins, or the one my parents tell me, which they perform really well, too. I stopped breathing at a certain point, and my dad, who was kneeling outside the ICU window, said, "Please, God, let my baby girl live, please, please, please . . ." He had a six-pack of Budweiser beside him, and as he drank the beer, it occurred to him: "My daughter is the size of this beer can. She is a beer can on legs." When he tells it he mimes holding a beer can, and mimics my legs sticking out of it, and we laugh. He was in his army gear in the hospital—he was stationed in Baltimore—and he put down the can and returned to his intense praying. "Please, please, please, Lord," he said, his hands clasped. "Let my little baby girl *live!*"

I then let out a scream, as if on cue.

The story, told to me my whole life, at every birthday, helped me imagine that my dad could get God on the phone whenever he wanted, that if my dad prayed hard enough, God would pick up his very important telephone and take Dad's call. Since I grew up Catholic, I imagined the saints and angels as holy secretaries, clambering to get to God, specifically for my dad, despite all the other work they had to do. There was Saint Christopher, who carried Jesus as a baby, without knowing who he was yet, and was made the patron saint of travel because he was just nice. He had to help everyone traveling, yet he could answer my dad's call to God the very moment I was born. There was Saint Anthony, helping people find their lost keys, and he, too, would drop his responsibilities in order to get the phone to God, because I was being born and my dad had persuasive powers.

My mom had gone in for a checkup at the hospital on Halloween. The story goes that the doctor felt around in her uterus and "shook his head in disbelief." Then he went to get the nurse, who came in and felt around, and she and the doctor started laughing. My mother, in the stirrups, was left out of the joke. Then the doctor told her she was having twins, which was a real trick-or-treat moment. I was born a week later on November 8, 1968, at 3:33 a.m., despite a due date of January 7, 1969. My mom was just twenty-two, a baby herself, and describes this time as being "completely over-whelming." I can imagine.

Excuse me, can I have a Diet Coke? Thank you.

My twin brother, Chris, was closer to the door on the way out. Hanging out in utero together would be the closest we'd be in our lives, and the act of being born was, of course, our first trauma. I'd later learn that my mother had been in utero with a twin, too, but that she'd lost her brother. My brother was first and jaundiced, weighing five pounds. I came out three minutes later. We were both breech and pulled out by our feet, and my mom was fully sober for all this. Can you imagine? She says, "I swear, I felt you come out from under my arm!" Maybe next year for Halloween I'll make a big hat that looks like an arm and just come as myself. No, I think a can of Budweiser would be too obvious.

One of my first memories—whether or not it's "real"—is of my brother being wheeled away from me on a gurney. The image is black around the edges and blurry, and I'm not sure if I created this moving shot or if it happened. After he was taken away, the doctor came into my mother's room and said, "Your little boy is fine, but your girl, we need a name. For the death certificate." Hearing this story as a child made me feel as if I'd already "made it," having gotten through being born—it was like applause.

So, my name: When my mom was eleven, she was a Girl Scout, and her friend's older sister had a daughter named Parker. Back then my mom thought to herself, "If I ever have a little girl I will give her a strong name like Parker." Her own name was Lynda, spelled with a "Y," and she always hated it. "The obligatory Y," my mom called it. Why, Y, *why*? So when the doctor asked for a name, my mom said Parker for my first name and Christian for my middle name, because they wanted the help of Jesus and of the Trinity: the Father, the Son, and the Holy Ghost. Posey was from my father, obviously. My mother says she thought the name Posey was silly, and it really is. I know, my name sounds made-up. I will most definitely make that arm hat for Halloween next year and come as myself.

I was just two and a half pounds and spent six weeks in intensive care, and the nurses' hands, enclosed in rubber gloves, held me inside the incubator. The first photograph I have of myself is of the moment I was brought home from the hospital. I'm in my mother's lap, wearing fake eyelashes. When I asked my mom why she put fake eyelashes on me, she said, "You were so small, I didn't know what to do with

---

you." She also said, "You were born a nervous wreck." She'd seen me in the hospital being fed by an eyedropper, like they do with baby birds, and I must've looked unreal to her. I look at home with these eyelashes, though, huh?

Later on, in my twenties, after a stint of playing too many roles in too short a time, the birth and death of those characters triggered my birth trauma. I crawled on the floor to my psychoanalyst, Mildred Newman, and sat at her feet and cried the trauma through me.

Nora Ephron was a former patient of Mildred's and described her as a white witch, but to me she resembled my granny, in an old-world European way. Mildred helped me through a lot, especially when I became more known and tried to isolate myself from my success, as if it were a catastrophe. Being famous is a birth into something else and some people can handle it better than others.

The diagnosis was simple to Mildred: if my good wishes came true, then my bad wishes could come true as well. My psyche was frozen in that battle. At her feet, I was in a trance, and she said, "Those nurses held you and looked at you with love and care . . . through a glass box. Now look at what you do." I felt her spell and my ice started to crack.

When Dad left the army base in Baltimore for Vietnam, Mom drove us down south to Shreveport, Louisiana, in her red convertible Fiat. It was still winter but we were kept warm on the floor in the backseat, close to the engine, where the humming vibrations soothed us, and where I developed a preternatural sense of smell for gasoline, which I've always loved.

We'd stay with my grandparents, Nonnie (whose real name was

Faye) and Glenn Patton, in their ranch-style house on Lovers Lane, where tensions were rife and fraught but disguised and kept separate in that Southern way—left behind closed doors and swept under the rug. My parents had eloped for a shotgun wedding and had no real home together quite yet, and Dad got drafted in a war that hippies were protesting and most people, including my mom, were questioning. To this day, she still says, "Why were we over there?" like a wife and mother. She became a student teacher in Monroe, Louisiana, and taught junior high. She lived in an apartment and made friends with her neighbors Pat and Duddy Garret.

This lasted for three years, with us back and forth to Baltimore, when Dad had breaks from the war. He was a captain liaison officer. Chris and I said "Dada" for the first time into a reel-to-reel tape recorder that my mom mailed him. We'd listen to his voice and she would point to the tape recorder, saying, "That's Dada." Once, when he came back for a quick trip to the base in Baltimore, my dad saw us "screaming bloody murder" and holding tight to our mother's legs. He called back to the stewardess at the top of the stairs and said, "I'd have an easier duty back in 'Nam!" We didn't recognize him because he wasn't a tape recorder, and the noise of the plane was fierce in our ears, but when he got close to us on the tarmac, my mom pointed and said "Dada" and then we started the "Dada" bit, which had become a song at this point, and Dad sang along and swept us up, carrying us to the car.

Nonnie knew a neighborhood girl named Missy, who was six years old and blond with pigtails and whose mother was a flight attendant. One day, Missy was walking alone in the neighborhood and knocked on Nonnie's door, asking for candy. Nonnie loved the gall of this girl but told her, "You'd better ask your mother if it's alright. It's not safe to knock on the doors of people's houses you don't know, so go on and ask your mom if it's alright and then I'll give you some candy." The girl went away, and Nonnie watched through her kitchen window as Missy stood at the end of the driveway for several minutes, alone and tapping her feet and swaying to pass the time. Then she watched as she walked back up the driveway and knocked on the door again. When Nonnie opened the door the second time, Missy said that her mom said it was okay to have candy. She had some nerve and was a good little actress.

Nonnie loved this story so much that she called me Missy, in tribute. But I felt something was amiss in my not being older and blonder, in not having hair long enough for pigtails. So I'd daydream about being someone else. When I was nine, I told Nonnie that I was going to be a movie star and she told me that she was going to be the president of the United States—guess I won.

3
Why Are You an Actor?

I'm an actor because funny things happen to me and shame flirts with me. I left my apartment once and I didn't tie my harem pants tight enough around the waist, so they dropped to my ankles while I was walking down Fifth Avenue. I found a stranger to help my shame and wanted to share a laugh. This lady was an older woman in her eighties with great style—big glasses, sharp quilted blazer—and I smiled, and turned my inner camera on so I could remove myself from the situation. I said, "My pants fell down," almost like "Hi, how's it going?" She didn't respond or laugh because she wasn't an audience member in my show. She grimaced, maybe thinking I was a streaker, and walked quickly past. So I said it again, to absolutely no one, but to the air around me and to the buildings, as I pulled my pants back up and tied them back together.

When I'm asked, "What's it like being an actress?" I always say, "It's like walking around with your pants down and around your ankles." It's somewhat of a stock answer so I was happy to experience it for real. Embarrassing and shamefully uncanny things that are at first humiliating and only funny later seem to naturally happen to me. I think this is a big part of why someone becomes an actor.

In my Chelsea days, in the nineties, I'd start baths and forget about them, flooding the beauty shop downstairs. But Kathleen, the owner, was laid-back and cool. "It's the third time in a month I've flooded the beauty shop downstairs! I forgot about it! How could this happen again?!" Like forgetting is something that happens to you and not something that you participate in or that you're like, you know, responsible for creating.

You're stressed out and your friend calls and says, "What are you up to?" and you say, "I'm looking for my phone!" You look for your glasses for ten minutes while they're on your head, or you're wearing them. I've slipped on banana peels several times in my life, and not as a joke. The door has opened when I'm in the bathroom many times because I haven't locked it, and the other person is more em-barrassed about it than I am.

I'll never understand how I could watch my hand casually toss my Nokia nugget into the gutter and into a puddle as I strode down the sidewalk. It felt like something out of *The Matrix*. This was made more absurd and uncanny in that it was the first of three times that I "lost" my phone that week. The second of those times, "losing" it just meant leaving my phone somewhere because I didn't want to be reached.

But the third time, I was at Madison Square Garden with my eight-year-old niece, Isabella, for the Cirque du Soleil Christmas show. Have you been to the theater there? It's huge, just . . . Wow. It holds around 5,000 people. Our seats were close to the stage, down in E or F of the first level, right in the center front.

We arrived at the perfect time for the theater, with less than ten minutes to wait—enough time to get some water, enough time to maintain our excitement and focus for the magical show, and enough time for me to wink at those who recognized me and wait for the curtain to rise. It was then I realized that my phone was missing. It felt like some bad joke. "Bella, where's my phone?" I asked. She said, "Didn't you just buy one on the way up here?" I had indeed, in Chelsea, when I hopped in a cab to swing by to get her.

So we're digging through my bag and looking under the seats, and the people in front of us and behind us are looking as well. I'm patting my pockets and shaking our coats. "This is the third time I've lost my phone this week," I share with the strangers around me. They're laughing, of course. Bella says I must've placed it on the bar when we got our water. I ask the kind strangers if they could watch my niece for a second and I scamper, all hunched and hiding as I run to one of the theater ushers. She points me to the security guard, down and up front, standing at the lip of the stage. "I've lost my phone," I tell the security guard, exasperated.

The guard points me toward the lobby, up the long flight of stairs. Should I stay or should I go? It was daunting. I would have to run.

The lights are dimming on and off, the intro music has started, and I am out of the gate—hauling up those stairs, two at a time. Panting, I ask the bartender if I left my phone there and he says no, but I can check the office at intermission. "Okay! Good plan," I blurt out, and start my hunched and speedy jaunt again, down the steps, where the lights have dimmed but the theater is not yet completely dark.

There's a spotlight on the performer playing a burglar elf, dressed in green spandex. He's dancing around, introducing the show in Cirque du Soleil fashion—animated like a court jester. He warns the audience of a pickpocket and instructs everyone to hold on to their purses and wallets. I'm breathless and shaking my head like a crazy lady as the spotlight catches me mid-gate and I freeze: 5,000 people laughing. The joke's on me as I run back up the steps to a security guard holding my phone out to me. Caught ●

Things like that, that just "happen," are the reason I'm an actor. David Harbour, who plays the cop in *Stranger Things*? I ran into him a couple of years ago walking with a crutch, in a full-leg cast. I was eating my pretzel croissant from City Bakery and he was going inside for a cookie. I asked what happened and he told me he had to back out of a production of *Troilus and Cressida* at Shakespeare in the Park, where he was to play Achilles, because he tore his Achilles heel. Sometimes you're in the play, but not the play you'd intended—and that's what's strange with a career in acting.

My mom was always burning herself in the oven; she said it was hereditary and that her father was always burning himself on the oven, too. "Is Glenn going to have a Band-Aid on?" we'd ask on the way to visit my grandparents, and when he did, we'd all laugh. In the house were lots of Band-Aids, peroxide, Neosporin, and, back then, Mercurochrome and Merthiolate, which we called "monkey blood" because it stained red. You'd blow on it if it was Merthiolate because it burned like hell and you'd beg Mom to use Mercurochrome because it didn't burn. All of us over the age of thirty have mercury in our blood—they later learned it was poisonous to the brain, which is too bad because the stuff worked.

Needles and thread at the ready for mending, and baking soda for stains. I liked the grunge period in the nineties when Gen Xers wore ripped clothes with safety pins and tied flannel shirts at the waist—shirts that looked like hand-me-downs from your older brother, with missing buttons left unmended.

When I was a little girl, I had a rag doll that got so dirty and worn from all my playing that she'd get thrown in the washer and dryer repeatedly. She was 100 percent cotton. When her blue felt eyes came off, my mom sewed new ones back on with black thread, making her eyes solid pupils. I called her Muffin—there's a nod to her in my *Waiting for Guffman* monologue, in the deleted scenes—and she had yellow yarn hair that was in a permanent up-swirl from my hand holding tightly on to her head.

I have a series of photos of Muffin and me, with my mom and dad and brother, from when we were five. We look picture-perfect, although the day had started badly, with me running away from the camera lens. I liked to say back then, "Don't look at me! Don't touch me!" when someone wanted to take my picture. I'd even splay my hand in front of my face and grunt as I said it. It was primal for me, but for others, it was funny. I know, look at me now.

The photographer didn't scare me, but the camera did. I think it had something to do with how my parents changed when the camera pointed at them, and that I didn't know my part in the scene. But also, I loved Muffin and wasn't sure that my parents would want her in the picture because she had weird hair and looked poor and dirty. But the photographer liked her, so eventually he led me and Muffin to a flower bush to smell the flowers. My mood shifted as I found myself in the scene everyone wanted me to be in, and I was comfortable in the frame of the shot.

I wore Muffin out so much that I got another one for Christmas. She'd lose her eyes again and get new ones sewn back on—big black pupils again, like the lens of a camera.

4

Nonnie's Fireball

There was no way Nonnie was going to be called "Grandma" or "Mee Maw" because names like that sounded old. She wanted to be called Nonnie, a name that no other grandmother I knew had. It's abbreviated from the Italian *nonna*, which has a ring to it and sounds lyrical, lofty, and traveled. Her real name, Faye, means "fairy," and she was very much otherworldly and wholeheartedly self-created.

Nonnie's mother, Sara Josephine Eskridge, was one of nine girls, all of whom went to college (and did cotillion and all that chic stuff women did back then). But Sara Josephine Eskridge married beneath her: a cowboy, a ranch hand named Jesse Thomas Baggett. Jesse did the rodeos, which was badass and cool, but the Eskridges couldn't stand him—not that he gave a shit. No, this wasn't in Italy. It was in Wichita Falls, Texas.

I wish I could say that Jesse loved Sara Jo, because it would have set a good example, but, according to my mom, they had two modes of communicating: pretending the other didn't exist (which is different from ignoring someone, although they did that, too) and fighting. Jesse doesn't sound like much of a conversationalist, since sometimes he didn't even bother to sit down to eat with his family, opting instead to pull a chair up to the fridge and eat from there. They slept with a sheet partition between them, which isn't usually a sign of getting along. Sara Jo chased Jesse around with a skillet, apparently, and a knife at one point, threatening to kill him. I hear she was a warm and loving grandmother but favored boys, like everyone back then. Mom describes the dynamic between the couple as "a showdown," and Jesse as "Texas tough."

When my mother was five years old, her family lived in Texas (this was before the move to Louisiana), and she remembers Jesse eating breakfast—three fried eggs with molasses on top. He stirred it all with a stick of butter, which he took a bite out of, like a piece of toast. They had their own cows and a dairy farm, so he could do with his butter what he damn well pleased. Thank God they had that farm to sell eggs and milk during the Dust Bowl days, when the sky turned black and dusted the very air they breathed, and during the Great Depression of the thirties, which decimated agriculture and left people starved and homeless. The weather alone was brutal and relentless year-round. It would get so hot in the summers that you could fry an egg on the sidewalk. As the radio DJ did just that, describing it animatedly and with humor, my mom would roll her eyes and think, "That's supposed to make us feel better?"

When Jesse barreled through the living room, outfitted in his cowboy gear (the gun, the holster, the whole nine), shouting, "Let's corral! Let's corral!" my mom and her two brothers, Tim and Jimmy, would spring off the floor. My mom remembers making eye contact with her brothers and her dad, all of them rolling their eyes at the ruckus and what a show of machismo Jesse made of it—that bit of extra that wild people take over the room with.

Glenn Patton was my mother's father and courted Nonnie when she was just seventeen. They met at a government-sponsored dance social in Amarillo, not too far from Wichita Falls. He was Irish and Scottish and was the seventh son of the seventh son. The religious connotations of this being something that gave him special powers didn't go to his head at all. It was by default in actuality, since one brother died of tuberculosis and the other at childbirth, but that still counted, right? I loved it when that conversation started.

Nonnie would gloat when she'd talk about it, saying yes, it did mean something, and it did count. We'd look at Glenn like he had special powers and he would laugh and shake his head, good-natured and reading his paper with a Benson & Hedges cigarette burning in his ashtray. He had a great sense of humor and humored Nonnie in her fantasy life. He had to.

Their courtship story is upstaged by Nonnie's older sister Lois's husband, though. His name was Elbert Higgens. Lois was also just seventeen when she and Elbert dated for a bit and then married. He moved into the house when Nonnie was fourteen and she hated him—he was even wilder and more primitive than her own father. Anyway, on one of Nonnie and Glenn's early dates, Glenn walked my grandmother up the driveway, where Elbert was hiding in a tree. When they passed under him, he farted on them and laughed like the crazy man he was. Nonnie hated his guts, and for good reason. I'm sure he tried to chase her down.

Glenn was a pilot and took her away from all that. He taught at the flight school in Amarillo, and his father had been mayor of Amarillo in the early 1900s because he was the "wet" candidate (translation: he was for booze) and had his own saloon. His name was J. H. Patton and he saw the first pavement laid on Polk Street. J.H. was charming and fun, liked to socialize in the public square and kept candy in his pockets to give to the kids.

The saloon was called the Old Forester, where you'd pay with cash in exchange for wooden coins you'd keep tight in your suit pocket for drinks and maybe even a glass flask of whiskey. Those coins are collectors' items now. My cousin Todd was on a website and saw an old bottle of whiskey and some bar tokens with our great-grandfather's name on them, but the guy who ran the site wouldn't sell Todd the coins or that old bottle. Maybe he held a family grudge and would take the memorabilia to his grave, along with some rifles—yup, don't mess with Texas.

Nonnie and Glenn settled for a bit in Amarillo and had children. My uncle Tim was first. As a kid, he remembers Uncle Elbert perching outside on the air conditioner in only his underwear, holding a gun. The family was having dinner and a prisoner had been released from Leavenworth prison, which was six hours away, so Elbert was on the lookout. One time, probably to entertain my uncle Tim (or maybe it was some ritual, since Elbert was a Mason), he stood on the kitchen table, unscrewed the lightbulb from the fixture, and stuck his finger in the socket to make his hair stand on end. He learned that from the carnival, where he met my great-aunt Lois. She was blond and beautiful, and at Elbert's funeral she had a broken arm. It was a funeral Nonnie was happy to attend.

When I was little, Nonnie was, for me, a queen: tall and thin with dark hair—a raven beauty. She dressed like a movie star and would go to Neiman Marcus for inspiration and return home to sew her own clothes. She had a movie-star way of talking, too, and of comporting herself. When she'd say, "I'm just a country girl," she sounded and acted just like Susan Hayward—not like a country girl at all. She'd sashay around in high-heeled boots, swaying her hips in pencil skirts, with nowhere to go except lunch at the Piccadilly, or bingo at the Petroleum Club, which served a delicious buffet dinner. The names of both places reeked of high class to me—and truly, even though the Piccadilly was just a cafeteria, it was a big deal to go there. Glenn would put the copper-colored coffee thermos on the table and Nonnie'd say, "Who will do the honors?" and gesture to the thermos like it was Waterford crystal.

At night, Nonnie added Sweet'N Low to her zinfandel wine—tapping the pink packet into her glass like it was gold dust—and she'd say, emphatically and with feeling, "I can't stand the bitterness." She always said it with profundity, as if it were the first time she'd realized this. I'd give her a new reaction each time, as if the cameras were rolling, each take better than the last. She prefaced the most mundane comments with phrases like "Forgive me if I must say so," and then would go on to say something that wasn't anything she'd need forgiveness for, which muddled my Catholic brain.

She let me stay up late with her to watch talk shows and old movies, and we'd sponge-roll our hair or pin-curl it and do our nails. In the morning, I sat on the couch with the Yorkies, Benji and Teddy, their framed photographs blending into the wood-paneled walls. We'd brush our hair out and she'd lament, "Why, I could've been a textile designer in New York. Mmhmm. I really could've." I would zone out staring at the dirty feet of the boys in a reproduction print by the baroque painter Murillo, which was the only other picture on the wall in the TV room. "Why, if I could do it all over again, Mittens, I would've married a man who'd give me gifts. Someone who'd take me out to places." I'd spin her globe, close my eyes, and stop it with my finger, then take it to Nonnie, and she'd tell me where I ended up. Glenn would be at work during the day, at Sunbeam Bread.

Nonnie sat in her rich leather chair in front of the built-in bookshelf, which mostly held the *Encyclopaedia Britannica*. There were other things to look at on those shelves that I liked: a tiny figurine of Ganesh, who when I asked about him, she'd say, "I don't believe in him, Mittens, I just like the aesthetics." She had regular playing cards that I got to use, and a double deck of cards encased in French provincial-style covered compacts, which she used for bridge. There was a Buddha and a sumo wrestler and a geisha woman and her fan, harmoniously placed. I liked looking at her book about ikebana floral arrangements.

She'd say things like "I love the Orient" as if she'd visited there, seen all the sights, and had a fabulous time. She would sort through the paper, cutting coupons, and say things to the newspaper as if people lived in there. "Serves you right," she'd say with her quiet genteel judgment. "Mmhmm, yes. Serves you right."

When I finished fixing myself, I'd put the pins or rollers away and move from the couch to the floor and do back bends or splits and watch TV. I'd watch Nonnie watching the TV, and I'd see how content she became as she placed herself inside it; she was happy and humming, swinging her crossed leg or shimmying her shoulders to the music. She'd throw her head back and laugh, watching Gwen Verdon or Liza Minnelli, and she adored Bob Fosse. "Mittens, why do you think homosexuals make the best choreographers?" she'd ask. Bob Fosse wasn't a homosexual, but she probably thought he was. I was around eight years old, so I didn't really know what she was talking about. (I got to meet Liza on a film I did called *The Oh in Ohio* and told her how much Nonnie giggled at the sexuality of Fosse's choreography, and Liza said that she'd made him laugh. "I didn't even know what I was doing was sexy! But he'd sit in the audience, just laughing at me." By the way, Liza needlepoints on set, in what she called jazz, or freeform, style.)

Nonnie and I played cards in our time together, too. She taught me how to play solitaire, a game she loved, as she was always happily self-absorbed. She enjoyed having conversations with herself—her interior life so loaded that snippets of dialogue would naturally come out. I loved it when she sang as she got dolled up, whether or not she had anywhere to go. She let me be, and I enjoyed that—playing with the plastic buttons in her sewing box, respectful of the "nice" scissors (the ones to cut fabric, not paper). I hummed along with her as she waltzed around, through the kitchen and into the bathroom, where the "good" towels were folded perfectly in the cabinet and never used. I'd open the cabinet and stare at those towels like they were King Tut's tomb. There was a soap dish in clear plastic wrap with decoupage flowers—never opened, never touched. Then I'd look at myself in the mirror. My hair, brushed out and curly, looked like a wig. It reminded me of Judy Garland and her movies on TV.

King Tut
(he coulda won a Grammy)
King Tut
(buried in his jammies)

At my brother's wedding, Nonnie danced the night away, and took breaks to alternately puff on a cigarette or her asthma inhaler—she was in her early eighties and still living it up. She kicked through the Charleston and said, repeatedly, "I could dance forever. I just love dancing." Since Glenn had passed away, she'd been partying it up with the Greeks at the Orthodox church in Shreveport and they loved to dance, apparently, so she had a fun group of friends. "I love the Greeks," she'd say, with the certainty and fervor of a politician. I'd picture her friends looking like Greek statues.

What Nonnie didn't love was her son-in-law. My dad didn't kowtow to her or treat her like a queen. She didn't find him charming or funny, which drove him to act even more provocative and obnoxious. She'd met her match in him. They both ruled any room they entered, but my father, with his sense of humor, could bring any house down, including and especially hers. They needled each other with mind games worthy of the theater. It was not boring, but it was not peaceful.

When the air was tense and drama was being whipped up—when the family spoke their resentments toward each other in silence, and when the drinks got made—I liked to sit on the floor in the kitchen and spin the double-tiered lazy Susan that held the canned goods. Green beans, asparagus, deviled ham—which came wrapped in white paper, a little red devil modeling with a pitchfork. The miniature Morton Salt with the girl on the label—she was my age and had a pageboy haircut and yellow raincoat. Her umbrella produced the rain under her parasol and she was happy on her walk. I'd spin that lazy Susan again and again, grabbing the cans and stacking them before they whipped away and back around. It was a game between heaven and hell: the can of deviled ham against the Morton Salt girl. She raises her umbrella and shoots the rain that drowns the devil back to hell.

Nonnie made recipes straight out of *Good Housekeeping* magazine. She'd make brisket or marinated crab claws, pimento cheese and artichoke dip, and she'd serve canned asparagus as if they were fresh. She exuded such intense imperiousness over everything that my uncle Tim didn't know she hadn't invented the BLT until he went to college.

She also adored Atomic Fireballs (those bright red jawbreaker candies), which she kept in a big white box on the island in the kitchen. My cousin Samantha and I would climb on the table to get to them when Nonnie wasn't looking and run them under water to let the heat out. We stared at the only picture hanging in the kitchen: a somber old man praying to a loaf of bread. When we asked who the man was, Nonnie said it was God. We asked questions about that— like "How can someone take a picture of God?"—and Nonnie would leave the room, which made us laugh. I took catechism, so I knew God made everything and knew everything and was *in* everything. It was inane to think that this man was God, because why would he choose to be photographed praying to a sad loaf of bread? And why look so glum? Jesus, it just didn't make sense.

One Thanksgiving on Lovers Lane, after we'd eaten and were sitting around in that post-turkey dip, my dad had this ingenious idea and put down his drink and went into the fridge. He snagged the innards of the turkey from the crisper and cupped them in his hands. Then he went up to Nonnie and said, "Nonnie, the meal was delicious, but"—*cough cough*—"I don't feel so good." He pretended to throw up and coughed some more and showed her his bloody hands holding the turkey remnant's entrails. If she thought this was funny, she sure as hell didn't show it, and I doubt she thought it was funny. She put herself above laughs that she didn't orchestrate herself. It was a Texan showdown stare-down, to be sure, and my dad won. Nonnie was "on a mad" for that number, stoic and beautiful in her resentments as she conversed with herself—holding tight and chewing all that bitter material.

The following day, when we were in the kitchen eating leftovers, my father started cutting the turkey, and it started rolling back and forth. He put down the knife and picked up the turkey and there it was—Nonnie's Fireball. It was smaller and not as bright red as it was before but still mobile enough to hold and rock a carcass with a knife. How the Fireball got under there is still a mystery.

In tribute to Nonnie, as well as to the Patton side of my family, I'd like to turn you on to the Fireball Cocktail. You can call it "Nonnie" if you'd like. It's inspired by the Manhattan cocktail (like my aunt Peggy likes) but has a Fireball thrown into the mix. When the Fireball releases its potency, it sweetens the drink and turns it red. A few dashes of bitters are balanced out by the pure sweetness of sugar. The drink takes beautiful shape, like a cosmos.

Fireball Cocktail, aka the Nonnie

1½ ounces Rittenhouse Rye

¾ ounce Punt e Mes vermouth

2 dashes of Ms. Better's Batch 42 aromatic bitters

1 Atomic Fireball candy

Lemon peel, expressed

Place ingredients over ice in glass and stir. Pour in shaker and shake (dance, please). Express the lemon peel's oil over the finished cocktail and drink. Then express yourself and get loose. Cheers to our lineage and being able to live on the planet at this time, and don't forget that resentment is poison. And good luck with your regrets; they'll leave you lonely and you can't dance with them.

5

Pansies Are for Thought

I spent time at my other grandmother's, too. Granny's name was Nautis DeLatin and she lived in Shreveport as well. She was the landlady of one of those old Southern homes on the corner of the street. It was three stories and had a huge wraparound porch. Off to the side where the traffic whizzed by was a bench swing, maybe twelve feet from the high ceiling, that hung by long chains. We'd shell peas and shuck corn together on the front porch as neighbors strolled by. Yes, she'd sit in a rocking chair and there was a metal glider couch, too.

I never saw her tenants but they lived around and above.

She taught me how to sew and embroider and I made a rag doll out of her old pillowcases and slept on a rollaway cot where I could feel the bedsprings. This was in the back of the house in a little screened-in porch room. When it rained I could smell the hydrangeas just outside and the damp air contained the scent. I'd wake up to look at them and notice how the petals had speckles of soft pink, like a watercolor brush had sprayed them.

Granny was the bohemian in the family, with relatives from the Netherlands. "Bohemian" was how my parents explained why

Granny had no interest in doing things like decorating or cooking or cleaning. She was diametrically opposed to Nonnie, who wallpapered even the light switches to match the walls and did her sewing on a sewing machine. Granny sewed by hand and painted with watercolors—flowers like irises and tulips. She liked her "stories," which is what we called soap operas back then, and the beauty pageants. She appreciated beauty without having to own it herself.

Before all this, when my dad was a boy, she was a CPA for an accounting firm called Frost and Frost. She wore Andrew Geller shoes and a fur collar and went to work decked out and ready for business. Once she flew to Mobile, Alabama, to set up the books for the branch's office and when she passed above them in an airplane, my dad and his older sister Peggy waved to her in the air. Peggy was in kindergarten and my dad was around two or three then.

Dad and Peggy had older siblings that they weren't as close to (they were really wild), and a housekeeper—"maids," they were called back then—named Mary Baker. She was at the Poseys' almost all the time. Mary's husband drove a cement mixing truck and once in a while, if he was in the neighborhood, he would dump a little pile of cement for them to sign their names in. She looked after them as best she could and was a great cook—she made things like chitlins and corn bread and collard greens with ham hocks.

The Bakers' home was a small shack, located in what was called "the Quarters," which was made up of dirt roads. You'd park on the paved street to walk into the neighborhood. My dad was born at night, and Peggy remembers walking to the Bakers' house with my grandfather. Paw Paw entered the house yelling, "Mary Baker! Get your party shoes on! There's gonna be dancing tonight!" He took them both back to the Posey house, where Dad was born and the next day was circumcised on a card table in the living room.

All the kids had a Red Ryder BB gun back then, according to my aunt Peggy. Once, when my dad was five or six, he was taking the heat off his Fireball jawbreaker under the water faucet in the bathroom. Peggy remembers hearing him hum a song as she stood in the kitchen. She called out to him, taunting and singsongy, "I'm going to shoot you . . . right between the eyes!" When he came out of the bathroom, there was Peggy, about twenty feet away, pointing her Red Ryder BB gun at him. They stood looking at each other, in a showdown, for almost a minute. Then she shot him right between the eyes. My dad walked around with a BB above the bridge of his nose until some lady noticed it and squeezed it out a week or so later.

This was around the time my dad had taken to playing with matches and lit the couch on fire. Peggy hid him in the wardrobe closet when the fire department came over, and they both got beaten for it—"whooped," as they call it, or a "good whoopin'"—which they laughed about as adults. Peggy and Dad were close and would discover much of Shreveport together, walking through the sewers in the neighborhood and then popping up and out of the manholes. They'd look around and guess the neighborhood, and then look up at the street signs, which they were barely old enough to read.

They also played a game at Granny's vanity mirror, where they'd place the other in a chair as one would stand behind. They'd stare at each other in the mirror, and the person standing would hold their hands just inches away from the other's face. Then the standing person would swing their arms wide as if to slap the other's face, and freeze their hands while having their stare-down. When they finally did slap, it was the other's turn to go. They'd play for hours and the game always ended in tears. But they'd make up, because they loved each other. And that was the fun of the game.

In the sunroom, Granny had an embroidery hoop mounted on an adjustable tripod that I'd sit at for hours. I'd look at her pattern book and copy the stitches onto the fabric. I liked the backstitch— the needle moved forward a few centimeters, then went under the fabric, pointing through and creating a gap to be filled—then traveled backward again to pull the thread forward, returning to the exact point where the previous stitch ended. With the stem stitch, you wouldn't see that gap because the needle threaded just barely a centimeter, under the overlap of the previous thread. The split stitch took the needle through two strands (if you doubled your thread) and could backstitch along to create branches. Granny sewed a map of the United States that included every state flower. It was made from a pattern, but still. Like Ophelia, she would say, "Pansies are for thought," and she liked to paint them, too.

My grandfather was named Youree Posey and we called him Paw Paw. He was born in an old railcar to David Posey and Ethel Maybell Gage, who went by Maybell. The Gage side of the family was Irish and David's father was too, but the Maybell Gage side was of Cherokee descent from the Trail of Tears. She was several feet taller than her husband and "towered over him," according to Paw Paw. These were such tough times with the Depression and, before that, the cowboys and Indians. I liked picturing her towering.

Paw Paw's dad was especially tough. One time, he put a knife in the fire to sterilize it so he could cut his own tonsils out. He followed through with it, too. He also shot and killed a man who trespassed on his property, which you didn't do back then, as it was against the law—both things. When he went to court he showed no remorse whatsoever. When the judge said that he was free to go, David volunteered even more information than needed and shouted, "I'd do it again and shoot him even more times, if anyone ever went on my property!" The judge banged the gavel—"Quiet in the court, quiet in the court!"—and my great-grandfather marched out of there, high on the waves of drama.

Maybell died when Paw Paw was thirteen. Back then, if you didn't have money for a hearse, the casket was put under a school bus and that's how my great-grandmother traveled to her grave. David got drunk and married another woman shortly after, but when he sobered up the next day, he ran her off. He married again, to someone named Miss Ruth, but that's all I know. I don't think she was a lot of fun or particularly nice. Not long after, when Paw Paw was fifteen and riding his horse in the country in Arkansas, he picked up an African-American boy, who was around six or seven, and called him Smokey. Smokey called Paw Paw "Yick," or "Mr. Yick."

David, for some reason, said it was okay if Smokey stayed, as long as he ate off of Paw Paw's plate and not his, and everyone in town came to know my granddad as the teenager who rode on his horse with Smokey at his side. Paw Paw even rubbed Smokey's head for good luck when he played cards. Both Paw Paw and Smokey were "dirt poor," but they were friends and loved each other.

Paw Paw was a great athlete and played basketball for the semi-pro league. This was in high school and it was a self-made team. He stayed in high school an extra year to play on the team so he could make money. He even had a German pseudonym, Youree Hans, in case there was press at the game. This way he wouldn't have to speak or cop to being overage and still in high school.

Paw Paw left his family when my dad was fourteen, and my dad was made "man of the house." He had to "grow up fast" and Granny "took to bed," to use my father's words. Granny even made him get her "feminine products," which embarrassed him. She bad-mouthed Paw Paw, because she was heartbroken, and she manipulated her kids with "call your father and tell him that you miss him."

North Louisiana had a pocket of Catholics, which was unusual in a Protestant "Bible-thumpin'" Southern town. The DeLatin side of the family were deep Catholics: Granny's aunt was mother superior at Saint Vincent's Convent School (Eulalie DeLatin was her name) and we had another relative in the 1800s who was a big Catholic, Monsignor John Van Degar. The names sound like soap opera stars, don't they? My dad loved the Jesuit school he attended; he loved that it was smart and strict and that he learned Latin. He was a star student and he found father figures in the priests there, and thank God, there was no weirdness. Aunt Peggy loved going to boarding school at Saint Vincent's and the nuns were fantastic and lovely. She watched them outside the schoolroom's window as they rode mules pulling the plow to grow vegetables and crops to feed the chickens and cows. Then they sold it all to Sears in the mid-sixties and she was rightfully pissed off.

When things got too heavy at Granny's, I'd sit in front of the gas-fire radiator and stare into it, then run to the bathroom to look in the mirror to see if the tips of my lashes had turned into ash. Granny didn't have separate soap with flowers on it like Nonnie did—there was just one bar, the unnatural pink of calamine lotion, which didn't lather much. She had rippled candy in Depression-era glass bowls, which were beautiful, and she had just a few demitasse cups, which she loved to show me. She'd sit in her rocker in the living room and sing the depressing cowboy songs of her childhood, like "When the Work's All Done This Fall," which she sang to her own children and made them cry so hard they'd hug each other. This particular song was a real guilt-ridden heartbreaker, about a cowboy who got stampeded by his own cattle and died, right before he was about to get all his work done and make it home to his heartbroken mother—who told him not to go in the first place. Don't leave your mama, boys.

Paw Paw would come over for Christmas to receive the bad vibes from Granny and the kids. Paw Paw was at the Office a lot—which was the name of the bar that he owned. He married a woman named Kathleen, who he loved very much but died, and then he had a lady friend named Helen, who had a pouf of light blue hair—a touch of magic, I thought.

When I visited Helen's house, which was tiki chic seventies style, she served us mixed nuts in bamboo bowls and had needlepointed cozies over Kleenex boxes. Everything was mostly brown and I dug the brown shag carpet and rattan furniture. One time, she put her hands on a table and repeatedly said, "Come up, table. Table, come up." She said this repeatedly and for too long, in the hopes that her magical powers would reveal themselves to us. They didn't, unfortunately. I really wish they had. I would've liked to have seen that. The gold lamé genie slippers, with the slightly curled pointed toes, reminded me of Aladdin, and with Helen's blue hair it wasn't a far stretch to picture a table floating up like a magic carpet.

My granny and my aunt Toni-Anne were much more grounded. They'd eat on TV trays in the bedroom and watch "the stories." When I was on *As the World Turns,* it made them very proud. "You got my widow's peak," Granny would say, before talking about how handsome Holden was. Holden was the hunk on the show, played by Jon Hensley. "He's really nice, too, Granny," I'd say. "You'd like him." I told her how, on my first day of work, the woman who played my aunt Barbara said, "Be careful who you share your secrets with because these walls have ears." Colleen Zenk turned on the waterworks like nothing I've seen in my life. Granny *loved* that dish. *As the World Turns* was one of the earliest soaps—its first airing was shot live in 1956. She loved Eileen Fulton, who played Lisa Grimaldi, and Helen Wagner, who played Nancy Hughes, both of whom were there in the beginning. I'd tell her how classy and nice they both were in real life, since they'd kept her company as she took to bed and martyred herself in her forty years of heartbreak. I told her how nice the producer of the show, Laurie Caso, was when he asked if I'd like to get out of my contract early because they needed to put Holden in a coma before Labor Day (his love story with Lily was huge and they needed to focus on that). I told her how Laurie hugged me like a dad and was so sweet that I cried. She loved all that.

I didn't spend as much time as I would've liked at Granny's house, though. During one visit, when I was only around seven, one of my cousins got me to put an "f" in place of the "d" for "duck," and I walked up the steps of the porch and said the F-word to all the grown-ups. That pretty much ended my solo time at Granny's.

When Granny was dying, she called Paw Paw on the phone. "Does my baby girl want me to ride in the ambulance to the hospital with her?" he asked her. He rode with her and held her hand and was able to pay for the funeral. When he died, he left all his kids money and my dad his prized coin collection. One of his neighbors wrote a piece in the paper about how kind he was to his neighbors. All he wanted to live for was to be remembered as "having a good name."

For the DeLatins and the Poseys, this apple pie recipe. It's really easy.

Skillet Apple Pie

1 stick of butter

2 pie crusts from the grocery store

Big Ziploc bag full of sliced apples

1 cup packed light brown sugar

1 teaspoon cinnamon

Preheat oven to 350°. Melt the stick of butter in a cast-iron skillet, then add one of your pie crusts. Fill the Ziploc bag of apples with sugar and cinnamon and shake. Pour the apple-sugar-cinnamon mixture onto the pie crust. Cover the apples with the other pie crust upside down, as a lid for the apples.

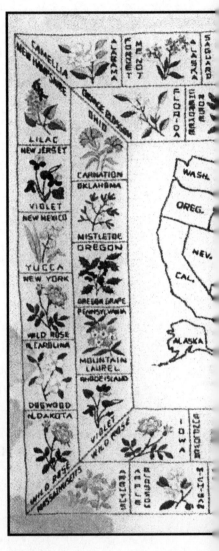

Put it in the oven and watch the butter bubble and cook the edges of

the pie. I think this takes about 45 minutes. May God bless America.

6
Indie Days

I can always tell the *Party Girl* fans because they look fun and some even tell me that they wanted to live in New York after they saw the movie when they were kids. When we made the movie, we talked about giving the kids something to dance to while they watched it on TV.

When I was doing press for *Party Girl*, I met a journalist from India who was so excited because it reminded her of Bollywood cinema, and I'd never seen a Bollywood film. She explained that characters in Bollywood films break out into song and dance all the time and that these breaks are shot like music videos within the film. Sometimes the breaks are fantasy numbers, or party scenes, or declarations of love or heartbreak. There's an air of performance to it all, which is why she thought I'd be a fan. And now I am. *Sholay* is the film I'd recommend seeing first. It's a classic.

Daisy von Scherler Mayer directed *Party Girl*, which she cowrote with her friend Harry Birckmayer. I've gotten few parts that I auditioned for and that was one of them. Auditioning feels like my real self has been punished and sent to my room, while my pretend self is forced to make nice when there is nothing that I've done wrong. At an audition in my twenties I spazzed out so much that the casting director asked my agent if I was on drugs. I wasn't, but just had lots of energy and was excited to be there. I *was* going out dancing with my friends a lot, though, so with *Party Girl*, I was cast in a role I'd been living.

I remember passing Sam Rockwell in a basement apartment in the East Village, where the auditions were held. We had met at a reading together, at a theater somewhere in midtown, a year or so before. I've always loved his vibe, it hits close to home—cowboy rodeo meets Chuck Barris from *The Gong Show*. He later played Barris in that movie *Confessions of a Dangerous Mind* and learned to lasso for Sam Shepard's play *Fool for Love*, a part he'd always dreamed of playing. I forget the name of that part. On closing night, I joined him and his friends backstage for a toast of whiskey, which I drank with added drops of oregano oil to fight a flu I'd felt coming on. Later they went out and Sam was still holding on to his role by lassoing people on the sidewalks.

We'd worked together in a 1995 film called *Drunks*, which was shot in a church in Harlem. It took place at an AA meeting, led by Richard Lewis's character, where everyone shared their stories of getting sober. The actors' "holding area" was in a room off the large congregation room, with individual dressing rooms separated by bedsheets. Inside these "rooms," which were about four feet in diameter, sat a metal chair draped with our character's clothes. I remember actors prepping their monologues in these rooms, which struck me as holy confessional booths, minus the priest. We'd all tiptoe around to respect each other's privacy because some of the older actors were sleeping.

There were maybe a hundred of us, total, all held in this church, so there was nowhere to go except outside, and it was cold. We drank lots of coffee and I smoked outside with Kevin Corrigan and Sam. Kevin has a similar essence to Christopher Walken—idiosyncratic and human. And Gary Lennon, who wrote the play the movie was based on, was receptive and cool and always around; he went on to write for *Orange Is the New Black* and won some Emmys. Pre–*Ally McBeal* days, Calista Flockhart was there and fully committed to her work. There was Dianne Wiest, who was luminous and truthful and beautiful, and Amanda Plummer, wholly authentically sensitive, and LisaGay Hamilton, who was just completely fierce.

I was a big fan of Spalding Gray, the monologuist, who performed his own monologue in the film. He'd stand poised and silent, sometimes by the doorway between the two rooms but mainly, almost always, close to the wall, like an insect. He'd glide around, peering over people's heads as if they were antennas for his own intelligence or creativity. Looking through us or above us, in his vacuum-land. He was never without his yellow legal pads and no. 2 pencils, which he held to his chest while walking and on his lap when sitting. I remember telling him that I was a fan, and he showed me his pencils and told me how he always wrote in longhand. That was the extent of our only conversation.

Faye Dunaway swept in for a few days for a monologue, and she had a birthday during the shoot. Everyone came out of hiding or solitude to sing to her in the back of the church. Before she blew out her candles, she said, "What should I wish for?" Her hands were held up, splayed in a court jester gesture, as if to say, "*You* tell *me*, fellas!" And with really good timing she said, "That I remember my *lines*!" and blew out her candles as we all clapped. She was touching the shoulder of a first AD named Burt or Burke, who she had worked with twenty-five years before. It was a long time ago, so I don't remember. I recall he wore a kerchief bandanna around his neck, like a wrangler rustling cattle. Faye Don'tRunaway.

I also recall that Faye and Burt/Burke seemed to have had a past. A rumor that they'd had an affair back in the day surfaced almost immediately, because when she entered the set the first day and strode in with outstretched arms to hug him, they were both laughing and he was blushing. She grabbed my forearm years later, seemingly out of nowhere, on an empty red carpet at the Golden Globes (we were both running late) and told me how much she loved

Personal Velocity, an independent movie I'd done with Rebecca Miller. She still cared a whole hell of a lot about movies, enough to grab my very arm.

Liev Schreiber got the part that Sam auditioned for in *Party Girl*, the part of the bouncer. We'd auditioned in another basement apartment, in the West Village. Liev came in fresh off his motorcycle, holding his helmet and exuding a strong actor's attitude. He acted like he'd just finished Yale School of Drama, which he had. This was before the *New York Times* said he was the greatest living theater actor of his generation, or something to that extent. He was the envy of so many of his contemporaries and treated the small part as a favor to Daisy, which it was. Liev is spectacular onstage. He later told me that he almost didn't do the part in *Party Girl* because I seemed like an idiot.

Independent filmmaking felt small-town, which was nice. There was congeniality and favors were granted if people had good relationships. Michael Clancy, our wardrobe designer, borrowed clothes from designers and friends to dress my character, Mary. Vicky Bartlett, Clancy's wardrobe assistant, gave me the shirt off her back in the first wardrobe fitting, which started in my closet in Chelsea.

Liev introduced me to his friend Greg Mottola, who wrote and directed an independent film called *The Daytrippers*, which is a wonderful movie all around. The production company's name was Fiasco, which was funny since on the first day of shooting the camera was stolen from someone's car. It was the fastest and tightest schedule I worked on during my indie days. It was only a nineteen-day shoot, and most of the movies averaged twenty-two or twenty-three days.

There was a scene where my mom, played by Anne Meara,

collapses on the sidewalk and we think she's having a stroke. I asked Greg if I could say "Don't go into the light, Mom," and he said I could. Liev groaned a bit, thinking it was dumb, and then when he saw the movie told me that it got the first big laugh in the film.

Greg did something really smart suggested by Steven Soderbergh, who'd seen Greg's short film at Columbia film school—it was shot in one take and called *The Party*. His advice to Greg was to write something contained, with not too many locations, and the locations you'd need could belong to your friends and family, who you could also cast. So we shot in Greg's parents' house, as well as in their station wagon, and in Campbell Scott's apartment, who also invested in the movie. We shot a party scene on Liev's rooftop in Brooklyn, as well as in his apartment—where Marcia Gay Harden was hysterical in a cameo. Greg wrote a part for his friend Andy, and we shot in *his* apartment, of course, while using Greg's place as a holding area since they lived in the same building.

Anne Meara I loved and adored so much because she could make me laugh without trying. She got mad at me once, though, in her close-up, in Greg's parents' kitchen, when I couldn't control myself. I was close to being punished and sent to my room. Watching her bend over to pull her panty hose up from her shins to her legs in Greg's cramped apartment, with nothing to hold on to but hanging clothes and an open doorframe, is something I'll never forget. She started laughing at herself, and then I started laughing at her, and then she was laughing at me laughing at her, as she tried to figure out which of her legs had the best balance. It was like watching a vaudeville routine—it was so pure in its humor and she was real and exposed and loved every second of it.

Films cost money and in those days, the budget went to the cost of the film itself and the time it took to edit—to cut and splice the film on what's called a "flatbed." Now films are made in digital and edited on a computer. I guess it's comparable to doing your dishes by hand as opposed to putting them in the dishwasher, where you lose the experience of seeing and feeling for yourself how the plate gets cleaned. But if it's digital, then the plate goes into a dishwasher, and when it comes out, it's clean, like too clean, so the technical team of engineers (on their computers) dirties up that plate so it looks real again—or as real as it can, since digital doesn't have the depth of field that film does. The digital cameras now are better than they were twenty years ago, but still, it's a whole other thing when they can push buttons to create the light of a sunset. With film, you had to be there when the sun was actually setting. I need to watch *Heaven's Gate* again.

Anyway, the focus and energy to shoot in film, which is costly material and not disposable, made the work happen differently. Everyone whirled like dervishes. Actors hit their marks, made their cues, and knew their lines—there wasn't time to spare. No dillydallying by the crew but horses at the gate, reflexes on, moving large equipment like C-stands and ladders and sandbags to blast off the shot as quickly as possible. "Time is money!" was shouted all day long. Sometimes, I'd sing back, "GE, we bring good things to life." "GE" is short for the grips and electric department—the ones doing the heavy lifting and loading of the lighting and electrical equipment.

In *Party Girl* and *Daytrippers*, this mode was full-on and it wasn't unusual to work more than twelve hours in a day, but sometimes being overtired frees you up and the commotion around you fades away. I was almost dreaming, while standing sometimes, holding the focus puller's measuring tape at my nose—the center of focus on the face. I'd release the tip of the tape from my fingers and listen for the sound of it snapping back. All the hubbub would put me into a fantasy where EMTs were trying to revive me: "Roll sound" was like "We have a pulse." The clapper in my face and the assistant cameraman shouting "Marker!" woke me, thinking, "Huh? Marker, Parker? I'm here." Then "Action," and I was in the scene.

I remember Daisy saying, "We have a hundred feet of film left, do you think you can do the shot in two takes?" I remember Greg Mottola was lying down in the back of the station wagon, recording sound, with barely any film in the "mag" (which is what the container is called). There was no room in the car for other crew except for camera, who yelled, "We're fighting for light!" as the sun was close to going down.

Something else that doesn't happen in digital is "checking the gate." This is when the camera assistant would shine a flashlight in the little window of the camera where the film was exposed, to see if any minuscule particles had stuck to the film. When the gate was dirty, the assistant camera person would shout, "Hair in the gate!" This meant that the last three or four takes held in the mag were ruined "in the can." "Don't shoot the messenger!" you'd hear a lot afterward. I'd freak out when there was a hair in the gate and act like a child. And like a child, I'd let go and move on and want to see the hair in the gate, which was not a hair at all but a piece of fuzz. That little piece of fuzz destroyed the entire mag of film? Wow.

They also call independent movies "guerrilla filmmaking" but it's more like punk rock because no one cares if the movie makes money and you're in it for the experience or for the art of it. John Cassavetes is probably the king of this and I got to work with his daughter, Zoe, in a movie called *Broken English* in 2006. The first time we met, we hung out on the grass at the Chateau Marmont from one in the afternoon until eleven that night, drinking wine and talking about the character of Nora, who I played, and the painful and funny stuff we'd get to expose of her. "None of that *cute* shit," Zoe would say. What does she look like when she's alone and no one is watching? That's what we were interested in.

We shot just two weeks later in New York. I lose things easily before I start a job, and of course left my cell phone in the cab on the way to meet Zoe's mom, Gena Rowlands. I would work with her the next day, in the first scene on the first day of production. I told her, "I have to tell you, to get this out of the way, but *Opening Night* is my favorite movie about an actress and your performance was so incredible . . ." She smiled and sighed, remembering, "Well . . . how do you think I felt when I read it?" And we sat there in silence for what seemed like a while and got comfortable being mother and daughter.

Zoe and her sister, Xan, and brother, Nick, grew up making sandwiches for the cast and crew of their parents' movies, because they shot all those films in their home. There's a documentary about John Cassavetes called *A Constant Forge*.

What it is to *forge*—where metal is heated and wrought to make malleable.

Zoe has the intensity of her father and the beauty and spirit of both her parents. She nurtured and inspired easily since she'd experienced home in that way. She'd hunch close to camera, disappearing with her crew in whatever setting we were all shooting in. I was in her story, feeling more like an extension of her—like an appendage, the fingers to her hands.

The woman's touch is drawn to subtlety and nuance, like emotions and instinct—and the space of expression between the words. That space is everything.

Hal Hartley has a similar scope and places his actors like dance partners with his cinematographer, as well as composing his own music while writing his screenplay. The notes of the music fill in emotions or transitions and that space says more than words or just as much.

Hal and I have done five movies together and the last time was in his movie called *Ned Rifle*. We shot in a prison and I asked him if he ever felt like he was going to be locked up and sent to jail. We were both raised Catholic and I wondered if the thought had ever occurred to him, if he felt guilty or needed to confess. He was emphatic when he said "Yes. Look at what we do. We *get* to make movies. We should be in jail."

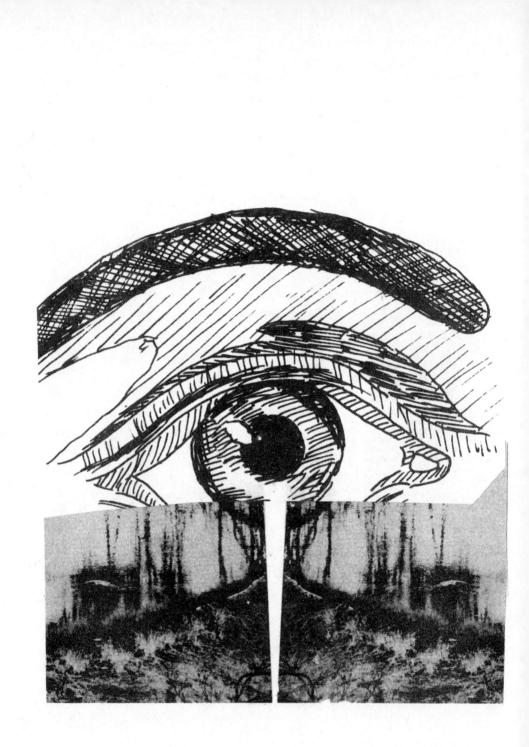

7

Earth, Wind, and Fire

I love New Mexico and got to work there in 2007 and visited the Hanuman temple in Taos. I was filming a movie in Albuquerque called *The Eye*, starring the beautiful Jessica Alba. It was a Hollywood movie based on a Korean horror film and directed by two Frenchmen. Jessica plays a blind violinist who gets a cornea transplant. The cornea she now sees with belonged to a girl in Mexico who had hung herself after receiving a vision of a horrible industrial accident she couldn't prevent. After the transplant, Jessica's vision becomes psychically blurry because she's seeing with the eyes of the visionary girl. The horrible accident keeps playing in her mind's eye as she progressively loses her grip. Therein lies the horror. I never saw the movie because I'm not a horror movie fan.

I liked the part I played of her sister, though, who shows up intermittently to tell Jessica that she's acting strange and to ask if anything's wrong. I was relieved not to know any of her horror, and I got to play a flight attendant, which I've always romanticized. I wanted to wear soft materials Jessica's character would find comforting, and since it was a gothic story, I thought playing guilty was the way to go. I threw on a comfy sweater but looked too much like a school-marm, according to the producer, Paula Wagner, who wanted me to dress more like her. I ended up getting fitted for expensive power suits that a flight attendant would never have been able to afford.

I was difficult for a day in wardrobe fittings because my character's clothes were less personal, but understood this was "genre" and I'd need to blend in with the dark color scheme of everything. I was grateful for the paying job, really. My last film, *Broken English*, had been at Sundance a few months prior and got good reviews, and I was hot enough for a second to land a Hollywood gig. Don't bite the hand that feeds you, I learned, and plus, I was already digging the horizon and the air and driving to my music, like *Don Juan's Reckless Daughter*. "We're going to come up to the eyes of clarity / And we'll go down to the beads of guile." Joni Mitchell and New Mexico went hand in hand—and the expanse of sky was like medicine. I need the wind.

There was an Ayurvedic café in Albuquerque called Annapur-na's, which is Sanskrit for "full of food" or "goddess of the harvests." I wanted to see if it would be my hangout during my downtime. I always check out the yoga or vegetarian places when I'm on location, because they attract people who are searchers, or looking to heal themselves (and in turn others), because they've suffered (or are suf-fering), which I think is deep and cool—and because I've suffered. No one gets away without it.

An Indian man named Prakash was the chef of Annapurna's. He was effervescent and liked to name-drop Julia Roberts, who'd been there a few times. I told him what Shirley MacLaine had said about her, that everyone knew she was going to be a big star when they did *Steel Magnolias*. Then I went into my spiel: "Why do these movies with these big actresses never have roles for her friends? What hap-pened to the funny friend in those movies? I always thought I'd be that friend. Rhoda to Mary Tyler Moore. Friend to Julia Roberts." Blahblahblah. I was still suffering in that gripe mode.

Prakash led me to the Ayurvedic Institute, where Dr. Vasant Lad taught Ayurveda—a belief system and practice of balance through food, movement, and the climate or place you inhabit. I went to the institute one evening to drop in on a lecture, which took place in a small room where everyone was sitting on the floor. The students were writing in their notepads while Dr. Lad was telling a story about a boy who'd received a kidney transplant from a boy who'd died. The boy found himself sleepwalking to the village where the deceased boy's family lived, and he knocked on their door. I don't know what he said and can only imagine. After introducing himself, he asked to use the restroom.

There was also a story about a man who'd been given the heart of a suicide victim. He reached out to the wife to thank her for this gift. Well, they fell in love; he married her and fathered her four children over twelve years. And then he killed himself in the same way her first husband did.

Dr. Lad explained that organ transplantation was not condoned in Ayurveda because it's considered taking a part of someone's soul and putting it into someone else's body. I thought, well, hey, you could get lucky, and the new soul could make your life more interesting and give you more of a personality or make you better at math. But it wouldn't be very Ayurveda of you. Ayurveda is more about psychological mindfulness solutions to illness, which is part of your soul and the diet that goes with it. It's not just about being sick; you have to get deep about it and think that it's teaching you something. It's not a "fix it" solution with a pill; it believes that illnesses are part of your karma, your path—and the actions you take can remedy the imbalance. I'm not saying I'm balanced, by the way, but I work at it.

"Ayur" means life, in the Vedic culture, and "veda" means science or knowledge. It's a five-thousand-year-old system, which says a lot. It's a belief that humans are a part of nature. How could we not be?

There are three fundamental energies to our nature, to our inner and outer life, that are dominant in particular body types:

there's Wind (Vata), Fire (Pitta), and Earth (Kapha). Or Earth, Wind, and Fire, if that's easier for you to get down with. We each have all three qualities, or doshas as they're called, and they each have different attributes that manifest physically. So, to give an example, a big burly man carpenter would be Earth (Kapha) dominant: he's slow and steady, and can focus in on a task. The Kapha-dominant person is grounded and can tell a long story without going "all over the place." Let's say that you have a Kapha contractor working on your house and he's overweight from drinking too much beer, but he tells great stories. Everyone has seen *that guy* (like everyone's seen a skinny bitch). On a good day, the contractor is doing his job and is content. On a bad day, he's gluttonous.

I am Wind (or Vata) dominant: I have lots of energy, am a small person, am changeable, and like to move. But when I'm out of balance, I move too much and spin out and have anxiety and forget what I'm doing; I'm prone to spiraling down or spinning out. Vata people eat a meal at the same time that they're walking down the street and talking on their phone—and while they're running an errand. I could benefit from burly carpenter/Kapha energy, and there is a whole system of vegetarian fare that will bring me back to balance. Right now, I forget what it includes.

Fire- (or Pitta-) dominant people are intelligent and ambitious and intense; if they're out of balance, they tend to be assholes and have prostate problems. Think of the skinny "live wire" comedians you've seen who do lots of coke and become impossible to be around.

Places, as well, carry a dominant dosha: New York City is Vata, Los Angeles is Pitta, the South is Kapha. I suppose Canada is, too.

Anyway, I liked the talk; it rang true. It reminded me of drama school and a teacher named Joan Potter who typecast based on physicality and essence, and would recommend which Chekhov character would best suit each of us.

One of the things that Dr. Lad said in class was, "We never see our own faces, we only see them in mirrors. We will never see for ourselves our own image." Maybe for you, this isn't a mind-blow but something obvious, but for me, it blows my mind.

Excuse me, I've brought my tea and thermos for some hot water, when you get a minute. This is a dosha-balancing tea from this place called Premium Steap. I got it when I worked in Philadelphia. It's a local company and the tea sommelier, Peggy Stephens, is really nice and cool.

I introduced myself to Dr. Lad after the class and told him about *The Eye*—that I was playing a part in which my sister had the eyes of a visionary who committed suicide. I told him I was an actor, but he wasn't a movie person, so he didn't recognize me, and he took what I said at face value. So I was taken aback when he made an announcement to the class that there was an actor in the room and singled me out, which made me feel exposed. He thanked me for the work that I do, and spoke of entertainment as having an important place in healing. Or something like that. I blocked out the flattery because I didn't want the other students to resent the extra attention I was getting—I wanted to be independent of *that*.

I sat in on some more classes and took yoga with the students. During one class we all lined up against a wall and kneeled down, facing front, eyes closed, with our hands behind us, against the wall, while making buzzing sounds, like insects. I heard the clank of keys opening the door, and I opened my eyes to see the mailman coming in to drop off the mail. Here was a room with thirty people, backed up against a wall, making loud collective insect noises. I couldn't stop myself from laughing, which I did, alone.

I went to a few house parties and sensed the different levels of tightness and silence that people exhibit as they are suffering. There was lots of looking down while talking. Mainly, though, I hung out with Prakash and learned some recipes from him, like how to cook bitter melon, which is extremely bitter, but once you get used to it, it's alright. And it's a great system cleanser, if you know what I mean. I also got turned on to this stuff called triphala, which is a plant medicine that *really* cleans your system, but not in a scary way. I took a tablespoon in powder form and shot it down with water while not breathing through my nose, because it tastes like ground furniture.

One day Prakash and I drove to Taos for the Hanuman festival. Hanuman is the monkey god in Hindu mythology, and he has a blue face and is extremely devoted to his own god, Rama, for whom he'll run errands and move mountains. Prakash told me that George Harrison brought the giant, however-many-tons Hanuman statue to America and drove around with it for some time while looking for the right home, which turned out to be Taos. I don't know if this is true, but I know the Beatles turned this country on to India in the sixties. There's a Hanuman pose in yoga, which is the splits as you hold your arms back together above your head to grab your foot. I can do this, not to brag. But I will go out on a limb to tell you I have had past lives in India.

Julia Roberts didn't show up at the festival, but we did—with a giant bag of lentils, ready to feed a hundred hippies and Hanuman devotees. When we opened the first bag, hundreds of bugs came out, so we walked into some open land and dumped the lentils there. Luckily, we had another bag, and I helped Prakash make dahl. We ended up having just enough for everyone, and it was such

a cosmic handshake that we were like, "Right on, brother." I live for moments like that.

What happened to people?

8

Vampires

About four years before *The Eye*, I was in *Blade: Trinity*, which is the third film in the series based on the fictional Marvel Comics character. When I took the first meeting for that film, I was like, "What's with these vampire movies? These are B movies, not serious movies, not adult human-being movies that people can relate to. Just *who* is going to want to see people with vampire teeth being all serious? It makes me laugh just thinking about it!" I didn't say it out loud to the writer and director, David Goyer, but that was my attitude.

I may have been wrong about a few things in my career, but who's to say, really? I passed on *Girl, Interrupted*, the Angelina Jolie part, and remember saying in my defense, "Who cares about a bunch of depressed white girls in the sixties? What about civil rights? Hello!?!"—an attitude I remember Liev Schreiber calling "self-sabotaging." It's alright, though; it's not like she won an Academy Award for that performance. At my *Speed* audition, I used a paper plate as a steering wheel as I "drove" the bus. I couldn't pretend to drive a bus by gripping the air, and the plate was just sitting there on the table. I thought it was a good choice, since the character was initially written as a stand-up comedienne, but the director wasn't laughing. Keanu and I became friends, though, and I think the movie did a lot for Sandra Bullock's career. I auditioned with Robert De Niro in a hotel room with a camera in it, and he taped me for *Meet the Parents*. There was a line I couldn't say, which was, "I'm not your Pam-cakes anymore, Dad." I wanted more lines to say, and the fact that *this* was my movie moment with Robert De Niro made me laugh and roll my eyes. I remember Mr. De Niro saying, "If you could just commit," and I couldn't. I think those movies did really well, and weren't there sequels?

So in regards to *Blade*, my agents were like, "It would be good for the studio to see that you want to participate. These movies do really well. It'll be good for your career." And I thought, "Hey, just because it's not my bag doesn't mean it's not in my makeup bag."

This was the beginning of everybody being werewolves and superheroes and living in Middle Earth—around 2004—in movies. Wait, maybe it wasn't only in movies. I was walking around thinking, "What's happened to people?" But when my agents asked if I would take *Blade: Trinity* seriously, I said, "Of course; I am an actress!" My boyfriend at the time thought it was rad that I was playing a vampire, and he was proud of me. He was younger and liked those movies (and video games, metal music, and Godzilla).

I was skeptical about *Blade: Trinity* but when I got my fangs, I got more into it. I put them on and ordered a sandwich at the deli and walked the sidewalks in the East Village, doing errands and acting natural—just another reason to love New York. I got on the phone with the wardrobe designer and shared all these ideas about what a thousand-year-old vampire would wear: talismans of various skulls of the people and animals she'd sucked the life out of, multinational monk garb, crucifixes, grunge Elizabethan, a monkey's head on some monk beads that she'd swing around like Bette Davis. I wanted to be a dirty and chic cavewoman with hair extensions that varied in length and texture—for *my* vampire to be moody and nihilistic, yet romantic and emotional. I went to set only to have all this nixed, and I ended up as a corporate vampire. I wore designer clothes and dyed my eyebrows blond, wore blue contacts, and sported mainly a tight all-business ponytail. It was actually enough of a change to get me going.

I was playing the part of Danica Talos, who the *Blade* Wiki describes as "an ambitious vampire, whose aim is to rule over the vampire world . . . She's violent and cruel, but she's also a strong leader." My first scene was with Wesley Snipes, who wasn't actually there, so I acted with his double. I asked David Goyer if I could say, "What's with those tattoos, do they mean anything?" and he liked that. Danica Talos was deep and dry and tired of being a vampire.

There was an art-imitating-life thing going on with *Blade*. Wesley was possibly losing control of the franchise to the younger (and whiter) Ryan Reynolds and Jessica Biel, who both starred in the third film. And even though I didn't get the full story, I knew it was intense because David had Triple H as his bodyguard. Triple H's arm was as big as my thigh and he was such a nice man. We actually did another movie together a few years later called *Killing Karma* or *Inside Out* and produced by WWE. He said all he had to do was swing his hair out of his face and fifty thousand people in the wrestling arena would scream and cheer. He was surprised how boring acting in movies was but he was good-natured about it. I remember talking about pergolas and how he liked Splenda in his Starbucks iced coffee because it melted more easily than sugar. And I did, too.

Wesley and I were both accepted in the acting program at SUNY Purchase. We went at different times, but had the same mentor, Joe Stockdale. Joe told me how remarkable Wesley had been onstage but was frustrated with the character parts he got because of his race, so he started a company outside of the acting program, which was nothing short of righteous. When filming started, I'd just finished doing a play myself, so I asked the first AD if I could visit Wesley in his trailer when he was around, to talk about Joe and to bring it back home for him—his acting, the theater. *The Waterdance*, an old indie movie he'd done in the nineties, was so beautiful. Wesley had an entourage of maybe twenty friends and sometimes at work I'd get hit on, like I was in a nightclub.

After I got the go-ahead, I knocked on Wesley's door and sat at the table in his trailer. I told him what Joe had said, and he laughed a little—at me? I'm not sure—and I could tell he was in battle mode, because his sunglasses never came off. He finally said something like "You don't understand, you don't understand the whole story." How can anyone understand the *whole* story, of anything? He was *taken* by the part of Blade and battling in a vampiric world.

Being a vampire leader, I wasn't afraid of either of them. He'd keep us waiting late into the night, and when he'd finally come to set I'd whine, "Where have you been? This has been so boring because we've been waiting . . ." He'd give me a "You don't understand," and I'd give him a "I know, I'm sure." Being a vampire sucks. I'd walk around set in my vampire getup and think, "I should make a calendar of Danica doing simple things like mopping the floor or playing solitaire." I didn't have a camera so it didn't happen. But one night, when we all went to a basketball game, I did start a cheer: "We say Blade, you say Trinity. Blade!" "Trinity!" "Blade!" "Trinity!" Can't forget to have fun!

One day I was acting out on set and gnashed my fangs at my makeup artist and she started crying. I hugged her afterward and told her I was joking and just acting out. That was a fun day. Then, the next time I flew to Vancouver, she'd dyed her eyebrows blond and sported a tight all-business ponytail. Since I already had a body double for stunts, this made the day even stranger because there were three of me there.

There's a fine line, I've found, between being playful and becoming inappropriate or even difficult. As the shoot progressed, I kept wanting to make things more sci-fi. Like, "At this point wouldn't Danica have developed a psychic skill to open this door with only her mind? So *why* press the intercom?" The idea got shut down like a bat seeing sunlight. There was also a seduction scene between Dracula and me in his bedroom, where a wind blew through a large gothic window lit by a neon moonlight. It reminded me of a Heart video from the eighties, as my shins caught the billowing lunar-blue sheer curtain and I leaned to catch the wind on my face from the giant fan, set up in the soundstage. My hair had been let loose and rocked out, as I stood bored and not feeling it that evening. To seduce me, Dracula spoke in that sexy and slow, hypnotic way and said, "I was around at the time of Jesus," and I ad-libbed, "Oh yeah? I was around at Woodstock." I was able to be sexy and serious about it but the whole scene got cut. I think David appreciated the commitment that I gave throughout the film. Who cares, really? No one. When I took my torture scene with Ryan seriously, though, I got a heartfelt hug from David and he thanked me. That was nice.

Even though we were working in a studio, there were a lot of night shoots because we were running behind by the end of the week. I zipped in and out of town for my part so it wasn't as difficult a shoot for me as it was for the others. I'd get tired, and my feet would hurt from stomping around in pumps, and my eyes would get dry from the contacts, and I'd get headaches because the dry contacts would blur my eyesight. If only complaining weren't so exhausting. One night, I filmed a scene in which I had to shoot someone on a balcony while gliding purposefully sideways and shooting a gun through the air. It was important to me that I appeared to be floating like vampires do. To prepare, I lay on the floor with my legs up against a wall to get my blood flowing and napped using my purse as a pillow. When they finally called the scene, I got it together, ready to glide sideways with that steady vampiric grace and intensity, ready to shoot, *pshew pshew pshew*, with my gun. We did a take, and the director came up to me after and said, "That was great, but you were making sounds with your mouth when you shot the gun."

"Really?" I said. "You could see my mouth move?"

David nodded. "And we can hear you."

"I'm sorry, I don't know what to do. I mean . . . that's the sound you make when you shoot someone. I've never shot someone for real . . ."

It was my last day—or night—and I got back to the hotel just before dawn. It was good timing since I was playing a vampire and there I was, watching the sun come up.

I was at
Woodstock.

9

The Death Star

I used to be with a big agency called CAA. "The Death Star," as it's called in the biz. When I hear "You know they call it 'the Death Star,'" it's been delivered in midstride, with excitement and knowingness—like Han Solo in *Star Wars*—and there's conspiracy in the air. Han Solo knows the force and the machine; he's in on the game and mission. He is cool under pressure.

I signed with CAA in the early aughts when I heard they "package movies." And the big stars were there, and stars get movies made, and if your agent is friends with someone else's agent, or if they like the same kind of coffee, you have a chance of being squeezed into a supporting role. And that's a crapshoot. What was also happening was "a paradigm shift," as those in the biz called it, in the types of movies getting made. *Whoa!* was me when I heard about *The Lego Movie*. I had a hard time wrapping my head around that one. I tried to imagine it: I'm going to my friends' house. They have kids and their elevator opens to the apartment. I step out of the elevator and see a bunch of Legos on the floor. I holler out, "You need help cleaning this up?" No, I know they made the Legos talk to each other. I didn't see it but I wonder if their teeth clattered. Anyway, yay for the plastic arts and new forms!

I went into one of the conference rooms on the Death Star and met with my agents and manager to talk about "projects" and what was "in the pipeline" and "setting up meetings" and what they were "tracking." This is agent-speak and my agents were cool. I liked them and thought of them like brothers—we rolled our eyes at the same-same-like movies being produced around town. They'd say rhetorical things like "Well, the studios need to make money," and "Making a remake guarantees an audience," and "There's a paradigm shift," and I'd ask rhetorical questions like "Why is it like this? Will it always be like this? Is it ever going to change?"

It's harder for agents to have creative agency since genre films—like horror or action films and kid-friendly movies—are what the studios want, since they make the most money around the entire world. I think about all this same-like and then about industrial agriculture and what it did to farmers and everyone's relationship to where food came from. And then I think about porn—terror porn, action porn, news porn—anything that speeds up our hearts and minds to consume and to remedy a quick fix, when there's nothing to fix. It all started with that gosh-dern remote control! It's nice to be up in the air and away from all that.

At the meeting, one of my agents had a dark orange tan, fresh from vacation, and I kept thinking he used a self-tanner as well as the sun. We all did. I think Ben Dey, my point-person agent, brought it up first and we discussed it for a spell, the reasons for the double-extra glow—perhaps to convince himself his vacation had lasted longer. We all poked fun and goaded him, "Are you wearing makeup?! There's a streak mark from your tan wipe!" I told him he looked like an actor in a cigarette ad from the seventies skiing down a slope to stop for a drag of a menthol, and I lit his imaginary cigarette. I liked those guys.

It was around this time that I ran into Nora Ephron at the airport, just after she wrapped *Bewitched*, a movie remake of the TV show from the sixties. I remember that trip because Gracie pooped in her travel bag from the hard drugs that the vet in LA had given her to relax her on the flight. *Valley of the Dolls* was a favorite book and movie of mine—Gracie's favorite, too—but these dolls were too much. Her eyes were glazed and she was swaying, like a drunk dog leaving one of those Dogs Playing Poker needlepoints. The flight attendant was exceptionally cruel and condescending about Gracie's being zipped up *all the way* in her bag before we took off. So much so that I started crying, and when we got to the altitude where we could walk around, he knelt down beside me to apologize. "I didn't mean to insinuate you were a bad mother," he said.

"But you did," I said, and blabbered how in our lifetime we're going to see people's need to interact with animals as healing beings that help us be calm, and especially on flights; they will help people deal and everyone will be nicer to each other because of it. I know he was having a bad day but my day was worse.

If my crystal ball hadn't been confiscated at the security checkpoint before that flight, I would've been able to tell him, "Just you wait, mister, you will see emotional support *ponies* on flights by 2018!" Now, there's a show I'd like to see, *Mr. Ed* style—that TV show from the early sixties where the star is a talking horse. In the remake, our pilot is also named Mr. Ed but he is a pony. What a small world it really truly is because, as fate would have it, he's the uncle of one of the other emotional support ponies on board. Her name is Make My Day and she and Mr. Ed have a nice conversation about her mother, Already-Winning, who's feeling better now that her master is coming out of depression and has started to leave the house for walks with her.

Make My Day could've helped Gracie when she pooped later on that flight back to New York. She could've helped me when I took Gracie, and her bag, to the bathroom, where the flight attendant cornered me.

"I'm sorry, miss, but the dog must remain in the bag."

"Really? Because she pooped in her bag, I have to clean her *and the bag*."

"It's not my decision, ma'am, it's airline regulations and she must remain *in the bag*."

We were standing outside the business-class bathroom, just a few feet away from each other and both talking in angry whispers.

"I either clean her *and the bag* or I go back to my seat and smell up business class. Now, which do you prefer?"

In retrospect, I can see that in his head he made me the bully and used me as an opportunity to finally berate someone. But I took it personally and defended myself: "I remember when flying used to be fun, don't you?" Our faces were as close to each other as actors' on a soap opera. I wish I could've marched away, slamming a door shut, but instead I clicked the tiny lock of the airplane bathroom and cried some more, and bumped around cleaning Gracie, trying not to get shit on my hands.

When I walked out, I saw that Seal was on the flight, too, so that "Crazy" song went through my head. "In a world full of people, only some want to fly, isn't that crazy? . . ." No, "we're never gonna survive, unless we get a little crrrrayyyy . . . zee . . ."

When I saw Nora walking out of the terminal, she told me that I had my shirt on inside out. It was a pajama shirt so it was fine either way, I explained to her. Gracie's bag smelled so I kept it swinging and away from us. I was also nervous about her behavior and feared security might administer a Breathalyzer test for Gracie, because she was not okay to drive. Nora looked fabulous, as always, and I looked like crap. She knew then what I know now, that when you can leave a place gracefully, do. No need to look like a bat out of hell if you can help yourself because it only inspires other people to treat you like one. We had both just wrapped—me, I don't remember, and Nora, *Bewitched*.

Around that time I ran into Nora's sister Delia on the sidewalk, and so directly she asked me, "How do you do it, Parker?" She'd written movies with Nora and knew how much movies had changed. "I stay distracted," I probably said, or "My denial skills are really strong." I said both those things a lot during that time. It was nice to be seen and supported. I was taken aback, really; when you're famous, people think everything's okay. We said good-bye and I walked down the sidewalk thinking about these things and about the missed love stories and romantic comedies that, despite the success of *You've Got Mail*, weren't easily financed and produced. It just became too much of a business, obviously. Stories of characters were swept under the rug, in favor of caricatures and stereotypes. I was feeling swept under the rug, too—maybe that's why I didn't care that I looked like a rug rat. It was difficult not to become jaded and feel left out when romantic comedies became bromantic franchises.

I'd had such a good track record with most of my choices for independent movies that I'd offer help to my agents in reading material. I couldn't produce my own material because my name didn't guarantee financing, but I could read stuff and know what was good, perhaps get a bigger star attached and shop a script around.

In the conference room, a young lady came to the door to drop off a script—hot off the press. She placed it right in front of me, on the huge table, and sashayed back out of the room. It was called *Sara's Cell*. My manager, Alyssa, and I perked up. Alyssa is a Harvard graduate, and her beige patent-leather Christian Louboutin pump was swinging her ankle in strides under the desk. She was sharp and smart and blond and a Hollywood native, so she was in her element.

"I'm sure it's awful," I said, aloud, and everyone laughed. I think my gripe shtick was amusing enough without being alienating or a full-on attitude problem. At least none that I was aware of.

I opened the script to see where Sara was, and I found her on the floor of a prison cell, naked and shivering with a guard throwing a prison uniform at her. "What am I supposed to DO?!" she yells. "I don't know," the guard's dialogue went, and then: "I don't care. I don't care if you shit yourself." Wow, gross. I stood up and marched to the door dramatically, swung the door open, and threw the script like a Frisbee down the hallway, the pages flapping at first like a seagull and then sliding as it surfed at least twenty feet on the white marble floor in the CAA mausoleum. We all laughed as I ran out of the room to get it.

On that same trip, I met up with an old friend, Joseph—we'd been dancing buddies in the nineties. He'd recently been made head of casting at a major motion picture studio and was casting a picture. The studio wanted a good actress to play the mom in the film, to help guide the thirteen-year-old actress playing the daughter into a good performance. It was a comedy, and I thought, "Cool! Studio job, comedy, residuals! If it's not too gross I'll do it!" I'd worked with the young ladies from *Josie and the Pussycats* and had a sweet time. I told my manager to set it up, that I'd be game for this. It was also partly an excuse to see Joseph again, because he was always fun.

I tried to read the script. It started out cute, until page 2, when the mom started making out with her twenty-something-year-old boyfriend in front of her kids, at breakfast, before they caught the bus to school. Then a page later, on the bus, our tweenage leading lady got into a conversation about a blow job with one of her girl-friends. Garbage pail, please!

I met Joseph at a new chic place off of Vine where they'd "paved paradise and put up a parking lot." It was a new building that seemed to have plopped down like a cemented island, surrounded by miles of concrete. The two huge potted plants at either side of the entrance doors were as big as statues and seemed to cordon off the place. They love that outsize look in LA, just like they do in Texas.

It was great to see Joseph. I congratulated him on his new job, and we sat down to eat before we headed to my manager's party across the street. After we placed our orders, he got into it, trying to convince me to take the part. I'd read enough of the script that afternoon to have a lot of questions: "Why does it have to be so inappropriate and gross? It's so weird that Hollywood makes this material sexing up thirteen-year-olds. You know that's why other countries hate us, right? And this is a conservative country, mainly, with religious people who don't want their kids even watching this, so who is it for? Is this for pedophiles? Do you want young girls emulating this actress, wanting to grow up faster so that they can give blow jobs, too? It's disgusting. Why does this material get made, produced? I don't understand, I truly don't. And it will never make money, I can tell . . ." Blah blah blah! The words just kept spilling out.

I started to sweat. The warm dinner roll I was eating became the texture of a soapy sponge, and I got a kind of cottonmouth. Joseph started talking, pitching me on it, and then he started laughing, admitting, "I haven't even read it." My insides were swirling (my head, my stomach) and nothing made sense as Joseph's face became a hypnotic spiral wheel. I needed to touch someone, to just hold the hand of someone fun and nice, which luckily I was able to do. "I need to get some air, come with me." I squeezed Joseph's hand and walked quickly outside, where I immediately threw up in one of the enormous potted plants. And then three times more. It was the perfect height, and I paused and felt *blessed*.

Joseph ran in to get a wet towel from the bathroom and when he came back outside he put a soft hand on my shoulder, and I started to feel a little better. He looked at me in an almost pathetic way but I could also tell he was suppressing a laugh. I relished the moment when I grabbed his shoulders and implored him to "*please* stop talking about that *awful* script." It was a perfect Hollywood moment. We pulled open the abnormally heavy dungeon doors of the restaurant, where I ran to the bathroom to gargle in the sink and to look at myself. A few young ladies withheld their concern, if they had any, and Hollywood types were arriving across the street to the party I would now not be attending, which was too bad.

I settled back at the table with Joseph and we got back to shop talk, which passed quickly. "Well, when I tell the studio what you said, your ideas, I'm sure it'll make them want to hire you even more," he said. We smiled at the system and I said I'd be game.

"If the studio wants notes, I'd be open to that. It would be fun to make it better," I said. I was leaving town the next day, so I didn't know how setting up a meeting could be possible. We brushed that off like it was something we'd worry about later, crooking our hands like otters in a lake.

Meanwhile, back at the Death Star, we were all still laughing when I brought back the script I'd thrown down the hall and sat down to look at it. "Where is it shooting, if the story takes place in Afghanistan?" I asked. My agent looked at the cover letter: Ventura. "Well," I said, "at least it will *feel* like Afghanistan in the Valley, where it's sweltering." I thought back to those TV shows from the seventies that shot in the Valley—Lindsay Wagner as the Bionic Woman, tackling rough terrain and entering into danger-lurking soundstage sets, full of empty cardboard boxes that she'd fiercely kick away. So many cardboard boxes served as obstacles, back then. Knives would stab the backs of "dummies" and they'd roll them down a hill, which any seven-year-old would know wasn't real. They really hammed it up back then and it was a little exaggerated, which was fun to imitate: a stab in the back, then hands flipped up, an "ugh" said in close-up, then the buckling of knees and a long shot from the back—rolling down a hill. As a kid, it inspired me to play in the yard, and I would pad myself with kitchen towels to roll down a hill.

"*Who* wrote this?" I barked. I flipped the script over: it turned out two brothers had written it. "Well, I want to meet these fellows and ask them what their problem is with women, why they want to put them behind bars and if they love their mothers or have any sisters. How is this torture porn even getting made? Don't even send me this stuff!"

It creeped me out and I asked, "Why do they think that I'm right for this?"

They all assured me they hadn't read it and I calmed down a little. I figured that one of them enjoyed the same coffee as another agent who knew of this movie, independently financed by who knows what person, and why or how.

We all laughed, like lovers after a dumb quarrel (how stupid we were! We love each other!), and Alyssa said, "When I looked at the title I thought it was a romcom about cell phones!" And we laughed some more.

Now, there's an idea. A romantic comedy about cell phones— starring me and Vince Vaughn.

Speaking of Vince, I met him at the Chateau Marmont a few years ago. I introduced myself and he hugged me. He asked how I was, like we were both war veterans or addicts out of rehab—this is not out of the ordinary, for actors to greet each other this way. I'd never met Vince Vaughn or at least that I remember, but we came up at the same time in the independent film world, so he knew the change, the "paradigm shift." He put his hands on my shoulders, like a good dad, and said, "You're talented. Don't lose faith. Don't get down."

I said something like "I think talent's a detriment. They don't know what to do with me out here . . . They think 'talent' is another word for 'crazy.'" Which it isn't. What do I know?

I wish I could tell you that we went back to my room and pillow-talked afterward, riffing on our own version of *Sara's Cell*, but that didn't happen. I went back to my dinner and watched all the women in their twenties who dressed like they were older, in escort-trophy fashion, with their hair the same length and blown out straight, having a good time in Hollywood.

10

In Line

I escaped New York in January of 2017 to live in Vancouver for eight months. There were fewer buildings there and fewer people on the sidewalks and more sky all around. I'm aware of how mundane and obvious that sounds. But even walking the sidewalks in Manhattan is magical. Looking down as I walk, I'm both grounded and hovering, the mica in the cement glittering like stars with the hardened black chewing gum looking like planets—and a piece of trash, an asteroid.

Vancouver's sidewalks were wide and more open, with less mica, and they're clean because all the trash finds its way into the garbage cans. I felt more free there while walking and less like a ping-dot navigating its way when passing people, as you do in a video game, with that constant practice of reaction and instinct from one destination to the next. I love the grid of the city and the energy it creates but I had just moved and wanted to stop.

Vancouver felt like a town *discovering* itself as a city and landing in the 1950s. It likes its trends and style, loads of people had tattoos, and the guys had beards that they groomed. There's a café culture that I'd never experienced, and I got a kick out of coffee sommelier talk in a barber shop/café/used furniture store called Space Lab. There was a newly opened sandwich shop called Say Hey, only a block away, where I met the owner, whose mother brought fresh flowers for the counter. A food truck could become a restaurant, like this place Tacofino.

One day, I was waiting in line at Tacofino, a restaurant in the cool part of town called Gastown, which was ten minutes from where I was living in Chinatown. There were enough tattoos at Tacofino to last a few days of storytelling. I wonder if an animated show starring the tattoos of people could be a hit. I was thinking of getting some teardrops coming out of my nostrils at one point. I'd get to say, "Laughing and crying, you know it's the same release" when anyone would comment.

There were a few "modern primitive" stretched earlobes in the place—one woman was sporting shiny silver gauges that made holes in her ears the size of silver dollars, large enough to contain a jalapeño. If she ever had a baby she'd get whiplash.

Two bearded fellows came in and one of them announced to all of us waiting, "There would be more room if we moved the line over here." He gestured for everyone to move against the wall, and stood there as an example.

They were dressed like timber cutters or construction workers from the fifties. If smoking pot was cool in Canada, they may have been stoners, but since it's legal and the sense of humor is laid back, it's difficult to know. What did it matter anyway? But their suggesting how people should line up and everyone's complying made me think of the fifties—of soda pop and greasers and rules adhered to.

I walked past them like a secretary taking a survey and said to the one who spoke up, "You must be the line guy . . . what is it like putting people in line?" I wagged my finger at him as I moved to the ladies' room. His face flashed in recognition as I did a quick thumbs-up and shut the door.

This mode comes from my father. I describe him as "a comedian without a venue," and he loves that. Restaurants, or any rooms full of people, naturally become stages for him, but if the room happened to be empty, he could flirt with a doorknob or entertain the wall, "no problem."

Later that night I ran into the bearded guys walking on the sidewalk in front of me and said excuse me as I passed them, stumbling in my clogs, not recognizing them from earlier. I was on my way to have a "dirty burger" at a place that's not advertised, because it's that cool, and they only have a select number of burgers per night because the beef, which they cook medium-rare, "American style," is pure. Cooking burgers medium-rare in Canada is almost against the law (the health department will shut you down), so the place was kind of taboo. You walked upstairs to a "hole in the wall" made trendy with a beautiful bar and gruffly handsome bartenders who asked what you wanted to drink as if they'd been out corralling all day, steering the grass-fed cattle from which you'd be fed. Prohibition hung in the air, although nothing was illegal. There were just a few people there because it's only ever crowded on the weekends.

I said, "Hey, Andre!" to the bartender, who'd seen me a few times before. I was always overly friendly here because the place had attitude. "We have only one burger left . . . he uh . . ." And he tilted his head toward a single man, sitting alone at the bar, and I completed Andre's sentence. "He took the last one? Or there's one left for me? Is that Van Couver?

"So there's one more and I can have it?" Andre nodded yes as if we'd bartered. I always felt out of place when I went there but then loved it—and Andre. Plus, the burger was perfect with its special sauce of mayo and onion, but mainly, like every burger, it was the fries that did it. There was one time that they didn't have a burger for me and I made a big show of my disappointment. "I'd like to speak to Van Couver about this, if he's around."

I was a stranger in a strange town. When I met people, if they weren't too shy for a conversation, they asked me, as a New Yorker, whether I thought Vancouver was a lonely place, or unfriendly. They got stars in their eyes when talking about New York, and told me, "Vancouver's famous for being unfriendly." Being a New Yorker romanticizes you, and the friends I made loved New York. It's not an unfriendly place, but I had been yelled at by cyclists for not using a turn signal—a few times, I got a kick out of that, especially since I was in the turn lane.

I was walking down a main street called Main Street as I passed the bearded fellows, another easy walk from Chinatown. The tripping in my clogs made a sound as I stumbled and they turned around and we recognized each other from earlier. "This is *so random!*" one of them said. "I didn't know who you were, but he told me, so I watched clips of your movies on YouTube." It really should be called MeTube.

"Thank you," I said, despite its not exactly being flattery, and wondered if they'd laugh. They did. "You guys must play video games," I said as a conversation starter, but it wasn't. They were of another generation. "I bet money," I went on, "that in our lifetime, it won't be weird to dress up in costume when it's not Halloween." People want to escape their skins. Is that why Comic-Con is so popular? Enter anyone, role-playing anywhere. It was a random thought I wanted to throw out there, since when people say "This is so random" it's usually not, and ends the better conversation people used to have before they'd say "This is so random."

I asked where they were going. To Boxcar, they told me—a place I knew about because one of my new friends, Ash, worked there. I'd met Ash at Mamie Taylor's, a Southern soul food place, not five minutes from where I was living.

Do you think that in another time, people enjoyed each other more? Maybe thought about death as more impending than we do now? That they realized that so much of everything is distraction, or a conspiracy, to keep us separate or guarded and locked up inside? Collectively, without realizing, we've let slack a present awareness. Maybe that's the context for the animated show starring people's tattoos.

Another new friend, Kristian, had a conspiratorial idea of such conditioning, and this kind of talk had me feeling seduced, counter-cultured, and fifteen all over again. Of course, I agreed. He and I were at Tacofino together when the bearded fellows came in and ordered us into line. Kristian was a blue man in the Blue Man Group, and he always wears a black knit skullcap, which he adjusts as he talks, as if it were a haircut he was shifting—bangs for a Beatles cut, or a side part for Morrissey, or covering the ears for a James Taylor shag. He's bald with a great-shaped head, and I loved this manner-ism of his when he gave himself different hairstyles. I'd met him at OX, an oyster bar, across the street from Mamie's. He was with his friend Gregory, who was working in the art department on a com-passionate documentary about the Menendez brothers. They talked about "fluidity" in relationships and in gender and this next wave of free-love relationships, communal living, dating multiple people, or being in a throuple. That's when a couple agrees to bring a third party into their union. I liked this talk, even if "throuple" to me sounded more like "trouble."

Gregory and Kristian invited me out for drinks, so we began walking, and Gregory admonished me for putting my cigarette out on the sidewalk. He was smoking a clove, like the cool kids did in college. Gregory was cute because he had freckles, but his facial fea-tures were angled and pointed, which matched his sharp and intense seriousness. "You know that goes into the ocean," he said when I flicked my cigarette to the pavement.

"I do stub them out and put them in my pack and in my bag mostly," I said, ashamed and exposed and somewhat flattered. "And besides, I'm quitting." He'd put me in line.

"There's so much antismoking these days," he went on, "but then you think about the Indians and how tobacco was used as an offering when they offered their peace pipes to the colonials. And the gift turned into capitalist gain."

Yeah, that's right, James Dean type, smoking is only as bad as you make it because we're all going to die anyway. He put the half-smoked clove in his pack and talked more about his home, an hour away, which was a solar-powered storage container for the boat he was building with his father, so he could eventually live in ports around the world. "Wow, I've never met an unavailable man like this before," I thought. He was interesting and authentic—in the fifties, they called them "loners" or "man's men." You know, that fifties mystique where real men are alone, or on an island—don't bother.

I had a brunch date with Ash on the following Sunday. He picked me up in his fashion-torn black jeans, a sleeveless Metallica T-shirt, and his motorcycle jacket (he rides, for real). His bright white Pumas with no socks were worn like a prized possession. I'd met him a few weeks earlier at Mamie's when I stretched out my back on a barstool and my leg went into an arabesque and brushed his side. I was unaware of this, of course, but he followed me out and got my attention. He said I didn't look like "someone from around here." I told him I was shooting *Lost in Space* and had just landed in town.

He started giving me the lowdown on Vancouver men, how their style is really important, that they spend hours in front of the mirror to get that casual look, and, a more heady esoteric toss-out, "In our lives, we meet the same four kinds of people . . ."

"Sure," I said. It made sense to me; I like the square of four. For me, it's more secure than the three of a triangle. If we're here to progress, let's get all math-mystical about it. A rockabilly chick with dark hair and a ponytail swooped in off the street and gave Ash a whack on his butt before entering the place.

He texted me that weekend about a drive he went on. I replied, "I don't like texting," and he texted back, "Me neither." He texted me a week later to see if I wanted to go on that drive, to see the seals. We saw dolphins that day and he said, "This is not something that happens a lot." I wish I could swim like dolphins swim. Ash got comfortable in his tight jeans and nice shoes as we sat on the incline of the cliff's rocks. He took out a flask and offered me a sip of whiskey, like Joaquin Phoenix did when we shot *Irrational Man*.

Staring out at the water, I pictured the decorative fluorescent gravel used in some aquariums. I'd had a vivid dream where I was swimming. There were two bodies of water: a swimming pool and the ocean. They were separated by a dividing rope with buoys—bobbing and bright enough to hold on to and close enough to let go of without going under and getting taken too far away by the current. I could, if I got up the nerve, let go of the rope to swim with the dolphins. The swimming pool was huge and the body of water calmer, but the ocean's water got darker with choppier waves and went on forever. I was in the middle, calculating the different sides: if dolphins could swim on the ocean side, that meant it was safe. I pushed myself out—excited to break away from the rope to swim with them. One of them was smooth and gray; there were some gashes from his being attacked and I hugged and pet him. He had lived long and hard, I thought as I swam to another one. She was more pink, like the dolphins I saw in Brazil, and when I pulled away, one of her eyes was cloudy and I thought maybe she was sick. My concern for her woke me up.

I showered and took a walk around Vancouver in the rain, and thought about what would happen if I joined Facebook. I was shooting *Lost in Space* now and more anonymous being out of America, so maybe this would be the best time to get in touch with all the people I've met and missed. I've met a lot of people, though. I'd met a woman in an airport between flights who'd said I'd worked with her father in Minnesota. I told her I'd never been there, but she assured me that I had. I couldn't bring myself to look myself up on IMDb to check the facts. I've been to so many places and traveled so much, it's best to keep up with today and tomorrow.

Ash was a new friend and about to start design school after being in the bartending scene a little too long for his taste. He was congenial while welcoming a guest to his city-town, his country. It was a really good time to be away.

He took me to brunch at a restaurant called Alibi, just a seven-minute drive from where I was living. The décor was Coen brothers, *Barton Fink* style. I curled up in a leather easy chair to release my lower lumbar, which was sore from wearing my space suit all week. There were typewriters and scripts behind me on a shelf and large windowpanes to look out through, and an unfinished papier-mâché work of art up in the corner, not fully expressed, and left with no worries, "no problem."

I asked him about a dance club called Celebrities where there was a Carnival dance party happening that night. My costar Ignacio, from Argentina, was going and I'd been feeling the need to let loose and dance around. You know, let my spirit fly.

Ash had been offered a job at Celebrities, for $500 a night, when he was in his twenties. He would have had to wear his underwear, cowboy or combat boots, and a tuxedo tie, and walk around with a tray of drinks. He put his hand up to mime this. "Think of all the gay uncles you'd have by now if you'd done that," I said. "And the stories . . ." We both agreed that this was a "regret" and perused our menus.

When the waitress came over, I asked for something sweet with brunch: "a waffle, a pancake, just something on the side, not a full order or anything." I put my palms out like the peaceful and suffering statues of saints. She said she'd ask the kitchen. When she came back, she said they'd said no. But she felt bad and said, "We have fruit and whipped cream," to which I replied, nodding, "Yes, it's not the same thing as a piece of French toast with maple syrup, though."

When she asked if there was anything else she could do, I said, "Yes, you can bring me a piece of French toast." Then I went into my mean-lady-at-the-country-club bit, uptight and jilted and patronizing: "I like something sweet with brunch. If I'm going to even have brunch, I'm going to go for it. Not a full order or anything, it's only a piece of bread, soaked in a scrambled egg. It's really the maple syrup I'd like, but I'd like some bread *with* it. If I'm going to eat brunch . . . "

I was flirting or entertaining her, as I do sometimes with waiters and waitresses, as it can be part of the exchange of going to a restaurant. Hey, if I wanted to eat alone, I'd have stayed inside and cooked something myself, to eat over the sink. And since it was brunch, which I think is weird in a city that's missing a country club (What's a provincial thing like brunch doing in cities? Are we living in the fifties?), I wanted a piece of French toast! If you're going to be about brunch, *be brunch*. Maybe I was being more French.

In Canada, they have these credit card machines that they give you after a meal, to pay for what you've just eaten. Don't try to eat it like a mint. There's no name for this gadget, this remote-control credit card machine thing that I begrudge every time a waiter or bartender hands it to me.

One night with Kristian and his friends, I ran up to the bartender to pay for my food and drinks, so I could go home. He was shaking his martini shaker loud enough for it to sound like tap dancing, which made me wince. So I did an "If you can't beat 'em, join 'em" tap-dance shuffle so we'd dance together. He didn't but handed me that thing to put my credit card in and I said, "This thing really gets in the way of a real exchange . . ."

"The exchange rate to the dollar is good," he said.

"That's not what I meant," I told him. "It gets in the way of the 'exchange' . . . *This* exchange . . ."

He looked at me like I was speaking another language.

Back at the Alibi, I followed the waitress to ask her where the bathroom was, and since she was standing by the open kitchen, next to the staff, I said, "Can you tell me where the *French toast* bathroom is?" and caught a few laughs. I got a bigger one when I shouted over my shoulder, "French toast forever!" as we left the place.

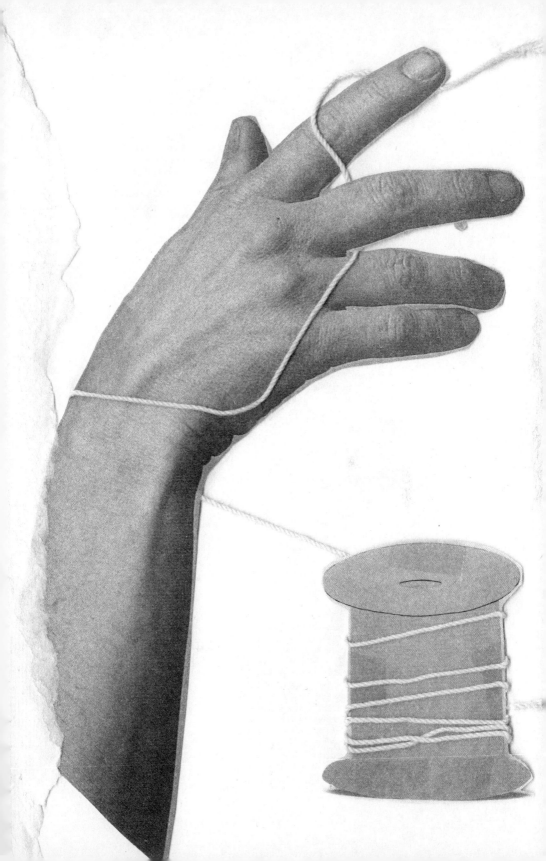

11
Louie

I'd only seen a clip from one of his early episodes but not the full *Louie* show when I met him. It was the one where a musician is playing violin on a subway platform and Louie watches him while waiting for the train.

The frame starts on four people standing and waiting for the train. Our eyes go to a blond woman in the shot, and then a few seconds later rack focus onto Louie walking down the stairs. The violin, the heart-stringed instrument, is being played by a professional concert musician. We're in the subway station, the metaphor of the underworld—where dark secrets unfold and knights are slain by dragons—blood and guts kept hidden from the rest of us mortals.

Louie walks past the musician and drops him a coin and then leans back on a column to watch. His face registers how odd it is to see this musician—young and wearing a tux and seemingly playing just for him. His cynicism ("What's a guy like him doing in a place like this?") turns into an appreciative beauty for a few seconds as he softens. Then a homeless man with something like twenty garbage bags around his feet barrels down the stairs like he's the king of the place. He's sloppy and crazy, and as the music starts a crescendo, he gets out a water bottle and starts to bathe himself with it. "Why is this homeless man ruining this music for me?" Louie's wondering. You can see that he wants to watch the violinist but the homeless man is so disgustingly scrubbing himself and is such a spectacle that Louie can't look away. The two characters start to meld as Louie watches and the music climaxes. When the shower is done, the crazy homeless man spits out the water like an ejaculation, and laughs—leaving Louie disturbed.

Louis CK is all three of these characters: he's Louie, the title character; he's the accomplished artist, in the role of the musician; and he's the homeless man, presenting no boundaries. He's the frame itself, as the director who composed it all. An artist given free rein to create exercises and test his limits—and ours. The more an artist can create, though, the more solipsistic they can become.

It's sad to think about how many men watch more porn on their phones than talk on them these days. These are not erotic times, to say the least.

We met at a reading of a play called *Beyond Therapy* by Christopher Durang. Frank Whaley, an actor I'd known for years, got this benefit reading together to keep the Cherry Lane Theatre open. It's a tiny theater and needed some TLC. It holds not even two hundred seats and the seats themselves must've been two hundred years old. The place was a silo at first and then a brewery in the 1800s; Edna St. Vincent Millay and her friends turned it into a theater in the 1920s. Playwrights like Eugene O'Neill, Edward Albee, Gertrude Stein, Samuel Beckett, and Harold Pinter—many of them writers of the Theater of the Absurd—housed their plays there. The Theater of the Absurd plays shared a point of view that life is absurd, pointless, meaningless—that words can't help us, and the afterlife won't help either, so live now and find something funny because it's a waste of time trying to figure anything out since we're all going to die anyway. You can go to Cherry Lane when we land and there will be a dramaturg to explain it much better than I could. The theater got a face-lift since the *Beyond Therapy* reading, with a new sign out-side even.

Louie's kids went to the same school as Frank Whaley's, which is how he got involved. And then other terrific actors like Nathan Lane, Marisa Tomei, and Mario Cantone (you may have seen some of their work) played other characters. Mike Daisey was the narra-tor, the wonderful monologist who just may have something up at the Public Theater now, which you could check out. You could walk from there to the Cherry Lane Theatre in twenty minutes. It's in the epicenter of the West Village, which branches short streets like a heart's arteries. I always think about that when I invariably get lost, despite having been to that corner many times.

A composer who worked on a Brecht play I did in college lived in the top apartment at Commerce and Barrow. He took me to see my first opera, *Don Giovanni*. Afterward, he showed me his one-bedroom apartment and made me tea and we listened to bits of the opera again on his record player. The cup was a hand-thrown piece of pottery, I remember—a large cylindrical triangle and glazed cream with patches of colored brushstrokes—late eighties New York style. Coffee cups were bigger back then.

I stood on the corner and looked up to the window and thought about his kindness, what a gentleman he was. I was bundled in Mil-dred's handwoven throw from Ireland that she'd given me one ses-sion when I was underdressed—it was wool, black mainly, woven with dark jewel tones and slit up the middle to be worn like a poncho.

It was on that corner and looking up at that apartment where I first met Louie and we shook hands, smiling and introducing ourselves. He was warm and bold and we walked into the tiny the-ater to rehearse. The reading was fantastic, as you can imagine with that cast.

Afterward, Louie said I was really good and should come do his show and play his therapist. I loved that idea. We had dinner at what used to be Grange Hall, with one of his comedy buddies, and put our numbers in each other's phones. We were both excited by the prospect of working together.

There was a place I liked to eat called Piadina, which was around the corner from where I used to live. It was a rustic place on Tenth Street, a neighborhood joint, not a "foodie" one, just west of Sixth Avenue. After 9/11, the business there improved as the locals wanted to feel grounded and unified, familiar. They were almost all Italian in there, and the owner always greeted me with a kiss on both cheeks, as is the custom. For the longest time the décor had warm exposed bricks and wooden spoons and forks and garlic hanging by string from the ceiling. An abstract painting of a naked woman, in oranges and reds, greeted you as you entered. They redid the restaurant and added a bar in the back and the brick was painted cream, but that's all gone now because it closed—due to rent prices.

I was eating there when Louie texted me and then joined me for several hours. We connected over our love of cinema. I observed him alternating his projections of me—between being engaged with me, Parker, and looking at me as if I were a character. "I know what I want to do with you," he said. Then he shared three stories of characters he'd wanted to amalgamate for a long time: one was an artist; another was a woman he'd met at an airport, who told him a story of her cancer and how she had to take care of her mother, who was freaking out over her sickness; the other was an alcoholic. He mentioned a homeless man, too, I remember.

"Oh, Janeane Garofalo lives here," he said when he walked me to my building. Janeane and I left each other funny stuff sometimes with the doorman—pumpkin seeds from Trader Joe's, some sea-salt-spray hair product. I asked if he wanted to see the roof, which was through the lobby. When we got up there, I stepped on the edge of a heavy potted plant to bend over the ledge and see the Empire State Building. "No, no! Don't do that!" he yelled, and I looked at him like he was crazy and saw his writer's mind working. He shared his mental note with me, saying that he'd read somewhere that the reason some people are afraid of heights is because the fantasy of suicide is closer to the forefront of their minds, and so the possibility of jumping is more at the ready—easier to make that leap.

He left soon after that. He was living on the Upper West Side in the same building Nora Ephron lived in, the Apthorp. After a few day dates, he picked me up in his car (I think a Porsche), and I helped him with Christmas shopping for his girls. We went to Purl Soho for sewing gifts, and he bought a table at a local store near Union Square. He had a bundle of hundreds with him, like a gangster, that he took out of his pocket and showed me and he told me a story that now I don't remember about a laundromat we'd passed. As his car pulled away from a stop, I shouted to passersby: "Louis CK's in this car, everybody!"

When I went over to his apartment to read his material, a friend asked if I would take some of the hairs from his bathroom floor for her. I didn't. I could have, easily, but instead chose to stare at the dust bunnies on the floor, along with the hair, and look at him like women look at those kinds of men and think, "Do you live in a *cave?*"

I brought over beets and salad stuff because he'd complained about being unhealthy. I was surprised that his kitchen was so foreign to him because on his show he wasn't scared of it. On television, he was totally adept at chopping vegetables, even while talking on the phone at the same time. It's sexy when a man can cook, but he was in some relationship drama at the time, which had him holding his phone, mainly. "No, you can't cut with *that*," I said, and pointed to his phone. I opened drawers and found what I'd needed, which was a knife.

The material he handed me was so well written that I fell in love with it. I played Liz, who works in a bookstore. Louie and I connect, have a night-long date, and then I disappear, leaving him searching. We shot it very quickly, spanning five days. On an early call at the bookstore where I worked, in Brooklyn, I remember waiting a few hours for him to show up. I'd brought my yoga mat, so I could lie down and relax if I needed to. I sang songs like Billy Joel's "Big Shot" to keep my spirits up and goaded Louis when he came in about arriving late, like a rock star—but he was a rock star and that's what rock stars do. I had seen U2 at the Universal Amphitheatre in LA on a Wednesday night, and Bono came out to a standing ovation and said, "It's so great to be here! On a Saturday night!" For rock stars, every night is Saturday night.

Louie did some really interesting things when we shot our bookstore scenes. For my first line, he wanted me to kind of take the words out of his mouth, so he mouthed the line while I said it aloud. The line, I think, was "Do you need any help?" or "Can I help you?" There was another scene in which he was coming up behind me to ask me out, and when we rehearsed it, he scared me and made me jump. He said he wanted to keep the jump and when we acted the scene for the camera, he said casually, "I'm a monster," before leading me to an aisle of books to ask me out. The line didn't make the cut, though.

For the scene where I'm telling him the story about my mother, when I was throwing up on chemo and comforting her at the same time, he said, "I'm gonna shoot this 'walk and talk' like you're talking to a ghost." He'd make his way into and out of the frame, so it seemed like I was talking to no one, to the air. I remember there was a full moon that night, the reflection of which was caught on a car across the street, and he was excited about that.

We ended that night's shoot with our scene in the thrift store, where I make him try on a ladies' sequined dress. We had to come back the following day to shoot it again because he couldn't zip it up.

It made the shame of being in the dress the next day even more authentic and he blushed, which was soulful and real and funny.

The shoot was seamless since he's such an auteur and knows every line he's written. I caught him once laughing to himself as he was looking at someone. I asked him what was so funny and he said, "I'm such an asshole," and shook his head.

I die at the end of the season, and shooting my death was really hard. There were real nurses there who hooked me up to a life support system, and who genuinely took care of me, saying I was going to be alright. They held my hand and comforted me with their protocol "You're doing great." In between the takes, I went into the bathroom and cried on the floor. I was upset that Liz was dying and mad at Louie. After the first take, he shooed everyone out of the room and we sat on the bed, side by side. He looked at me with intense concern and it seemed that it was difficult for him to find the words to say what he wanted.

"What? What is it? What am I doing wrong?" I asked. We were staring at each other. "You can tell me." My voice had become small and worried. Then he said something I couldn't understand:

"I wrote a death scene but you don't get to die."

"What? What do you mean? How does that affect what I'm doing? Can you be more specific?"

"It's before the last scene of the season when I leave for China. This will be a continuous shot with Steadicam and no cuts, so it has to be shot in one." My breathing was shallow and I wanted to just die and get it over with. We did the small but brutal scene around seven or eight times. He'd look at me with disappointment and regret. I'd mumble, "I don't know what you want. Was that take better? I don't know what you mean. I'm sorry."

In the scene, it begins outside the hospital, where the nurse tells him that I don't have much time or something, that I'm going fast. And then he just comes in and I say, "What's happening? Am I dying? I'm not ready. What's going on?" It's just a few words and I especially now don't want to watch it again to tell you what I said exactly. But before I die, I just say, "Bye?"—and it was written as a question.

In between all of this he reminded me I had wanted to die—the actor part of me was into it—but now I was strongly feeling, *But I don't want to.* I got so mad at him that I couldn't remove myself, couldn't not take it personally. It was difficult not to, lying on a hospital bed. I'd get out of the bed after "Cut" and run to the bathroom to close the door in agony.

No one had ever written a part like this for me and it was the kind of character I thought I'd be playing my whole career. He'd captured my voice. That's probably why he wrote a scene where he realizes he forgot to ask me my name and I tell him, "It's Tape Recorder." It was his voice, not mine, played back to him. Is that what he meant when he said that I didn't get to die? Because he created the story? Had I forgotten that it was dance?

There's the Minotaur myth, where the god Zeus sent a bull to Queen Pasiphaë and she gave birth to a half man/half bull. Her husband, King Minos, the king of Crete, was embarrassed about all this so he had a labyrinth built for the Minotaur to never escape from—he was a monster and slayed people and literally devoured them. There was all this Crete-and-Athens drama going on. The king of Athens, King Aegeus, had a son named Theseus, who wanted to kill the Minotaur—he had lost a lot of his friends who'd been sacrificed to the bull and was determined to end this feud between his dad and King Minos.

King Minos's daughter Ariadne is struck by Venus and falls in love with Theseus. She wants to marry him after he kills the Minotaur. She gives him a sword and some red string to tie to the entrance so he can find his way out. This labyrinth is pretty much inescapable but Theseus finds his way and slays the Minotaur. When he is free, he doesn't run to find Ariadne, though—by reasoning of the gods or more obligations to his father or he just wasn't in love with her. She's left on the bathroom floor—crying with a red piece of thread—which is where I was.

After I had died several times, Louie was nowhere to be found and I heard he'd driven home. "He's not going to give me a ride home?!" I shouted, abandoned and furious. "After all that?!" I was shaking with rage. Then the makeup artist asked me to put fake blood up my nose to record it for him, to see if it would be believable for the next day's scene. I shook my head and looked to my babysitter, Blair Breard, from Monroe, who also happened to be the producer of *Louie*. I'd run into her for the first time in more than thirty years at Bigelow pharmacy when she was shopping for something decorative to put in her hair for an awards show where she was nominated. She was leaving for Hollywood the next day and we hugged and I wished her good luck. It must've been three years prior to the moment we were sharing now, where I was deranged and saying, "What? What?! This is acceptable to you?" over and over again, and laughing in that horrible angry way you do when you don't want to cry—that passive-aggressive way. I snatched the plastic funnel-tipped bottle, squirted the blood-red Karo syrup up my nose, and looked into my makeup artist's iPhone to record it. "Is it believable? Is it believable?"

The next day began with setting up the shot in the bus, which would take place before the scene we'd shot the night before. I had called Louie once I got home, to make nice—I was upset she had died, I explained, and was just sad and troubled it had ended so abruptly. I could hear that he was in his cave/labyrinth and his voice was low and disconnected from himself, like he was very tired. I hoped the tensions would be dropped for the next day of work, but they weren't.

He was confused that morning as to how he was going to shoot the scene where I magically run into him on the bus. In it, my character is happy to see him, and I say, "Louie!" and go to him for a hug. Then my nose starts bleeding and I collapse, holding on to his shoulders. He had his camera lenses out in front of him at the back of the bus—lenses he was proud of and knew so well. I heard them talking about setting up a dolly track for the camera, which seemed like a bad idea. "A dolly track on a moving bus probably won't work," I said, to no reply. I went on, "Since the bus will be moving . . . over the bumpy roads . . . all the construction on the Bowery." I was met with blank and confused stares and a heavy mood of disappointment—or was it remorse? In the end, the shot was handheld and made less complicated.

I got to end the day with a shot from an earlier episode, where I was screaming at Louie and somewhat cheering him on, leading him to a view that I want him to see. He's out of shape and winded, and directed me to *really* shout at him, which I said would not be a problem. I shouted the lines "Just do it! Breathe! And step! Breathe! And step!" as we climbed the many flights of stairs to the rooftop, which mirrored my own heavy climb out of this realm. I got to tell him, as I sat casually on the ledge, that I wasn't going to jump. That *he* was scared of my jumping because it would be so easy for him to jump, but I would never do that, because I was having too good a time. Then a wave comes over Liz that's imperceptible to Louie (and us)—an unknown darkness too intimately confusing to be shared or expressed, and he's become a curious witness to that. It's then, when she's retreated into her own cave, that she can walk slowly and say her name, her voice low and disconnected—a ghost of herself.

I wore my own clothes in the episodes and my hair was in Heidi braids, like Ruth Gordon in *Harold and Maude* or like Liv Ullmann, Ingmar Bergman's main muse, sometimes wore in Bergman's films. On the night we met at *Beyond Therapy*, Louie had said he liked the scarf I was wearing. They were all my own clothes, so I could bring Liz back myself. I could have my friend Jack record me on his iPhone, on a moving bus, wiping blood from my nose and smiling, happy to be alive. I'd keep my job, at the bookstore, as a zombie. I'd remember the day he brought his Bolex camera in and shot me on black-and-white film. His Super 8 camera, which shot me in color, also on film. How he made me say "I love you" directly into the lens of the camera. It was a shared love of cinema or a pact that I'd given my heart.

I pitched "Zombie Liz" to the FX guys to no response. When they said they'd get in touch when something came up that I seemed right for, I looked at the posters of all the male-driven shows in their office—the Western show *Justified* stands out in my memory. "I don't really know if I'm right for any of these shows." "I'd want my own show," I told them in a small defeated voice. One of them said, "*It's Always Sunny in Philadelphia*," and I turned to look at the poster, thinking, "How can it always be sunny in Philadelphia? That's ridiculous," and crossed my legs, which seized my lower back into a muscle cramp. I shared this with them and we talked about back pain for a minute—"It's all repressed anger," I said. One of the nicer gentlemen walked me out, as I was limping, and we stopped at a desk to make an appointment with his acupuncturist.

A few years later, Louie texted me to invite me over for Thanksgiving. My oldest, dearest friend, Tanya, came with me to his place in the Apthorp. After talking to the doorman, we found out that Louie didn't live there anymore. We stayed talking to the doorman for a bit because it was Thanksgiving, but also because we wanted to make sure he knew we weren't crazy. It was a pride thing, too. Louie wasn't answering my texts, so we walked across the street to a diner with my big bowl of beets and Tanya's bourbon. We waited almost an hour for him to give me his new address, which was way downtown in the Village. It was snowing and the streets were beautiful and empty with hardly any traffic, so we sped along. He answered the door, smiling and happy to see me, and me, him. "I'm so sorry! I'm so sorry!" He put his hand to his head and scratched it in the "I'm such an idiot" gesture. "I can't believe I told you the wrong place. I'm so sorry." We were laughing and hugged, then separated.

"You didn't tell me anything because we haven't talked in two years!" I said. "I thought maybe you forgot where you lived!" Tanya and I told him how we had to do "that doorman thing," where you overcompensate and ingratiate yourself to the doorman, and the doorman accommodates this. It could've been a scene from his show. There's a particular kind of dialogue a scene like this produces, where it's mainly all subtext, and Tanya and I found that hilarious and laughed about it on the way downtown. It's a New York thing, when you go to someone's place who lives in a doorman building. Doormen hold the keys to everyone inside, and they don't let the wrong people in; they're keen to furtive glances. An inspired doorman knows everything about the whole neighborhood.

There was so much food on the dining room table because everyone brought something to share; it was so bountiful that Louie'd mention giving what wasn't eaten to the homeless shelter. He'd lost weight and looked content—the vibe was chill and we all enjoyed each other's company. I met Ellen Burstyn, who I'm such a fan of, and we talked about *The King of Marvin Gardens* and she said how all the actors hung out in the same hotel a few weeks before filming began—and how pre-planning for actors to chill out and get to know one another doesn't happen anymore. I told her I read her memoir and that the chapter about *The Exorcist* was so scary that it made me believe in monsters—how people can be possessed by dark forces they can't control. Art is the medicine the monster produces while trying to survive the labyrinth. When he or she is set free, the story is told and made human. Louie would squeeze past me and gently put his hands on my shoulders, like a good dad. He was out of the labyrinth and my thread was no longer.

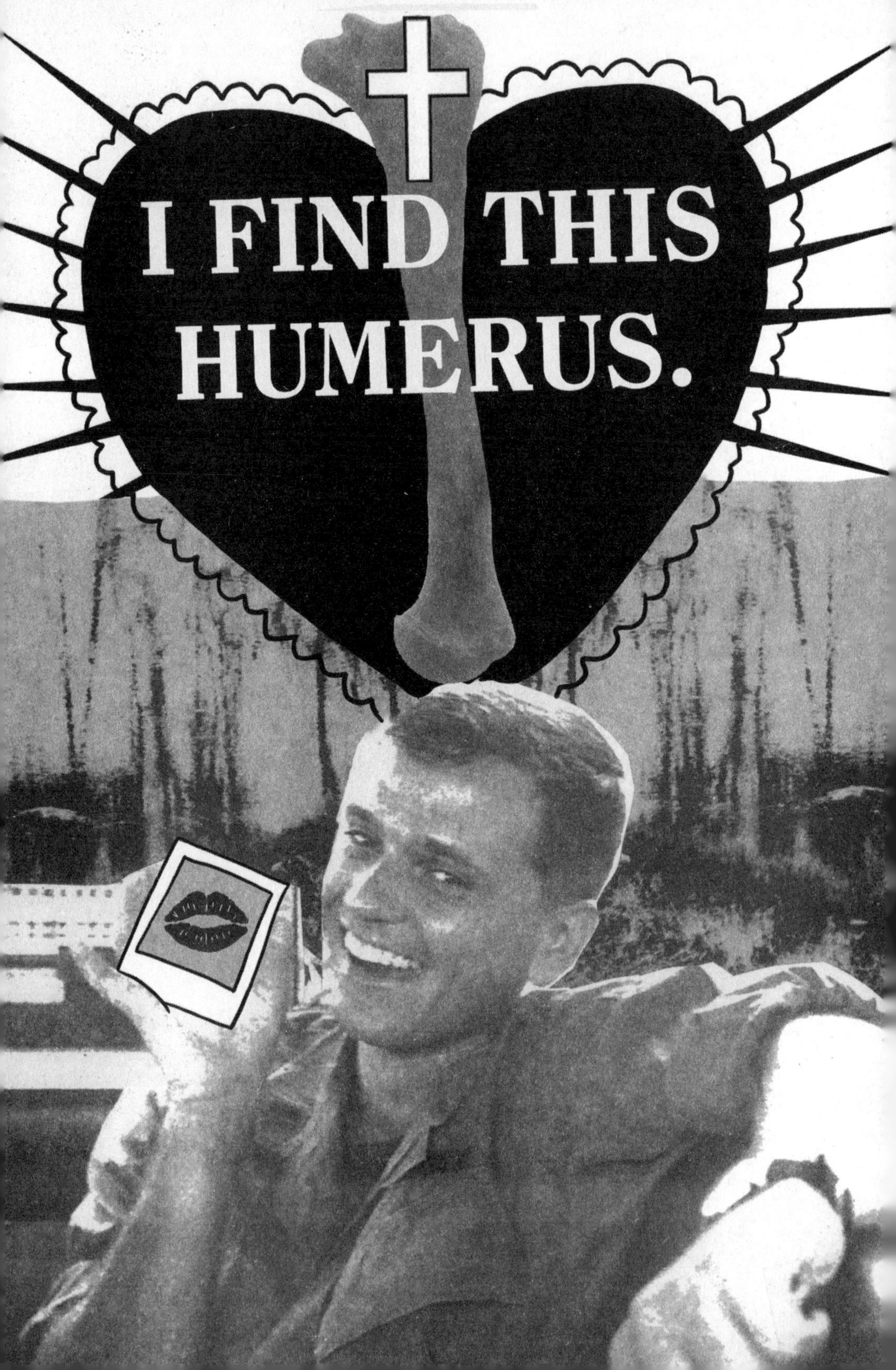
I FIND THIS
HUMERUS.

12

Dad and the Stage

I have a black-and-white picture of my dad in Vietnam, where he's sitting by a window and holding a photograph of my mom up to the camera. He's laughing or mocking the whole thing and angry underneath it all. A bullet going through his helmet, missing his head by centimeters, made him think, "Why would someone want to shoot me?" It didn't make sense to him, even though that's what war was, is. My uncle Tim, my mom's brother, was there at the same time and the news of his daughter Samantha's birth was radioed to him when he was in the line of fire, after he watched his fellow soldiers die in front of him. When he'd retell the story, he'd imitate the "krrrr" sound of the static on the radio . . . "Mr. Patton, *krrrr* . . . you have a baby girl . . . *krrrrr*." He makes a run for one of the barracks: "Congratulations, Mr. Patton, you're a father! Over and out! *Krrrrr*."

Whenever I heard a helicopter when I was playing outside, I got nervous. "Choppers," my dad called them, which made sense because the heavy sound would chop my heart's beat with its heavy vibration and the loud noise would shake the air. If it landed, the propellers would blow a wind so strong that it would stir up dirt that hit my eyes and almost knocked me over, like it did on the naval base in Baltimore when Nixon landed in the backyard and we all ran out to see him. My mom cried to the TV when all that shit went down but Walter Cronkite looked so comforting, like Santa Claus's brother. "Watergate" sounded like something magical in the backyard.

My dad brings the "never met a stranger" phrase to a whole other level. I've met people on the sidewalks in New York who say they had a great time with my dad on a flight or in a restaurant somewhere—they go out of their way to tell me this. He's so charismatic and seductive that he once gave an impromptu chiropractic adjustment to someone he'd just met at a business party, in San Diego. No, he's not a professional chiropractor, he was a car salesman. He got that lady to lie on a table so he could crack her neck. When we saw her rubbing her neck, looking like she was in pain as she walked to her husband, we tiptoed, running, out of there. When he'd try to sell a new car to a potential buyer, he'd put a fake poopy diaper in the trunk to "break the ice"—that kind of shit. He could sell ice to water.

Once I fell off a pier in the bayou and he pulled me out of the water by my ponytail. He'd forgotten I knew how to swim. I stepped directly over a boa constrictor in the funnel of a swimming pool when I was five. My dad stood at the end of the pool, saying, "Come directly to me, directly to *me*." He was intense and frustrated but whether or not he was angry with me, I couldn't tell. When I made it out of the pool, he ran to me and scooped me up and pointed to the snake—which even curled up was bigger than my body.

Another time, we went deep-sea fishing in Florida, on a giant boat, and when I got seasick he said, "Come on, let's throw up," and he took me by the hand and then grabbed my ankles and turned me upside down over the water to vomit, shouting names of foods that he thought would make me sick: "Eggs! Rotten hamburger meat! Sardines! Hog's head cheese!" I ate hog's head cheese once, for a dollar, and to impress him.

I drifted out of my body over the water. It gave me an aerial view of the scene: the fast-moving boat, the crashing waves, the gorgeous water spewing into my face. It was both exhilarating and terrifying and when I landed back on my feet, everyone clapped. This was the year *Jaws* came out and even if you hadn't seen the movie, you knew the theme song; kids would imitate it—"buuuum bum, buuuum bum, buuuum bum"—pointing their elbows up out of the water like a shark's fin and then ducking to swim under to pinch you. The older kids would run from the water and scream, "Shark! Shark!" pointing at the ocean and scaring the crap out of us. It was the summer I learned to put meat tenderizer on jellyfish stings, when a lifeguard rescued me—the summer when "everybody was kung fu fighting."

When I was five, my dad was shooting hoops in the driveway, and I walked out of the house with a cigarette.

"What are you doing?" he said.

"I'm smoking," I replied.

"Smoking's bad for you," he said.

"Well, you do it," I said.

I'll never forget how animated he was when he took his cigarette pack out of his pocket, walked to the garbage, and exclaimed, "Now I don't!" and threw them away. He made a big show of it and I knew this was a performance, that he'd get the cigarettes out of the garbage once I went back inside.

When Dad went to work, my brother and I had a routine where we'd chase him out the door saying, "Daddy, where are you going?" And he'd say, "CRAZY! Wanna go?" And we'd all do a crazy dance and be silly for him. He liked to ask, "What if you never got any taller? What if you just stayed the same size?" His face held a ponderous and sincere question—deadpan. He called us "the yard apes" because we were always climbing trees. When monkeys would come on the television he'd say, "Missy, Tophy! You're on TV," and we'd act like monkeys, climbing on him, and he'd throw us high into the air.

My dad told us so many stories, and I wasn't sure if they were true or not, and it didn't matter then. He told us that there was a tiny repairman, Mr. Manny, who worked inside the TV. When we were five or six, my father drove me to his house. A woman answered the door and I asked for Mr. Manny. She said she was his wife and that he wasn't available, that he was asleep inside his matchbox. I was too shy and stunned to ask anything else, like how she could be married to a man who was so small and did he really ride on record-player needles for fun and did he fix telephones? Did he know the little people that lived in the bookshelves on *Captain Kangaroo*? How did he make himself so small that he could go inside the TV? Because I really wanted to go there.

Another of my dad's favorite stories was about how we were made. "Well, God made you out of clay," he'd say, and then he'd start to mime this. He'd roll the invisible clay between his palms and "show" us an invisible tiny ball between his index finger and thumb. "God rolled a piece of clay in his hands to make a ball for your head." I was mesmerized since he was a good mime. "Then for your legs"— he'd rub his palms together, smoothly and gently—"he took more clay. And the same for your arms and fingers . . ." He'd place the invisible parts on a surface, for us to "see." He could really rearrange reality.

Another thing he could do was make other peoples' warts go away by rubbing them; he said it came from his Indian blood.

In kindergarten, the teacher asked us to tell the class what our fathers did for a living. My brother raised his hand and said, "My dad was an Indian a hundred years ago." This wasn't true; he was a salesman at the Van-Trow Cadillac dealership owned by his uncle (Granny's brother), Truman Van Veckhoven, who went by "Van," and his friend Toby Trowbridge. Van was a self-made man who never finished high school; he played golf and ate at the country club. He shouted "Ketchup!" when there wasn't any on the table, and was so charming that everyone laughed. He said things like, "Life is a pier and you walk down it like you own it." He invented his life and then died of a heart attack on the golf course after he told a joke; he died laughing. I don't know a better exit. I had another uncle, who died in a bathtub (after a heart attack) with a prostitute, before I was born. Bravo! Bravo to both of them.

My dad's father figures were his uncle Van, William Faulkner, Bob Dylan, Catholic priests, and God, the Father. And Atticus Finch from *To Kill a Mockingbird*. Who didn't want Gregory Peck as Atticus Finch for a father?

We had a nightly prayer, my brother and I, that started with "I love you, Jesus, help me be better tomorrow" and then asked God to bless our family. We ended the prayer by saying, "And help Father handle his job." When I was old enough to understand the real situation, my parents told me that we were praying for Father Rogers. The whole time I thought Dad couldn't handle his job, but Father Rogers was a priest in the parish and was having trouble getting through the sermons sober. He was cool and we all loved him.

I had some sweet nuns as teachers, but I had a mean kindergarten teacher named Mrs. Sweet. She once grabbed my brother by the arm and pointed a finger in his face for playing tackle instead of touch football. I marched over to her and pointed *my* finger in *her* face and said, "No one talks to my brother that way," and got sent to the principal's office. Sister Mary-Louise called my mom, who was so touched that she cried.

In first grade, Sister Mercedes was our teacher and she was truly sweet. On Fridays, we would line up from shortest to tallest and walk down the hallway on our way to Mass. The girls would reach into the cabinets for bobby pins and round black doily veils to pin to the top of our heads. We'd walk very slowly, "heel toe, heel toe, heel toe," focusing on our hands tight in prayer and standing up straight, as tall as we could make ourselves. I'd occupy this time by feeling guilty that Jesus was nailed on the cross and there was nothing I could do about it; the spooky organ music could be heard while we made our way through the cafeteria—grades two through six lined up behind us. Ash Wednesday was the most intense and ceremonious. "Remember, man, that you are dust and unto dust you shall return," the priest droned as he made a cross out of ash with his thumb on each of our foreheads. It was cool to keep the ash on your head as long as possible and the mood was extra somber and intense on that day—that was "the look." Classes were lax and we had more playtime to be morbid. "We're all going to die anyway" is fun on a playground.

Jesus was my first crush. How could he not have been? In those days, I tried to see him. As it got dark, I'd sit in my bedroom, on the floor and against my bed, far enough from the window to see a reflection in the glass if he should appear. I'd watch the lamp in the window's reflection get brighter or more clear as the sun went down. I never saw Jesus and I was sad about that.

My dad comes up to New York to Sloan Kettering for his prostate cancer that he's had for more than twenty years from the Agent Orange in Vietnam. He flies up here on a private plane owned by an industrial chicken farm that flies patients out of goodwill and because they can afford to. Last time he was here, he told me his doctor called him a "drama king" and I told him I think she meant "drama queen." He persuaded his neurologist to come to the hotel and have a drink with all of us (me, my mom, her brother Jimmy, and my aunt Catherine) and even got the doctor to remove the bow tie he was wearing because it was too uptight. Like a king, he wanted to arrange a marriage, and like a queen, I wasn't having it.

Part II
As the World Turns

13

Dazed / "Sweet Emotion"

I was a fan of Rick Linklater's before we shot *Dazed and Confused* — we all called it *Dazed*. He made the movie *Slacker*, the seminal Generation X movie, and no one had seen characters like these in movies before. Nothing seemed to happen in the film, because there wasn't a real plot, but if you were the black sheep, or the white sheep, or the "weird cousin" in your family who wasn't conforming to what everyone else was doing but was instead philosophizing about how weird everything was, then you could've been in *Slacker*.

I got a call from my agent at the time, Brian Swardstrom, who said Rick was casting a movie he was directing about kids in high school in 1976. I was excited about it; the nineties had a seventies counterculture nostalgia and I already had platforms and bell-bottoms of my own to wear. I was also really young, twenty-four, and confident.

Don Phillips was the casting director for *Dazed*, and he'd cast *Fast Times at Ridgemont High* and was a character; so much so that he was made into one in David Rabe's play *Hurlyburly*, which I ended up acting in years later. Eddie was his character's name; the one with the heart and coke problem. Don is pretty special—they broke the mold when they made him. A good casting director is like the vibrant aunt or uncle to a film, or maybe even more so the godfather, since they're the ones with connections to the agents. If your agent and the casting director have some vendetta between them, then you don't even get "into the room" with the Don.

I belonged in the room and had the right attitude. I remembered the seventies really well because I looked forward to growing up when I was little and still loved the music. We talked a lot about music in that first meeting. Rick said a lot of the budget was going toward getting the rights for songs like Bob Dylan's "Hurricane" and Aerosmith's "Sweet Emotion," and most everyone knows the title of the movie is taken from the Led Zeppelin song. I told them I wanted to play Darla, the main hazer, because I wanted to be a bad girl. I wasn't one in high school but loved Rizzo in *Grease* and that's what they said the Darla part was akin to. My aunt Peggy had some hazing stories, which I told them about—like having to swallow oysters knotted together by dental floss, only to have them pulled out of her stomach by one of the seniors. There were the Farrah twins, from back home, who'd keyed some cars of ex-boyfriends in high school, which I thought was crazy and pitched the idea, I guess. None of us, or at least none that I could remember, were rich kids; we were all more likely to have grown up around Harleys and good music.

So, they flew me to Los Angeles for callbacks and that's where I met Joey Lauren Adams, who played Simone; and Deena Martin, the blonde in the movie who could barely zip her jeans, who had lived around the corner from me in Chelsea; and Marissa Ribisi, who played Cynthia, and liked to sew and make things. We all hung out. Anthony Rapp played Tony, who was best friends with Adam Goldberg's character, Mike Newhouse. Marissa would be their best gal pal and she was already sporting a cute red 'fro. Nicky Katt played Clint, Adam's nemesis in the movie, and I'd meet his mom later that year. She had a parrot and was a free spirit living in

California. After we were cast, Rick sent us all mixtapes of the music he wanted in the movie. I still have it somewhere. I think it starts with "Cherry Bomb."

Dazed shot in Austin and we all stayed in that hotel by the bridge next to the Four Seasons—I forget the name of the place, but now it's something else anyway. I was on *As the World Turns* at the time, fresh from dropping out of college after three and a half years on probation, mainly for a bad attitude because I didn't like rehearsing scenes, preferring instead to wing it. I had a lazy attitude for things I didn't feel were important, like circus class. I didn't have the guts to be a real clown and already knew how to juggle. I skipped class to clown around and kept my probation letters in the freezer, for some reason—an act of self-preservation, maybe.

There were around twenty of us in that hotel in Austin, and for the first two weeks of rehearsals and cast bonding I was hardly ever there because I was doing the soap. I'd gotten cast in *World Turns* on April Fools' the year before, so I flew back and forth several times. It made sense for the character anyway, since she was a bad girl with a rough upbringing, I decided. She made her friends do things they'd regret the next day, like drink too much and say something they wished they hadn't—or go to the drugstore and swap the hair dye in the boxes, or put Ex-Lax in a batch of brownies, or Nair her dad's hairy back while he was passed out, drunk. She was one of those "my feelings are facts" people—one of those drama queens.

If she and her best friend, Simone, weren't on-screen for the party, they were in the woods, kickin' it with the older crowd. Joey and I wrote a casual scene where we were squatting in the woods to relieve ourselves but it was shot wrong; they were supposed to fake that our pants were down but you could see that they weren't. I don't remember if there was a scene with one of the guys going in the woods but we'd never seen a girl go (in a movie) and of course we had in real life. Joey and I were best friends for a while and we both had strong father figures, which makes girls more like tomboys and less like girly-girls.

She lived in LA and liked building things, like a platform for her bed and a swing that hung from the ceiling in her living room. The vibe was Topanga Canyon–like and she'd helped a boyfriend of hers build a shack there, so Joey knew her way around a hardware store. Joey's character was the girlfriend of Pink, played by Jason London; she's the pretty blonde who says, "Fry like bacon!" to the freshman girls as they shake on the ground. We were like sisters, and since neither of us had one, that was nice. We listened to Leonard Cohen with Rory Cochrane, who played Slater, and watched the bats come out from under the bridge at sunset. Chrissy Harnos, who played Kaye, would join, as would anyone else who was around. The hotel was like a dorm, really. We went dancing down Sixth Street on weekends, and ate Tex-Mex breakfasts early in the mornings after we wrapped. Typically, the girls hung with the girls and the guys with the guys. They shot guns at the firing range and we decorated our rooms with scarves from the thrift stores. Here's a bit of synchronicity: After Wiley Wiggins, who played Mitch (the younger kid whom Pink takes under his wing), finished working on Rick's animated film *Waking Life* (like eight years after *Dazed*), he worked as a troubleshooter for Apple. Jason London had just gotten a new Mac. Wiley answered the phone—"Hello, I'll be your helper, this is Wiley"—and Jason goes into his software troubles and Wiley's like, "Jason, is this you? Jeremy's twin brother? *Dazed and Confused* Jason?" And they're both like "What?!" It's all connected, man, cheers. Come on and take a free ride, yeah yeah yeah yeah yeah.

There was an actor in the film you may have heard of, named Matthew McConaughey? Well, we were a few weeks into production when I flew in and went straight to work from the airport for an all-night shoot. Jean Black was our makeup artist and there were Polaroids of some of the actors taped to the makeup mirror. What can I say but wow? This Polaroid of Matthew was freaking great: Ted Nugent meets daredevil Evel Knievel and just as gorgeous as Jesus Christ. We died. Jean had her arms in the air like she was the next contestant on *The Price Is Right*, like a Baptist taken by the Holy Spirit, and we screamed with laughter at how genius his whole look was. *That* guy, yes! I got made up as quickly as possible and went straight to set to meet him in person. I asked Rick if I could stand outside the pool hall for Wooderson's entrance into the party scene. The scene was set to Bob Dylan's "Hurricane" and I loved that song. I listened to all his albums as a kid—my love for Bob Dylan's music was one of the best things my father gave me. We'd talk about the stories of those songs and I'd sit on the floor, close to the record player, and listen to his albums repeatedly, holding and pressing those huge padded headphones to my ears, though they were too big for my head. "Hurricane" is about an African-American boxer named Rubin "Hurricane" Carter, wrongly accused and convicted of murder. It's almost nine minutes long and a masterpiece. Oh man, I'm such a fan of Bob Dylan. Well, I guess it's just something you have to grow up with.

Rick's laid-back. He's from Texas and lives in Austin. He's charming and nice, and he's a dude's dude, a sports guy, and a dad and the real deal as a filmmaker. So, yeah, I ran to set and asked him if he could throw me into the scene and he said yes. I introduced myself to McConaughey and explained Darla real quick—that she grew up with older brothers in a broken home and is tough but fun. We rolled soon after and when he and his posse strolled in, he came into the joint and slapped my ass and said, "Hey, Darla." That's what guys did back then, and in those days, it was a compliment.

I called my agent Brian right away and told him he had to sign this guy, that he was going to be huge star, but he didn't listen. I see Brian every few years and mention McConaughey so we can share a rueful moment.

Wrapping *Dazed* was bittersweet and the experience gave me the meaning of the word. It was the high school we felt we belonged in. When we weren't working we watched the other actors and everyone was just so good. I'm thinking now of Adam Goldberg and Nicky Katt during their fight scene, the shot of Jason London looking around when he was on the football field at the end and the music that made it all what it was. Rick called the music another character in the movie but it was the soul.

In 2003, there was a ten-year reunion for *Dazed* in Austin, and around twenty of us from the cast were there. It was a trip, and a few thousand people showed up. Joey hit the mic with "Fry like bacon" and I shouted out "Air raid!" McConaughey breezed onstage and everyone flipped out. The screening was in a park and people brought blankets to sit on and partied with the movie; some even stood up to dance when a song came on.

We all sat clumped together on the grass and there was one scene, of Mike and Tony and Cynthia getting out of their car, that had a boom mic in the reflection of the windshield. I looked over at Rick, who noticed it as well, and ran over to him. He was laughing and said, "I made a drive-in movie!" like it had just occurred to him. The extreme close-up of the keg was especially funny, as people got on their feet to cheer at it.

Rick was in New York in early 2016 for his "spiritual sequel" to *Dazed*, called *Everybody Wants Some!!* I was invited to the premiere by the publicists, and they put me down as one of the hosts. I walked the twenty minutes it took to get there, in the fast stride that the early spring gives you. I caught up with Rick for a few minutes and said hi to Ethan Hawke, who was there to introduce the movie. After posing for some pictures, Ethan said, "You should come onstage with me," and I said something like, "I would start talking and then say too much."

I walked over to the after-party, which was in a small Mexican restaurant on the Lower East Side, with David Cross joining me, who's always been too cool for school. I met Maria Semple almost immediately when I got there. Rick's new movie, *Where'd You Go, Bernadette*, is based on her book. My agent had been "pursuing the project," "chasing it," "tracking it." Making sure I was "on everyone's radar." I ordered a drink and was eating the chicken quesadilla and nachos that were sitting on the bar. She asked me what I was work-ing on, and I said, "Other career options, new media ideas, new forms, courage, a positive attitude, gratitude." I told her I loved her script, and how rare it was to read something where the characters feel like you and your friends. She was super nice and said I was on the list of actresses to play the nemesis of Bernadette. I was more right for the lead, I told her, but knew how the system worked. She mingled away after that, which was a defeat to my bad attempts at mingling. You can't be direct while mingling because that's not what mingling is and I've never been good at it.

I got pulled over by the publicist to take a photograph with Rick in front of a mural of McConaughey, airbrushed onto a brick wall. He was leaning against his car, as Wooderson, and Rick and I leaned against the wall to join him there. After the shots, Rick asked what I was working on, which is the same as "How are you?" in showbiz-speak. I said, "Other career options, gratitude, courage . . ." I felt like crying, for so many different reasons, and sensed he caught a tinge of the particular pain that comes with love or nostalgia. He has nice, kind eyes. "Aw, Parkey," he said. "I hope we get to work together again."

During my walk home, I found "Sweet Emotion" on my iPhone and wished I still had my Rollerblades. There's no better intro to a song. Where did those Rollerblades go? Did they leave without me?

We're cruising at the right altitude to take our seat belts off.

14

Southern Gothic

When I was a baby, I'd calm myself down by rocking back and forth on my stomach for several minutes at a time. Years later, I'd take a kundalini class and do that same thing but for ten minutes; it's called Bow Pose, and it keeps your energy flowing. Kundalini yoga is the one where they wear all white and sport turbans and get high on breathing. They reach this blissed-out state by doing lots of "breath of fire"—where you hold one nostril closed with your ring finger and breathe four times (focusing on the out breath) and then do the other nostril—pushing your belly in sharp, like a punch, and forcing your breath out to the count of four. It's like alternating leg lifts with each of your nostrils and it's not pretty. But rocking through Bow Pose as a baby helped me process what I'd been through, what with being born and all. Looking back at that time, it was preparation for when I'd be able to stand up to deliver my first performance. I'd work myself up so much, crying and shaking, that I'd stiffen my body and clench my fists at my side, like rigor mortis. These fits were simply entitled "rigors" by my parents, and when company came over, I'd perform them. It was up to me how long they lasted, but everyone knew that when I'd bite my own arm that the show was over. And then there would be applause. So, that's when I started performing, age two going on three. It's sad to think it was some of my best work.

The whole family would join in on the show: Paw Paw would take his teeth out (which brought the house down), and Nonnie, over at Lovers Lane, would get on the floor and do one of her tricks, like hike up her pencil skirt and pull her leg up to wrap her ankle around her head. She didn't know this show-stopping trick was the yoga pose called Eka Pada Sirsasana. If you have trouble pronouncing words that sound like a sneeze, you can call it Foot-Behind-the-Head Pose. I can do this one, too. Did you know that "yoga" is Sanskrit for "look what I can do"? That's my friend Jason's joke.

Glenn, my grandfather, taught me how to whistle with my fingers—it's good for hailing a cab and I think of him when I do. Nonnie could spit through her saliva glands. I don't know how she did this. I've tried and am bummed that I didn't get this gene, but she'd stick her tongue to the roof of her mouth and then a muscle would somehow activate and spit would fly out, like a spray from a water gun. We begged her to do this trick all the time, but she wouldn't often oblige, because it wasn't very *ladylike*. When she did, she'd excuse herself afterward, as we applauded and screamed. She'd come back into the living room while we were still clapping, like any professional actor returning for an encore. We called my uncle Jimmy "Uncle Eyeballs" because he could flip the tops of his eyelids up, and keep them there, and still look at us. He'd also get his teeth cleaned by asking one of Nonnie's Yorkies to clean them: "Benji! Teddy! Lick my teeth!" And they would stick their tongues in his mouth for a full-on session. He was also very gifted at making fart noises under his armpits—various kinds of noises. My brother inherited this gene, and when he does it, he'll call out things like "French horn" or "question mark" or "silent but deadly." When *Hee Haw* came on the television, the entire family knew we could upstage anyone on that show, were we ever called upon to do so. It was a tough house and we felt good, watching it all together, because we knew that we had better material.

My dad says that as a child I reminded him of Stan Laurel of Laurel and Hardy. He refers to a time when my brother and I were in the bathtub and he heard a scream. When he came in, Chris had a bite mark in the middle of his back. When Dad asked if I'd bitten him, I said no and stared deadpan at him, like Stan Laurel. I almost got to be in a movie about Laurel and Hardy as wife to John C. Reilly's Oliver Hardy. John and I met on *The Anniversary Party* and he knows all the words to *Jesus Christ Superstar,* as do I, so we rocked out in my room at the Chateau Marmont—"Must die, must die, this Jesus must, Jesus must, Jesus must die!" I love that guy and would have loved to have played his wife on-screen, but I got *Lost in Space* and wasn't available.

When I was four, I left the bathtub, completely naked, to knock on the neighbor's door for a visit. I loved hanging around old people's homes and perching myself on their armchairs or sitting on their kitchen counters. That was my vibe. There was a single lady who lived next door and was pretty, with long dark hair and a tiny poodle named JoJo. When JoJo was sick, my neighbor would crunch up a white pill and put it in the center of an Oreo cookie to feed him. I thought that was cool, being a single woman with a poodle. I've had Gracie for fourteen years and as much as she would love an Oreo cookie, she doesn't get one. I'll give her the occasional Tic Tac though—mint. She likes mint.

My first time on a real stage came when I was almost eight, at a camp called Strong River in Mississippi. The counselors picked me to come up with a show, or "presentation," really. I made up something about Little Red Riding Hood uncovering the case of Goldilocks and the Three Bears. Telly Savalas from the show *Kojak* was my muse, and I walked onstage with a red tablecloth wrapped around my head and a Tootsie Pop, saying, "Who loves ya, baby?" That was Kojak's trademark, and when everyone laughed I remember thinking, "This isn't funny. I am a detective." I maintained character and waited a few beats for the laughter to die down and then went on with my next line.

I'd take the stage seriously when I was nine and started ballet. It was expensive and I was glad my dad could swing it. I couldn't tap-dance on our wooden floors but there was some tile in front of the fireplace on which I could "shuffle off to Buffalo" or "shuffle, ball change." It could be annoying for my parents so it was best to wait until I was alone. I couldn't be bothered to count in order to learn the routine for the recital, so I was sure to be close to the wings to shuffle-ball-change my way offstage. I only really cared about the tumble routine to the *Star Wars* theme that year, anyway. The following year, my teacher Ms. Linda and her assistant held auditions for chorus dancers in the company's production of *Coppélia*. Ms. Linda was both elegant and strict, and when I auditioned, I looked directly at them, which made them laugh. She said, "The audience is in the mirror, behind us. You can't look directly at us!"

My mom was there, too, standing to the side of the room when Ms. Linda told her I had charisma, and when I asked what that was, Ms. Linda said it was talent. I was relieved to be called something that was good since I was a devoted daydreamer and adults often interpreted this as meaning I was developmentally challenged. My parents had had some doctor come over to look at my brother and me when we were two, who said we were going to be "retarded" and to hold us back a year in school. My parents laughed their heads off when they repeated this, because the doctor was quite the character and they thought he was out of his mind. I don't remember him at all, but my "rigors" made them wonder. Everyone knew I came out half-baked or undercooked and should've stayed in longer, so maybe there *was* something wrong with me. But everyone enjoyed the rigors and I enjoyed performing them, so there you have it. That doctor was a dork.

I spaced out in grammar school, so much so that my dad went so far as to attach jingle bells to my notepad so I wouldn't forget to write down my homework. This embarrassed me, but so had my red cloth shoes at kindergarten graduation, which stood out from the suggested, but not mandatory, expensive white patent leather shoes that all the other girls were wearing. The red shoes were cuter because they had flowers on them, and since they were cloth, I could wear them again. My mother could make things beautiful.

The night before first grade, I slept in my uniform. Up until that point, I'd just worn my own clothes to school and was excited to wear the jumper, like it was a costume. In second grade, I wanted to lie on the vision test so I could get some eyeglasses, as a prop. My parents started to think I might have a learning disability so they got me tested at the college in Monroe. I colored with the ladies who ran the program, who said I was creative and there was nothing wrong with me.

Ms. Linda accepted me into the ballet company, which meant I could go on pointe by age eleven. I danced *Coppélia* for the recital, putting on my own makeup and false eyelashes like Nonnie did, and like my mother did to me on that first day home from the hospital, on the army base in Baltimore. I made the local paper at age eleven when a Turkish man named Tanju Tuzer came to teach a three-week class. He was gorgeous and graceful and had body odor, which made him stand out even more, in my mind, as someone "serious." We made the paper together. In the picture, I'm pointing in tendu, and Tanju Tuzer is holding my hand, and the girls in the background look intense and focused and maybe jealous because he'd singled me out to Ms. Linda as having talent and promise.

We had to move the next year, though, because Dad got an offer from Uncle Van to have his own dealership. I got my first slip that year, when I was twelve, which made my mother cry. I wore it under a dress for our going-away party. I also wore her sandals, which were a half size too big, but it was fine because I took them off to dance around in the backyard as the boys played football. At one point, I said, "Well, I can do *this*," and grand jeté'd through their game.

We left Indian Mound Road and the house with the empty carpeted room off the dining room area. John Lennon had died the

previous December, and I'd been glad to be alone in that house to listen to his song "Woman," which played repeatedly on the radio. I cried without any knowledge of what a woman was, but I'd seen pictures of Yoko Ono and she was almost an adjective in my mind for someone who was different. Blondie's song "Rapture"—"I said don't stop, to punk rock." We left Monroe in a packed station wagon, as two dogs humped in our neighbor, Maw Maw's yard. I was hold-ing our new poodle, B.B., and Dad said "Cover B.B.'s eyes! Don't look at that" and we laughed as we cried, as I tried to cover her eyes.

We were moving to Laurel, Mississippi, a quaint, old Southern town, much smaller than Monroe, that still had the provincial *Gone with the Wind*–ness of the Old South niceties, where "Don't you look cute" sounded to me like that was all that was expected. It was a town where you *had* to belong to a church, and being Catholic was weird to other Christians because we worshipped Mary, drank wine that we called "the blood of Jesus," and also ate his body in the form of a wafer cracker. People in the town took their religion so seriously that there was an ongoing "my church is better than your church" drama. There were forty-one Baptist churches, and the two most popular ones, Highland and First Baptist, had competing bumper stickers. "I found it at Highland," and, touché, "I never lost it at First Baptist." Found what? Lost what, exactly? In seventh grade, there was a rumor that the magnetic strip on the back of credit cards was a code written by the devil. The girl that told us this was freaked out and pleaded with us to tell our parents not to use credit cards because they would go to hell. She had no idea then that she was a burgeon-ing anticapitalist—now she was just a homewrecker.

My dad took my brother to a KKK meeting when we moved to Laurel because he wanted to show Chris how crazy it was. I had wanted to see the idiots, as my father called them, but I was a girl and he didn't want me there. I was a ballerina at this point and this town was breaking my vibe.

One of the churches in town had a Christmas pageant, and God flew in a carpenter/actor from Florida to play Jesus. The minister's wife ran away with him after the show, so she got saved finally. She found it, and was no longer lost. I think as the story goes they lived happily ever after in the hair salon they shared together in Florida.

That summer—the summer we moved—Tanju Tuzer suggested I apply for a six-week summer ballet class with the University of North Carolina School of the Arts ballet company. I got in and had the time of my life the following summer. I auditioned to enroll as a full-time student but didn't make the cut. My dad knew I'd be devastated so he called the dean to ask him what he should tell me and he said, "Tell her she's an actress." I think the dean was called Dean Irby and

he said I'd almost gotten in based on my personality. When Dad told me this, I was shy about these ambitions because I didn't want to upstage my family, and being a professional actress, I invariably would. My dad was the star of the show, always. He'd do things like place a fart machine under the seats at check-in at the airport and we'd wait for reactions when it sounded off. His performances were nonstop. He'd introduce himself afterwards and make small talk with strangers—sometimes they laughed and sometimes they didn't.

I'd go back to Laurel, where I starred in *Little House on the Prairie* in my living room, opposite the television set. I'd seen many episodes, and when Melissa Gilbert cried, I cried along with her. I could almost guess the dialogue. My mom and I loved to watch *Mommie Dearest* together. We got the "camp" of it and would imitate it for fun. "Clean up this mess, Christina!" "That's *just* like my mother!" she'd say, and we'd laugh.

I liked when my parents would go out on a date so I could be alone and put on this black lace turn-of-the-century dress that I'd gotten in a secondhand store in New Orleans. It was like something Madame Defarge, from *A Tale of Two Cities*, would wear, the knitting old crone in her rocker who knew all the details of the tragedy. Or Miss Havisham from *Great Expectations*, another great part. The dress had holes in it and smelled like cat urine. I washed it in my bathroom sink, which made the water turn brown, and the smell never left, but I wore it anyway and played depressing music on my record player and cried. That was my idea of fun. I'd put ice in the sink to wash my face and then get into bed to read or write a letter, or watch *Pee-wee's Playhouse* on a recorded VHS tape in the TV room. I have no idea what happened to that dress.

I opened the door of a moving car once when I was around eight. I was in the car with my dad, sitting in the back with my brother and his friend. We were just going around the corner from our house, so my dad wasn't driving that fast. I simply opened the door, swung my feet out of the car, and held on to the handle, like I was water-skiing on the pavement. I don't remember why I did it, but I remember thinking I could put a stop to whatever the stress or noise was if I just opened the door and stepped out. It didn't last longer than a few seconds and Dad slowed the car down enough for me to coast. He was laughing when I got back in. "*Why did you do that?!*" I shrugged and looked down at the burned rubber on my sneakers. The tracks on the bottom of my shoes had worn down and I felt the loss of them with my fingers; the smoothness and heat of them made me smile. "And you hip-hop and you don't stop."

I stood under a tree in the rain and thought about lightning striking me and fantasized about being kidnapped. Maybe it was just me or a child-of-the-seventies kind of thing, or the simple kid drama of wanting to be special. Patty Hearst was kidnapped and I was too young to be afraid or to see it as something *real.* To me, she was a woman in a car being whisked away. It must've resonated with that early Catholicism and her being a fabulous martyr cast out by her father and left alone to suffer in her outlaw state. She wore a beret.

There was a pervert who had a kids' show. His name was Mr. Wonder, of all things, and he molested kids. My parents rolled their eyes at his name while gritting their teeth in anger. And there was Mrs. Banks, some bat-shit day-care woman who chased kids around with flyswatters to whack 'em with, when they were just playing. She had some cultlike nap regimen where we'd drink red or purple Kool-Aid and go to our mats and nap, even if we weren't tired. My brother told my mom about it and we didn't go back; I think we were four or something. It was the beginning, I guess, of not liking banks or being good with money. A few years later, Jim Jones had Kool-Aid and people drank it and died.

I had a crush on John McEnroe as a kid. When I saw him get so upset on the tennis court, it pulled my very heart. I wanted to make him laugh or bring him something I'd made, like a rock with the word "Jesus" painted on it. I prayed for him.

My cousin Samantha and I would get out a sleeve of Ritz crackers and play Mass, getting all serious and somber while staring at each other, a Ritz cracker held up with our fingers: "Take this, all of you, and eat it. This is my body, which will be given up to you and to all men so that sins may be forgiven. Do this"—pause—"in memory of me." And then we'd rock out playing the *Jesus Christ Superstar* album and singing and acting our hearts out. "My mind is clearer now. At last, all too well, I can see where we all soon will be . . ."

When the locusts came and dried out on the trees, we'd unstick them to decorate our shirts and even our hair like crowns and jewelry; the roughness of their skeletons made it easier to stick to us—the legs were slimmer than a toothpick, a few strands thicker than a hair. We'd take the tails off fireflies and stick them to our fingers to make rings, marrying the fireflies. When it flooded, we played in the ditches. The boys rode bikes in the water and popped wheelies, or up and down the mounds, not ten feet above the bayou. And all this was ten minutes from our house. I'd sit on top of the mound to watch them ride while I dug in the dirt to find the clay, a patch or swirl of smooth in the dirt. If the locusts came again, I would still put them in my hair and on my clothes and say to passersby, "The end is nigh."

THE END IS NIGH.

15
Sacrifice

I wouldn't give my right arm to work with Woody Allen so I gave my right wrist. I broke it three weeks after being cast in *Irrational Man*. When the bone surgeon in the city came into the room I lifted my arm up like an opera diva, saying, "I got a big *break* being *cast* in the new Woody Allen film." He didn't think it was funny because he knew what was ahead. He would numb my arm out of existence in order to attach miniature door-hinge hardware with seven tiny screws to the tiny bones inside my wrist. This was two weeks before the camera tests and the pain was so severe that I stayed up through the night chomping the maximum number of Percocets prescribed and begged him for morphine the next morning. I told him I felt he betrayed me by not preparing me for the pain—that he tricked me. I asked him if he was sure he'd done it right because it felt like something was wrong.

He ignored my pitch of a morphine patch: "I'm sure they have one, right around the corner, at Bigelow pharmacy." I tried not to sound like I was begging, but it didn't help that I answered the phone with "I'm a *basket case* of pain."

"It was good we went in there," he said with a bedside manner.

"The break was a lot more complicated than we initially thought. An X-ray doesn't show the individual cracking of the bones. A cast might not have set it properly, so it's good we performed the surgery."

"Yeah, it's good we went in there," I said. I apologized for blaming him and he told me to take Aleve, along with the Percocets; we hung up and I ran to the bathroom to throw up.

The night before, my right arm had been dead but had come alive in the sensory map of my brain and made a double of itself where I'd feel my fingers caress my face—like babies do when they're sleepy and content. A soothing gesture that I've noticed my mother and I still make.

I broke my wrist in the house upstate. I'd starred in a Pepsi commercial with Jimmy Fallon that paid enough to get the mortgage. It was an old farmhouse that had been a sheep farm during the Underground Railroad days and had disappeared off the market but came back after the buyer wasn't able to sell his place in the Hamptons. I'd seen only two or three properties before it, none of which were right, and then I got a job I don't remember, and when I returned to my search, that's when I saw it. "I've seen this place before," I said when I walked in. My friend Jim had forwarded me the listing, saying it looked just like me, around six months before. It was Tatum O'Neal and John McEnroe's house, and I'd run into her over the years socially and ran into her again just days after signing the ownership contracts for the property. We ran smack into each other at a dosa place in Soho. We were shocked and both stumbled back and hugged, and when we parted we were both crying. She'd spent some sweet years up there with her family and was sad to let it go but was happy I was the one who'd bought it since I'd made her family laugh with the Christopher Guest movies. I was crying because I was grateful and dreamed of a country house in nature.

At the time I broke my wrist, the pipes had frozen and burst and flooded the first floor. It was one of those out-of-the-blue freezing nights and I didn't have a Nest device yet to sync up the heat but I have one now. My neighbor across the street, Wes, saw smoke coming out of the chimney and came to the rescue. He knew I wasn't home, that there was no one there. I don't know how smoke was coming out of the chimney; I guess it was an electrical fire? I have no idea, but it signaled. He always helped me if I needed it, and he loved the house since it had belonged to his great-grandfather. He found Gracie when she ran away a few times, once clawing her way through a window screen when she heard a gunshot during hunting season. My sweet little lamb, my little sheep (she's snoring now). So Wes brought a few of his contractor friends over to meet me. It was a true disaster, and I was in shock. I started to block out the things I'd miss, like my albums I'd had forever, now destroyed—especially the records that were probably impossible to find, like the Catholic folk parish band the Dameans. They were a band of five priests from New Orleans and they were really cute and their songs weren't spooky because they didn't use an organ. Their voices harmonized so well with one another. It was patriarchal good-dad, tree-hugger music because they'd include nature in the songs. The lyrics were something like "I know the Father loves me, for he told me in the rising sun. I know the Father will care for me, for he told me in the smile of a certain someone." There were holes in the house now, and a kitchen to be reconstructed, which broke my heart because I loved the one that was there already—hand-built by Bernard Springsteel, a previous owner before Tatum O'Neal and John McEnroe's family. He'd made it all in my bedroom, which was then his woodshop, with wood from the lumberyard just down the road. He made doors, cabinets, shelving—even the curtain-rod holders. His countertop would have to go and the cabinets were ruined, but the structure at least would remain intact. I left, leaving it up to the gods—and magically thinking the producers of this had a vision and supported the director and it would *all work out*. Contractors can be tricky, though, like actors. One simply bailed, but sent me a nice email saying, "I'm sure you're gonna be angry with me . . . ," but he had another job to do and was leaving for Vermont. I wasn't angry, I was inspired that a line of work could actually include getting paid for doing nothing and then apologizing with an email. I loved his bit, though, in the beginning, of the sweet uncle good ol' boy coming to the rescue. The other one had started hanging around but was unable to complete the simplest of tasks and was always complaining about other work that had caused him pain. He would ask things like, "You have anything stronger than Advil, like a Vicodin?" My friend noted that he went by three different aliases, which most likely meant shady business. At first I thought he was just so adored by three groups of friends that they all gave him special nicknames, but when I thought more deeply about it, having three names was probably a good idea for someone who needed people who didn't exist to put the blame on.

I painted the walls myself after the countertops were in. I was furious that I'd gotten screwed over, and my adrenaline was pumping as I flew around my kitchen with a roll of blue painter's tape on my arm, like a bangle bracelet. I'd whip the tape off the roll with my left hand and swiftly tear off a piece with my teeth, like a fruit bat, and place the length of it to its edge on the wall. Flying around like a maniac, I fell off the ladder while reaching for an edge.

Thank God my friend Jim was there. We'd been close for more than twenty years, and met at Georgetown, where my brother went to college, and danced together at a place called the Tombs. And by "danced," I mean silly dancing, dumb dancing—we really made each other laugh. Jim moved to New York in 2001, right after 9/11, thinking that life was too short not to fulfill that dream of living in a city he'd always wanted to live in. He had great luck finding an apartment right around the corner from me, in Chelsea. "I used to have this girlfriend known as Elsie, with whom I shared four sordid rooms in Chelsea."

I loved his place. If you could have taken his ceiling off and looked at the apartment from above, it would've been a perfect square. It reminded me of those pink compact plastic homes I played with when I was little that you could shut and carry around, like a suitcase. The layout was a perfect circle: open the front door, the bathroom is directly in front of you, to the left is the living room, to the right is the bedroom; walk through the bedroom and go left through the kitchen, then you're back in the living room.

My place was a railroad flat, which was falling apart: the bathroom had a big hole in the ceiling that rained down plaster every now and then. I covered it with a garbage bag and duct tape because it was better than dealing with the super, who I'm not sure I ever met. (I probably did but my instincts told me it was best to just deal with stuff myself.) I put in a loft bed with Keene, a high school friend of Nadia's. She has a good dad story, too. Nadia Dajani's an actress and she never knew her father but grew up with older brothers who were baseball fans—they were all latchkey kids in the West Village and her brothers would pick her up from school and and she'd do her homework on the train to Yankee Stadium, which she called her "childhood living room." She had a poster of the pitcher Ron Guidry in her bedroom growing up, and when she was around twelve, she wrote him fan letters and sent him birthday cards. At around fourteen, she got up the nerve to write to him, asking him to wait for her until she turned eighteen so they could get married. He sent her a small black-and-white photo, which in her mind meant yes. There was a bio released soon after, and she saved up her babysitting money to buy it and flipped to the pictures immediately at Barnes and Noble. She was crushed and started screaming, "No, no!" when she saw the pictures of him married and with a baby. She was madly in love and devastated. Anyway, her friend Liz invited her to a benefit gala for Camp Say, a summer program that raises money for kids who stutter, and it was there she met Brandon Guidry, who was on the board. She mentioned that it was funny that he had the surname of the man she was supposed to marry. "That's my father," he said.

"He's my password," she told him. "Your father's my password and when I travel I take a framed picture of him to put by my bed."

"Well, now I know your password, and he's here."

Brandon brought her over and Ron called her darlin' when they met. She told him they were supposed to be married and his wife

laughed. Brandon became like another one of Nadia's surrogate siblings and invited her down to Lafayette, Louisiana, for New Year's,
where Mr. Ron would say, "Make yourself comfortable here, eat
what you want, there's food in the fridge and make yourself at home."
She'd be floating in the uncanny realness of the events that brought
her to Ron's home, and when she was asleep in one of his huge guest
rooms it would only dawn on her after he knocked on her door in the
morning, saying, "You have a thirty-minute warning to get ready for
brunch," that it was all *real*. She'd hear his heavy footsteps walk
down the plush carpet of the hall, away from her, and take that mys-
tical moment to her heart. Nadia lived close to me in Chelsea, in the
West Village, in a building she called a "witch's hat" because of the
pointed cone on top.

I was living on the second floor with a fire escape railing outside
my bedroom/living room not twenty feet off the ground. I could
easily ask one of the guys in the McManus bar to boost me up if I'd
locked myself out, which I'd done a few times. I was so close to the
sidewalk that I'd wake up thinking I had guests in my apartment,
but it would just be people talking on the bench of the beauty shop
directly below. Every few years a neighbor would play "Red Red
Wine" on her boom box repeatedly for hours. It wasn't a conventional home and felt more like a sleeve or a place I could be tiny in.
A friend said my paint choices were tonally "Easter egg"—light blue
and yellow walls, lavender trim, and a cream line for the molding.

I hover around the idea of a conventional home and I think that's
why I fell.

I knew my wrist was broken because it looked like an upside-down
ankle and because it hurt. I was a brave and calm soldier, like Brody
in *Homeland*, who came to mind immediately since I'd been binge-
watching the show. "Jim, there is a Vicodin stash in the first-aid kit
in the downstairs bathroom," I said. "Get me one and take one if you

want." I squeezed and carried my wrist to my truck, yelling back at him, "My iPhone, my purse and keys are on the table. Shut the doors, so Gracie won't get out, and the windows."

We both remained calm and alert, like I'd imagine people in a war zone to be. I sat in the passenger seat and dissociation started to kick in, like a drug. And then Jim told me that he wasn't comfortable driving because of his recent eye surgery. Jim has nystagmus, which is a vision condition causing his pupils to flutter involuntarily, affecting his vision.

He was working at Google then, and I'd joined him there for lunch the day before he was to leave for surgery. We sat outside and he grieved the old sight he would lose: the floating garbage bags in his peripheral vision that looked like "fluffy bunnies," the fading degradation in color of the fuzz around objects. All that cozy haze could become sharpened and cruel. What could this new way of seeing stir up and bring back?

He came over after the operation. We had both moved since our Chelsea days but were neighbors again on lower Fifth Avenue, under a ten-minute walk from each other. He'd called before he came and was groggy from the pain meds but wanted to see me.

When I opened the door, I saw that the area under his eyes was bruised to his cheekbones; the whites of his eyes were red with blood. We hugged and he walked slowly through my door, as if landing on another planet. He said, "It looks so clean in here," and looked around my apartment. He gazed at me, his pupils no longer shaking or shimmering and his shoulders no longer hunched with the strain it took to look so closely at things. "You're so pretty," he said, crying, wiping his tears with his shirtsleeve. He was trying to catch his breath. "It took me longer to walk here. I kept stopping at the newsstands to look at the papers." He was viscerally shaken by the newness of it all, the edges now distinct for him, and what I imagined to be a release of the unrealized burden he was born with.

The day that Jim stood outside my truck, I was in the passenger's seat and slumped over in teeth-chattering pain, taking his hands to touch my head to console myself out of this and making his hands my own, alternately squeezing my wrist. "Hold my head tight with both of your hands," I said. He did. "Now pet my head." He did that, too. "Now hold my head with both your hands, please . . ." Which he did. I started talking about *Homeland* and evoking Brody to come rescue me. "Soldiers feel this pain and it's so much worse."

"You're gonna be okay, punkin," he said.

I said, "I'm not dying," and we laughed a little. I said many "oh my Gods," swaying to rock myself. The minutes in pain go by so slowly and so fast at the same time, but according to the clock, we waited half an hour for the ambulance to arrive.

They drove down the gravel driveway, which had needed repair for years now, and the paramedics got out of the ambulance unfolding the gurney and shot me up with morphine once I got inside, where the drive up the bumpy driveway had me bawling, but there was a new hero to hold on to: Indiana Jones. The ER team went through the protocol—"What is your name? What happened? How did you fall? What day is it?" They asked me the same questions again, minutes later, and I had to say it all over again. "What horseshit," I thought. I said, "I told you already, ugh, I told you." Someone asked if I was still in pain and I said, "*Yes!* Look at my *arm*," and they stuck me with another shot of morphine. I asked for more morphine when they made their final stop to wheel me into the hospital because they were about to ask me, anyway.

The hospital, which struck me as sad, made me even sadder when I was told there was no bone specialist in the building. The doctor on call was animated. He liked that I was a celebrity. "I know who you are," he said, and I cried harder. How could he know who I am? The presumption of *that*. "I'm not sure if you have any movies coming up, but you have a serious break." *Yeah, I know!* I started to really wail, like Julia

Louis-Dreyfus in *Seinfeld*, and looked around for a laugh track. Then he said, "We can't do anything about it here"—hold for laughter—"except remove that blue tape around your arm to try to get an X-ray." I knew what he was saying, that he was going to break my wrist *back into place*.

"I know what you're going to do!" I cried. I wasn't born yesterday.

He waited a beat and said, "Do you need more morphine?"

Of course I did. "YES!" He gave a nod to the nurse and I reached out with my good arm and we high-fived.

Jim was there for that show, and would squeeze my foot or shin softly and smile in that way that's reserved for hospitals, with queasy love. He was there for the bigger show, too, when they pulled that blue tape roll off my arm to reset my wrist, and I screamed bloody murder. He was there for the taxi ride to the bone specialist, further into town, a visit I don't remember at all, because it was a blackout—the stage was dark and no one was home. I like to think the bone specialist was Quincy, from the seventies TV show *Quincy M.E.*, played by Jack Klugman.

When I came to and regained consciousness for a minute, Jim and I were sharing a taxi with a motley crew of teenage boys (not a lot of cabs in the country) and they were getting their Saturday night party on in the afternoon—laughing and bobbing to the loud bass of rap music, their arms pumping to the beat, not even aware we were there. I was holding my cast arm at the elbow, like kids who know the answer do in class, but I was a mess. We scampered out of the taxi feeling like invisible teenage losers and we were glad we weren't made fun of or beaten up.

Sitting on the curb, waiting for our friend Mindy to pick us up, I called Lowe's to check in on some twin bed frames for the house I barely owned and that was sucking me dry financially. But since I had the Partridge Family fantasy, I wanted very much to keep it alive. It would have to be rented to help pay the mortgage.

I nodded out on Jim, slobbering on his shirt, for an hour and a half, because that's how late Mindy was when she arrived. There were two streets that had the same name for some cockamamie reason. She was so shocked that I was so wasted that she still blushes when she talks about it. She drove us back to my house and left as I swayed a few feet from the front door by the TV room: "I'll just sleep down here and watch these shorts I have to judge for the blardy blar festival . . ." And then I touched Jim's shoulder and he must've thought I was going to say good night and thank you and "I love you, what would I have done without you?" but instead I threw up on him and myself. He ran upstairs to get towels, which I threw up into some more. I was cogent enough, though, to blurt out where the washing machine and dryer were, and able enough to make it to the bed, where I was out like a light.

The next day, I woke up to a fresh cup of coffee, a Vicodin, and a cast on my arm. A couple of my girlfriends, Leana and Keetja, had come upstate to get away from the city and the demands of being artists in the fashion world. They were just barely surviving the "Big Apple," which was more the Big Applebee's (wait for it), "home of the crave and the land of greed!" They sat in my screened-in porch, relaxing with handmade scented candles and essential-oil perfumes that Keetja had made—sandalwood, ylang-ylang, wild orange, lavender. They were like me and could land or plant themselves anywhere.

I sipped my upper, swallowed my downer, and back up the ladder I went. My friends couldn't stop me and it was the last bit of work—with my left hand I painted and I kept my right arm raised above my heart, like the doctor said—like I knew the answer in class. Fonzie charged through the front door and do-si-doed with Jim, who made a fast exit.

Fonzie barrels into every room he enters. Several months before, he'd barreled into my apartment—throwing his carry-on bag to the floor, and hugging and kissing me, "Darlingdarlingdarling." He then stepped back from me, with intent, like an animal in the jungle listening for predators. He circled his arms three times in the air, like a magician doing "hocus pocus" but even bigger and faster. After the first time, he said, "My bag," and looked around. The second time, his arms swung fast again, "My bag." The third time, bent even further,

"My BAG," in umpire position. I'd never met anyone who'd forgotten a bag at an airport, so this was pretty funny. We'd drive to the airport the next day and what was lost would be found.

Fonzie did take very good care of me before we went to the city to see a "serious doctor." We watched the Woody Allen documentary on Netflix and I built fantasies to fend off my fear of working with him. Penélope Cruz talked about how she thought she was going to be fired. There were scenes on set of Woody directing, and Josh Brolin looked handsome and brooding, sitting in a kitchen while Naomi Watts laughed at Woody and batted her eyes, looking thin and gorgeous and blond. She gushed about the letter she'd received from Woody, asking her to act in his movie, so charming and witty that she'd had it framed. I'd gotten a letter, too, but my letter wasn't frameable at all. It was very meh. Naomi's was one hundred Watts.

Fonzie had brought me plastic Academy Awards that he'd gotten from LAX: Best Actress, Best Woman, Best Sweetheart, Best Secretary, Best Mother. He drove me to my wrist surgeon in a downpour (he'd driven an ambulance in his twenties) and even found a servant's bell for me to keep at my bedside. He got me ready for baths and stacked towels for me to prop up my elbow with. He was at his best in a mode of high stakes—an emergency where he could come to the rescue. The high-stakes mode was familiar and special for both of us.

He reminded me of Erich von Stroheim, the great silent-film director. He was an actor, too, and played Max von Mayerling in *Sunset Boulevard*, the former director, husband, and servant to Norma Desmond. He was arguably the greatest silent-film director there ever was. There's a great documentary about him that you can watch on You-Tube, called *The Man You Loved to Hate*. His cinematographer said that he loved realism so much that he made his actors hate him. He'd scream at them, "Fight! Fight! I want you to hate each other as much as you hate me!"

He was interested in how men and women conquered their passions or how their passions conquered them. This was racy stuff back then and it's racy stuff now, but he was an artist and realism was his passion. He even shot in Death Valley, when it was 125 degrees, and everyone had to stay there, obviously. No one could sleep because it was so hot. One of the caterers died there. This was the movie *Greed*, which confronted systems of capitalism and marriage. I saw it at the Film Forum in New York—the studio version. Stroheim hated the edits the producers had enforced and said of it: "The man who cut my film had nothing on his mind but his hat!" His version was ten hours long and although he knew he was making a masterpiece, he also knew he was making a financial flop. And he didn't care.

He met Gloria Swanson when she produced and starred in the silent film *Queen Kelly* and asked him to direct. There is a scene where Swanson and a group of nuns from a convent pass a cavalry from some mythical kingdom and when they meet the prince, they curtsy. Well, while shooting the scene, Gloria Swanson's pantaloons happened to drop down around her ankles. She was of course mortified and all the guys laughed at her, but she rose to the situation with her dignity, and stepping out of her pantaloons, then threw them at the prince. He caught them and then put them to his face and smelled them, saying "Ah" and smiling. Stroheim loved this

moment, so this is what the scene became. I mean, that would probably be scandalous today, right?

So, the next day, at dailies, they watched it with the investor. He
asked the cinematographer what he thought and the DP said he'd
liked it, and got kicked simultaneously under the table, by Swanson
and Stroheim. Gloria Swanson was concerned about the censors at
the time and Eric von Stroheim wanted to challenge the censors—
he'd already shot orgy scenes that had nothing to do with the original story and turned the nuns to prostitutes, which was probably
really artful and punk rock for him. I'm sure he got out of hand.

There's a scene where she marries a man, and the part of the groom
was turned into a drunkard. They were setting up the shot and Stroheim had wanted tobacco juice to drip out of this man's mouth and
onto her hand when he proposed to her. This was Gloria's limit, and
she excused herself from set and went to her bungalow to call the
bankers and share what the process of shooting had been like so far.
She explained that Stroheim was manipulating the story and she had
not planned on playing a madam at a brothel but a nun in a convent.
How would that get past the censors? The slobbered tobacco juice on
her hand from the man she was going to marry wouldn't get past the
censors, either. They'd only shot twenty thousand feet of film and if
they continued in this way, the film wouldn't be completed for a year
and it would cost over a million dollars more to finish. They'd already
spent $600,000. And so the bankers flew to Africa the next day to
shut down production. Can you imagine? Gloria Swanson produces
this silent film and it's taken from her and turned upside down and
inside out. What was Stroheim thinking and what was in his twisted
genius? Where was his wife during all this?

When Swanson and Stroheim met on the *Sunset Boulevard* set,
they hadn't seen or talked to each other in twenty years. Stroheim
had reservations about taking a small part in a film, and questioned
whether it was beneath him. He had become a character actor after
the experience of *Greed* and lost much of his dignity as an artist, but
luckily they welcomed him in France, where he worked with Jean

Renoir as an actor in *La Grande Illusion* and collaborated with other French filmmakers. But in regard to this part, he concluded that the pain he had experienced as a director, having not worked in twenty years, was just as painful as the part of the butler, so he was on board.

At this point, Gloria Swanson had also been forgotten about, so they shared this fall from grace. They met now, laughing and hugging each other, with respect and appreciation for one another, and excited about the experience of working with the great Billy Wilder, who directed the film. I love that the small part wasn't too strong a blow to Stroheim's ego, and that it didn't prevent his attraction to playing it, or any of his creative ideas that would go into it. Gloria Swanson talks about this in an interview I watched on YouTube. The **STOP TALKING** script was yet to be completed when they were filming, so Stroheim had many ideas for his character and the story as a whole. He was back at his beginnings, when he'd worked for D. W. Griffith as a first AD and character actor. He'd made his small characters memorable with distinct traits and wardrobe, things like an eye patch. He'd created so many villains that people loved to hate him—he was actually spat on and thrown out of restaurants, but he loved this persona since it created the necessary power and force to become a great director.

He'd pitch his many ideas for his character to Billy Wilder, and Mr. Wilder would reject most of them because they didn't "further the story," which breaks my heart. I would've loved to see another *Sunset Boulevard* from his character's point of view. He had a lot to give, and the one idea he had that made it into the movie was that the fan mail Gloria receives is all letters written by him. This idea made his character the heart of the movie, not only with his silent and tragic unrequited love for her, but as her final director within the film. He's there at the very end, standing behind camera as she walks down that huge stairwell and into the lens and to "all those wonderful people out there in the dark," on her way, through us, to the mental ward.

If only I could weave baskets for the rest of my life. My psychoanalyst, Mark, says every director has a touch of sadism. I've been seeing him for well over a decade and when I tell him my experiences, he says very simply, "The business you are in is perverse." Like politics is corrupt, showbiz is perverse. People lie in politics and there's perversity in showbiz. Period.

I was nervous to work with Woody Allen, since he had been so steadfast to his psyche—both creatively and in his life. "The heart wants what it wants," the pronouncement he made on *60 Minutes* about his love for Soon-Yi. It could be an aria from an opera, couldn't it? Any person left by their mother in childhood has an enormous weight and longing in their heart and soul, with a life spent recovering. If I didn't believe in the complexities of another's heart and soul—their story, their mystery, their truth—then I really would have to weave baskets. A culture that loses this becomes unhinged; it's the chewing gum, Mark calls it, that holds us together.

Mark would compare Woody to Lewis Carroll, who he knew a little about. I didn't know Lewis Carroll suffered from a stammer, did you?

Order in the Court.

16
Gracie

She looks like Falkor, the dog from *The Neverending Story*, doesn't she? Her ears flap up and down when I walk her down the street, like she could almost take flight. I have this rope leash that I can clamp to a belt loop and I think of it as an umbilical cord and of Gracie as a white shadow-creature pulling me into pleasant thoughts and encounters. She is a bichon frise/poodle/Maltese mix, according to the vet. She is the energy in every situation we're in together, and people react in almost always positive ways. She deflects negative stuff coming toward me and I see people's faces light up at how animatronic she looks, like she could start talking. Then they reflect this happiness walking past me, and I hear "That dog was smiling at me" a lot, which is the bichon part of her genes. I learned that from the Westminster dog show.

Gracie sits in my chair and watches me work on set, sometimes in the director's lap, where she fits perfectly at the monitor, and sometimes curled up in her bag, where she doesn't block the view. I am in love with Gracie because that's what she's there for. She is a vessel of spirit for dark gaps in people, places, and things. Trained on wee-wee pads, she goes on corners of welcome mats as well as rugs. Her

early years were spent in hotel hallways, where she'd catch air as she leapt like a gazelle in her supreme agility, as I'd lie on the floor and she'd hurdle over me. In dog runs and parks, she sits next to strangers and cuddles up or places her paw on them to show her devotion. She likes to stop at nail salons and barbershops to look inside because she's a poodle and likes hair and nails. She likes makeup stores, like Bluemercury, and prefers sitting at the entrance of doorways, like the Anubis jackal from Egyptian mythology, the central figure in the journey through the underworld.

The paparazzi adore her. The "papps" or "paw-perazzi," as she refers to them. Strangers ask to take her picture and she gets a lot of hits on Instagram. I put her into the arms of people when they look like they want to hold her. So yeah, she's working all the time. She was attacked by the press, though, and suffered greatly after being unfavorably written about in Gawker—she called the site Barker, saying it was "all bark and no bite," but I knew she was hurt on the inside. They called her a "devil dog," and to this day, people still say that they heard she was mean and it's clear that she's not and wasn't. Lena Dunham told me that they called her dog a devil dog, too. We were in the works to start a protest called MODADO-COD, which stands for Mothers of Dogs Against Defamation of Character of Dogs, but people got in the way of it.

Gracie stayed indoors for weeks after the shame of that fake news and became eccentric for a while and started wearing wigs. She took the bait of the hate-talk and started biting back, but this was when she was younger and took things personally. It sounds crazy but the other's voice became her own so easily that it would wreck her spirit, as she chewed the wedge cork heels of my favorite slipper shoes. "I'm not a devil dog! That's not me!" she said, almost foaming at the mouth. She was upset and angry. "'Dog' spelled backward is 'God,' what blasphemy!" She started to cry and I picked her up and said, "Calm down, blessed creature, little lamb . . ." I held her by her armpits and looked her in the eyes. "If you let them hurt your feelings, you let them win, Cake Batter." She loves when I call her this but she was still devil-dogging and twisting and turning.

"Listen," I said. "They have to keep their website going because old-school journalism is almost out the window and they're just trying to make a living in this strange culture we have right now. Just see the big picture and don't attach yourself to the fiction of what they wrote. It's all fiction anyway, Gracie. Keep working on the *Ruff Times* blog, about your early years in the puppy mill, and make your own fiction . . ." She let out a growl and I lifted her high into the air with one arm in the "I'm the boss" position. She was still frustrated so I calmly said, "Relent and restore your spirit, Gracie. Recover, Butter Bones . . ." She started to let go of her anger and her body became softer as she felt the sadness.

"Why do people like to read about things that are made-up and mean?" I was holding her like a baby at this point and swaying and twisting, humming to her. We were in the bathroom because she'd said she wanted to wash her face and put on makeup. In the reflection of the mirror I saw the pills that were stuck in the crevices of her paw's pads. I squeezed her wrists to release her grip and flushed them down the toilet. She said she just wanted to take the edge off and had no intention of doing anything drastic.

She's much more mature now. She's fourteen and in her regal years and still does her job beautifully, being devoted to me and to other people. She was somewhat of an impulse buy but I'd been pining for a dog and looking at websites like Fur Babies to rescue a pet and was well into my "expecting" years. I just didn't know when she'd appear. My boyfriend at the time, Ryan, wanted a cat. I'd given him a "sleeping cat" from Chinatown for Christmas, the kind made of rabbit fur that has its little eyes closed and comes curled up, forever sleeping.

For a few weeks, the cat was asleep on the windowsill, until he slept on the wall in my bedroom attached with Velcro, high up and flying in the air, holding a piece of red yarn with the big ball of yarn stretched six feet away from his paws. It was not good feng shui per se, but it was my feng shui at the time. I'd wait around late nights for my rock star boyfriend to come home while he was out, catting about, making music. *Ryan Adams*, not to be confused with Bryan Adams; he makes beautiful music.

He'd recently fallen offstage and broken his wrist and needed surgery, just like I'd have years later. His right hand was filled with pins and screws, and he'd had to learn to play guitar again, which he would have no problem doing, and go on to record maybe ten more albums.

Anyway, it was snowing and we bundled up and journeyed out to a game store in the West Village to buy a puzzle and there was a pet store next door called Groom-O-Rama. Ryan wanted to look at the cats, but I was allergic to cats as a kid so their mystique never interested me. It was there, in Groom-O-Rama, that I saw Gracie, nestled in her cage. I couldn't believe she hadn't been taken and asked to hold her, and she pressed up to my very heart like a magnet and whimpered, longingly. It was time to have a baby, and so I did. At 5:02 in the afternoon on October the eleventh, 2004, I became a mother. It was an easy labor, there in the pet store in the West Village, where it was fated to be. Gracie is a Libra, with a moon in Scorpio, which is my sun sign. She traveled on subways, in her bag, as soon as she could. I was determined not to raise a nervous wreck like I was at her age, and I didn't.

I guess Gracie was around eight when I ran into a friend on the sidewalk in my neighborhood—a very reputable woman, talented and not "woo woo" at all. She was carrying her beloved dog, Bitsy (not her real name), who was sick. She had taken her to the vet a few times but decided to meet this pet psychic, Claire, who came highly recommended by other people, and I'm assuming by dogs as well. Anyway, Claire diagnosed Bitsy's health issue. My friend was mystified and relieved, since the vet had gotten it all wrong and this psychic hadn't. I, of course, asked for Claire's number. It was the holiday season and for Christmas, I wanted to hear what Gracie had to say.

There was nothing wrong with Gracie, but she did bark a lot when someone came over, and I'd have to say to my guest, "Sit down in a chair so she can greet you." When Claire came over, she was so nice and ethereal. (How can you not be, when you can hear dogs talk?) She started her work right away and was miming chewing and moving her mouth around and asked, "Does Gracie mainly chew on the left side?" She does. "There's a tooth that bothers her," Claire said, and then sat down on the couch with us and Gracie sat next to her, putting her paw on her knee. She explained that Gracie had been a seven-year-old English girl in her last life and that manners were very important to her, and whoever came into the home needed to sit down first and basically start telling her fairy tales—and put the kettle on for some tea and make her a crumpet or cut the crusts off white bread for cucumber sandwiches.

...crumpets

Claire started licking her lips, like she was tasting something. "You know what really makes her happy? Peppermint candy. She has a sweet tooth." Now, when Gracie was a puppy, she was compulsively sniffing gum off the sidewalks and trying to remove it in order to chew or eat it. I tried for a while to train her to chew gum and spit it out but after she swallowed it a few times, I stopped. She would get into my purse, or a friend's purse, and chew their mint gum. Claire said Gracie loved ice cream. Well, guess where I take her when it gets warm out? Down the street for a dollop of my own peppermint ice cream at Sundaes and Cones, where I share some with her. Please don't repeat this, I'm only telling you this because we'll never see each other again, but I'm at the window seat, so I'm the dreamer. What person doesn't want to imagine a dog's thoughts? I introduced myself to this actor (who's on a big show) at Sundance (I'm not saying who it is) and he goes, "I've seen you walking around the neighborhood. You have a *weird* relationship with your dog."

I could've said, "Well, you have a *weird* relationship with women," but I didn't, even though I know he does. I don't trust people who don't like dogs but I trust dogs who don't like people. When people say, "I'm not really a dog person," all I hear is, "I'm not really a person."

Some actors are like snipers who hide in the trees and wait to undermine you with mind games as they fight for close-ups or ruin yours and are having fun while they're actively conniving, like some kind of reptile person. There's something so dark and twisted about them and because they're so good at being this other thing that's not really a person, people love watching them.

I worked with one of these snakelike sniper actors and experienced the black cloud that came with him and the ravens that flew around him. He really created an energy of deep perversion. I saw him again when I was trying to meet Johnny Knoxville because I had a script I was trying to produce about Ted Kaczynski. It was at a premiere party at the Jane Hotel and I sat on the floor, in front of the fireplace. Johnny never showed up to the thing. I had planted myself in Michael Shannon's roped-off area and met Mary Stuart Masterson, from *Some Kind of Wonderful*, who was happy and kind and told me about a film production facility she was pioneering upstate, to boost the local economy up there. It was a different kind of movie party than we were used to, filled mainly with suits and indiscriminate but loud music and hardly any familiar faces. People used to have fun at these things and let loose but now you were easily watched and even monitored. Michael Shannon arrived with his friends and I stood up to introduce myself and asked if it was alright to sit in front of the fireplace and he was cool about it. He's a big handsome presence of sensitivity and force and sat low in the velvet couch like a king, with his hands on his knees as they jutted out. He asked how I was and what I was working on and I told him, "New media ideas, new forms," and I may have mentioned my dogs-playing-poker idea, and remember asking him to "imagine what it's like being an actress, to be like you but a woman in these times?" It was good their drinks came, and while I was sitting there, not thirty feet away, I saw the sniper snake man. His reptilian head slowly moved and I read his lips: "Is that Parker Posey?" he mumbled to the woman next to him. My hand swept a big wave, like I was on shore, and I said loudly, "Yeah, it's me!" I kept waving my arm back and forth as I registered his face turning me to camouflage. I got up and as I walked over, I watched him pretend to rack me into focus and said, "Yeah, it's me, Parker. Hi!" He acted surprised and I quickly introduced myself to the woman and then excused myself, saying I was going to the bar.

Standing at the bar waiting for the bartender, I saw a producer I'd worked with recently. When we made eye contact, his face showed no recognition, so I said, "It's me, Parker!" He was deep down some dark corridor and said darkly, "I know." It was going to be one of those conversations that took some work. I said, "We've worked together." The corners of his smile lifted with an effort of curling dumbbells. He introduced me to his friend, a much younger actress, and his spirits brightened. She didn't recognize me or my work, despite a long list of movies I spouted out quickly, and then, to lighten the awkward situation, I pulled out my iPhone, saying I was going to IMDb myself. Then the producer said, "She's coming around." People say such weird things to you when you're famous, like you're not a person but something else— like a cardboard cutout version of yourself wearing a mirrored mask. I could've passed out onto the floor, as if waiting for an ambulance to arrive. That way, he could've looked up to the party people while holding smelling salts under my nose to say, "*She's coming around.*" He could have lifted my wrist in the air, like an old boxing veteran—"She *was* a champion, back in the day! *She's coming around!*"—and I could've lifted my arms in a rah-rah gesture or fist-pumped the air. I could've said, "No, I'm not 'coming around.' I'm  the ghost of Christmas past, but you don't recognize me because it's not the holidays."

I could've stuck my elbows out and windshield-wipered my hands, twisting sharply and saying in robot voice, "Your credit card is not working. Your credit card is not working," as many times as I wanted and until everyone left. But instead I said, "Aw, I wish they allowed dogs in here." And then I felt the tug of Gracie's rope leash pulling me at the waist, to her dog's star, Sirius—the brightest star visible from any part of the Earth.

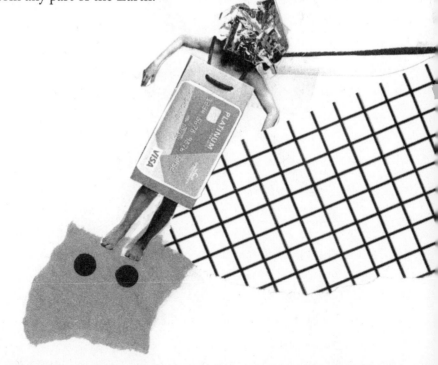

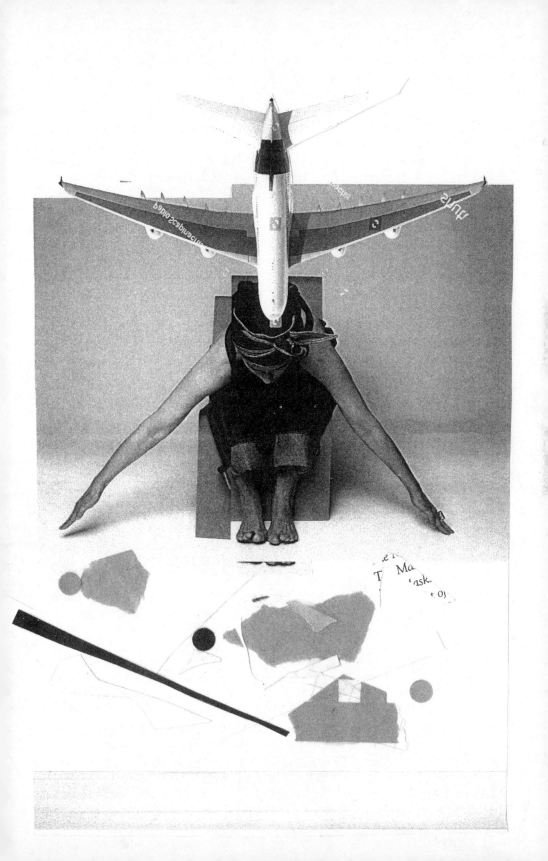

17

Garbage on the Beach

I learned the Mysore practice of yoga when I was in Berlin, working on Hal Hartley's movie *Fay Grim*. Yeah, you do get sore from Mysore but it's the fundamental "self practice" yoga, which, if you learn it, you can practice anywhere, all over the world, and since Mysore is the basis of all yoga, if you can do Mysore, you can do any other yoga class. Oh my, I'm sore. My teacher's name was Andreas Schnittger. He was in his early thirties, had trained in India with Pattabhi Jois (who founded the practice), and was intensely dedicated. He always wore the same thing to practice: tight black sweatpants with a white shirt and black sweatbands on both his wrists. And if this wasn't cool enough, he played jazz drums in an experimental, avant-garde jazz band. When I asked if I could come to a show, he said I probably wouldn't like it, that it was mainly "noise" and very loud. *J'adore!* A dedicated yogi makes-music-I-wouldn't-understand avant-garde jazz drummer. Far out! He was so cool.

I started with "the primary series," which is where you begin. Learning when to breathe and how to breathe is an integral part of yoga: there's just so much breathing. Yes, that's right, we are breathing the air at this moment, but I mean conscious breathing. Andreas spoke English really well but carefully, and he liked to say, "Free breathing." I think he must have liked the elongated *eeeeee* sound, because German's not a language that relaxes its vowels—when I tried to speak it, I had to purse my lips and push the O sound to the front of my teeth, and I did that terrible thing where you imitate the accent of the country you're in and it's annoying for everyone except yourself. Maybe that's why I wasn't invited to the jazz club. Anyway, Andreas said "free breathing" a lot.

After a few sessions, he caught on that I thought this was weird, and he said, "You don't like it, 'free breathing'?"

"I do, it's nice," I said. "But breathing being free? I dunno. It's not like you charge someone, like money to breathe. In English, it can sound like you're talking about commerce."

But he loved it. "I like it. Free breathing."

"Like breathing is in jail, and we need to free it from jail? Like put it on a protest sign?"

"I like it," he said again. "Free breathing."

"Of course it's free. It's breathing."

We eventually dropped it. Put it on a protest sign.

Andreas taught me private classes. When I wasn't working on the film, I'd walk to the studio, a few blocks away from where I was living in Mitte, and take class with not even ten students. This was in wintertime and Berlin was cold and snowy. The city didn't pour salt on the sidewalks, because they were sensitive to the dogs, whose paws would bleed if salted. So the snow never melted on the sidewalk and you'd see people sliding and slipping and their dogs trotting along. Hardly any dogs had leashes, and they were allowed in restaurants and bars and it wasn't a big deal.

My apartment was small, which I liked, and had efficient recycled modern-type furniture: a shower curtain made of sewn-together plastic bags, a bed on the floor, and a chair made of plywood that looked like it would break if I sat in it, which it did. Yeah, I leaned back and it broke, so I didn't have a chair anymore. The place was simple, and it was a relief at that time in my life. I had broken up with Ryan and suffered a betrayal when a girlfriend slept with my ex, and another friend was having drug problems and was being needy and crazy. "Bye-bye, *mein lieber herr.* Farewell, *mein lieber herr.* It was a fine affair, but now it's over!"

So it was a great time for me to eat alone and listen to the music of a language I didn't understand, and get my body moving to the Mysore Ashtanga yoga practice.

Samasthiti, or Mountain Pose, is the starting position: you stand at the front of your mat with your hands at your sides and your eyes closed, neck aligned with your body, imagining a line or string of energy from the cosmos to the top center of your head, traveling directly down, straight to the center of the Earth. Don't stick your belly out and become a hill. You find your center and pull it in, like a strong mountain. Be still. I'll show you.

Now you start the breath-
ing practice: Breathe in on
the count of four, in what's
called ujjayi breath, and then
breathe out. Do this through
your nose only. If you don't
know what ujjayi breath is,
contract your throat to
sound like Darth Vader, and

breathe in. Now breathe out, still sounding like him. Do it right now. Oh, who cares, you'll never see these people again.

On the last count of this "ocean breathing," at the end of the breath, in that space before the final exhale, bring your hands to prayer position at your chest—your "home," or "heart center," they call it. This is where you start the moving of your hour-and-a-half "practice."

When you move, your body becomes an architectural form traveling through space: angles, symmetry—harmony on the earth. It becomes a vessel, which the elements of nature pass through within the mind's thoughts or meditation. Yoga is the practice of the body so that it can become light, providing your thoughts with light so they don't stick to ideas that the mind creates for itself. You want your mind to float, or to at least create more distance from its attachments.

In class with Andreas, when I put my hands to my chest in prayer, my mind got quiet enough to hear a meditative voice say, "You're home. You've been running so much." Tears fell down my face and onto my mat, like rain. This is not unusual and if you're not drunk, I think it's kind of fabulous to be free enough to cry in front of other people. Yeah, it's written all over you that you cry when you fly.

There's a quote from the writer Joseph Campbell that I love because it's easy to remember. "I don't have faith, I have experience." My uncle Tim turned me on to Joseph Campbell with *The Power of Myth* with Bill Moyers, which was on PBS when I was around eighteen. I really dug it. Uncle Tim died of an overdose when I was in my twenties. He'd become addicted to opiates over the years and the trauma of Vietnam had been like a powder keg inside him. He also raged against small-town religious conservatism and returned to Shreveport to confront Nonnie—to find the mother within—but she wasn't easy with her heart because her feelings probably scared her. She'd become an icy queen.

As I stood there in Mountain Pose, more memories and repressed feelings came up. The biggest thing, probably, was that I recognized myself—or my life. I stood there in prayer, with hands at my heart center, and just felt my life up to that point. I saw the speed of my life and all this running. How I'd grab on to parts and my work as if it were real, as if it were something I could hold on to. I just wanted to be distracted and absorbed at the same time and have it be about something or someone else. I was reaching outside myself, mostly. It's so weird because really I want to disappear and acting allows for that; but at the same time you can see me on the screen on this airplane. Anyway, I started to realize stuff.

I heard my inner voice saying, "It took you so long to get here, but it's okay."

"It takes courage to live a life" is something Mildred would always tell me. You have to take the courage, though; it can't just be an idea. "Hold on to yourself," she said repeatedly, and anyway, it was on the yoga mat where I held on to myself. Stop digging when you find yourself in a hole. Just cut that string. "Free breathing." Put the shovel down. Isn't the dirt great around this mountain? Isn't this view amazing?

So the first movement you will do is part of what's called the "vinyasa flow," and it's the Sun Salutation. Okay, I'm getting up.

Your hands move up while you breathe in on the count of four (with your still-steady ujjayi breath), and you reach your palms over your head: your arms have made the circle of the sun. The movement or gesture is a worship to the sun. Again, a slow deep breath.

On the next count of four, you bend forward as your arms brush down and pass "the landscape" in front of you.

Then your palms are placed directly in front of your feet as you fold into a sandwich bend (a completed bow to the sun).

If your palms don't hit the ground, don't worry, it's not a competition; be calm about it. You see your limit and acknowledge it, and get over it.

On the next count of four, look up to "see" the "horizon," and then bow your head down on the next count of four, forehead on your shins again. Another bow to the sun.

The first big move comes next: your feet step or jump behind you to a push-up position, or Chaturanga, or "chat to Rhonda." You somewhat float down to the floor, for just a millisecond, landing with your torso an inch off the floor, your arms and toes holding you up. You scoop up to a back bend, with a long inhale, and then you're positioned facing up, like a seal.

On the count of four, the breath of your nose comes shooting out again, like water from a whale's spout, and then you push your butt into the air and make a triangle above the earth: you settle into Adho Mukha Svanasana, or Downward-Facing Dog. I met a standard poodle named Jackie O at the Chateau Marmont who did this posture on command.

In this posture, breathe four long breaths again. If you were going to practice with Pattabhi Jois, the father of Mysore, you'd spend months practicing only the Sun Salutation.

The next move is the first big sweep with your foot. It begins with the right foot. With your left foot planted at a solid quarter turn, swoosh your right foot back (the sound of a wave), then swing it forward, and plant your foot in front of you in a forward-facing lunge. Your arms come up, tight to the head, palms in prayer—

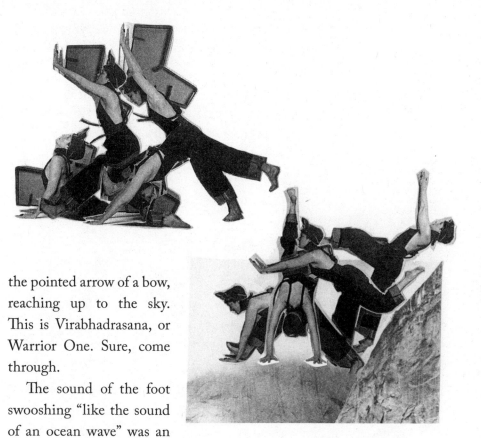

the pointed arrow of a bow, reaching up to the sky. This is Virabhadrasana, or Warrior One. Sure, come through.

The sound of the foot swooshing "like the sound of an ocean wave" was an Andreas touch, from his own teacher. I like it. The body can be fluid: all that's inside us moves around like water.

You hold Warrior One for four oceanic, *Star Wars* ujjayi breaths. Then slide out to Warrior Two for another set of ujjayi breaths.

Okay, I'm going to sit back down. At this point, it may not sound like it, but you're already sweating. This whole time you've been "cleaning the garbage on the beach," as Andreas would say. The voices that chatter with those awful scenarios and the voice of judgment, like stale, hard gum—spit it out, with the other garbage on the beach. The waves come and wash that gum away, along with those faded Budweiser cans and strips of

dirty plastic beach crud. Then look at the horizon. Look at the view. Oh, ugh, the garbage on the beach has come back again: my shit, my work, my stress, the beach is a mess, this world is a mess—clean this garbage on the beach!

And then you get calm again, centered. A nice wind, while in Warrior Two, has come to blow the garbage away, allowing inner peace. Leaves blow by not indigenous to this tropical climate—c'est la vie, auf wiedersehen. *Tschüss!*

One day, during my moontime, Andreas led me through a private yin class and guided meditation. In yin class, you hold postures that are mainly on the floor but you still get sore.

He'd brought over some yoga blocks and blankets and an eye pillow. I sat cross-legged in meditation pose, on the yoga block, so I wouldn't hunch. I closed my eyes. "I want you to picture yourself as a five-year-old sitting in a chair," he said. "You are looking at your-self in this chair. When the child moves, it's a thought coming up. You ask the child to sit in the chair." My five-year-old self was monkey-brained, examining the chair, walking around it—curious, distracted, laughing, crying. This played on a loop, quickly, in my mind's eye. I found myself telling the child to sit in the chair over and over again, holding her little hand, walking her to the chair, gently gesturing for her to sit and be still.

Before I knew it, the hour and a half had flown by, so there was peace found. When I opened my eyes, I saw Andreas looking at me as if in a daydream. His teacher position had dropped. "I'd like to follow you for a day," he said, "to see what it would be like to be you, with your dog, and to be free."

Not long after returning from Berlin, I'd come home from a baby shower for a college friend, and I was feeling sad and blue. At the shower, I'd seen an acquaintance, a woman around my age, a writer, and she'd seen me in something. Anyway, she blurted out, about the other actress in the film she saw, "Why does she wear a wig when it makes her look old?" She quickly covered her mouth, embarrassed, and said, "That was an awful thing to say." I shrugged and made it alright despite spiraling into thinking about all the talk that goes on behind my back. "She probably just likes the wig, and, you know, doesn't want to sit in the makeup chair every morning and be fussed over. Someone pulling your hair at six in the morning for an hour, sometimes for months at a time . . . it's not that fun." Then I decided to be more direct or honest, and told her how I remembered seeing Susan Sarandon talking about aging on television, how after the age of forty, women are just ignored. She ended that conversation and said, "Well, you were great in that movie," and I said thank you.

The snowy night in the city had me feeling like a lone figure in a snow globe and when I got home that night I couldn't wait to cry. The suffering produced some garbage on the beach: I want to hide forever, New York is competitive and harsh and it's not the same anymore; everyone wants something; everyone has to be so smart, interesting, or fascinating. Why do some conversations feel like I've given blood? The wind was dramatic and then settled and then I saw an IV tube and went to the ocean to rinse it. Oh, look, there are

Andreas's black warm-up pants and his wrist sweatbands. I went online to find a local yoga class.

There was one at Jivamukti, with a teacher I didn't know. I took a fun class at a workshop there once and on the last day, the teacher had us close our eyes and find the tops of our mats with our feet and then stand on tippy-toe, and click our heels three times and say, in unison, "There's no place like om, there's no place like om, there's no place like om . . ." I joined in for half a second and then just looked around to see if anyone else thought it was too silly or was too cool to do it and exchanged a few looks.

I started at the top of my mat, in Mountain Pose, Samasthiti. Then I started my four breaths on the count of four: earth, wind, fire (father, son, and the Holy Ghost), and water.

I put my hands to prayer at heart center: "home."

Then came the Sun Salutation, arms up to the sky, "the sun always comes up," my hands reaching out over the space. Then down on the count of four, bowing down, "the sun goes down." I put my head on my shins, jumped back, Chaturanga; swooping up, my back bent like a wave, "the water rushes out." I looked up and my emotions, like a wave, splashed out into the air. Good-bye. I pulled back into Downward Dog and receded from them as I breathed it out.

Next came four long Darth Vader breaths, "I am your father," and on the count of four, the first big sweep into Warrior One. I brushed my right foot against the mat, making the sound of the ocean like Andreas taught me.

Well, the yoga teacher was standing directly behind me and his legs were open in a standing V and during that oceanic brush, the arch of my foot, the shape of a curved wave, briefly cupped his package, and I thought, "Sea anemone." I fell to the floor, grabbing my belly and laughing so hard—rocking with laughter.

I looked around to share the moment but no one did, or they pretended not to. I was in the back of class so I knew people saw it because they'd have been looking through their legs when it happened. The yoga crowd can be a tough house. I said something to the teacher like "Never in my life," and he said, "Well, there's a first time for everything," which made me laugh even harder. "A first time for everything"? Like "Laughagainasana"? There is no place like om.

18

Imavegan

Places hold a certain karma when you visit them and I like to think it's written in the stars. Neosporin is good to stick up your nose when you're flying because it prevents germs, but no matter what precautions I take, when I spend time in LA, I can almost guarantee that I will throw up while I'm out there, whether it's a bug in a salad or some germs on a doorknob. The place has weird karma for me. The stories are always funny later, of course, and if you're with someone with a sense of humor, they're laughing even before you get sick. Like when I was dating Harper Simon and teetered in front of a yellow Lamborghini outside the Roosevelt Hotel and he joked about throwing up on the car. I knew the minute I ate the Roosevelt's delicious hot rolls that some dirty bug had got me. But the tables turned on Harper when I jammed a wax earplug too far into my ear and he spent a good half hour digging for it with a pair of tweezers. It's such a small world that I bet you know someone who has seen me get sick in LA.

I was needlepointing on a flight to LA once and chatted with a flight attendant who also needlepointed, and then ten years later, maybe more, I met her again on a sidewalk in the desolate outskirts of Salt Lake City, where loads of flight attendants live. She was taking a walk around the neighborhood, and we met after a physical therapy appointment for my wrist. She recognized me and smiled, saying, "The needlepointer."

The mountain was so close in proximity—in Manhattan, it would have been as far as the distance between the Village and Midtown— it was majestic. She lived in an apartment complex built in the fifties, by a tiny dentist's office where a large smiley-face sign on the front lawn jutted up to the sky. We chatted about the small world and she recommended a vegetarian place that I never made it to.

I tried being a vegetarian—so many cool people are—but I guess I come from too many ranch hands. I don't eat meat all that much, and make a lot of soups and salads, but too much food talk starves a good conversation. Kale isn't as popular as it used to be and I don't know why that is.

I don't go out to LA as much as you'd think but I do for meetings every few years. During one trip in the aughts, I would hear, "I don't really eat," just minutes after being introduced to someone. It started to seem like a surname for beautiful, young actresses. It's different today, isn't it? Back then, that was the jargon. Women are starved, the culture is starved, and minimum wage is starved. Maybe all the food talk has to do with the amount of shit sandwiches everyone in the biz has to eat. You know what a shit sandwich is, right? When you have to eat the bad news (the shit) but it's made with the best bread and cheese available. Sometimes it's served to you with so much crap that you don't even know you're eating it. "They love you" is probably my favorite baloney made of crap that I've eaten, because it's said a lot and sounds so good.

"Imavegan" started to sound like a surname, too, and I'd be smart to start practicing my vegetables. I started to do this thing, by substituting the word "kale" for "care," as in "I don't kale where we eat. I kale too much, is my problem."

I also started doing this thing when I drove around, that is completely obnoxious or funny, depending on who you are and how you feel: I'd roll down my window, get a person's attention on the sidewalk or crossing the street, and call out, "Excuse me! Are you a vegan?!" Or I got the attention of someone in a car at a stop sign and said casually (but a little too loud), "I AM A VEGAN." This was more fun in the passenger seat, when I'd get to hang out of the car. It was good clean fun—unlike veganism, which is hard work.

I get this from my parents—doing silly, unexpected stuff. One time we went on a trip and my mom wanted to stop at a mall for a shopping fix, so we went into a store called Spencer's and bought some plastic masks. My dad wore a Nixon one, I remember, and my mom was a pig. They'd put them on as they drove, and we'd see who they could freak out, laughing until we made ourselves tired. It wasn't cool anymore to drink in the car, so that's how they replaced their fun. Not really, they still drank in the car, but in moderation.

I really did try to live out in Los Angeles, for a few months anyway, but I'd read too much Dominick Dunne and books about Manson, which made LA not a friendly place. Being a New Yorker by this point, I wanted to see more interaction with people on the sidewalks and would think, "Where did everyone go? What happened to everybody?" When someone asks to go on a hike, which happens a lot out there, I get suspicious and a little scared. When they say "take a hike," I walk away.

On a recent visit, I'd just landed and was waiting for my friend Craig to get back from therapy. He lived in one of the 1930s Beachwood Canyon apartment buildings that housed actors back in the day, and I sat on the grass in front of his building, in the sun, with Gracie. You could see the Hollywood sign when you drove up that street. I recognized a neighbor of his walking his dog (we'd met on the sidewalk on a previous visit), and we chilled out, having that New York-vs.-LA conversation.

Eventually, one of us noticed that some man had his car parked up the driveway outside the building's garage. He was sitting in his SUV, and it looked like he was staring at us hatefully, like a murderer or a Quentin Tarantino character. It was so intense that we both denied that he was staring at *us*, and we looked behind to see if he had to be looking past us at something that had possibly angered him, giving him that sour look. But there wasn't anyone there. He was looking at us.

We made up excuses: his car's stalled, he's having trouble seeing . . . We chatted a little and looked again. Maybe his window was tinted so dark that he was squinting to see through it? We chatted some more. Wait, he was wearing sunglasses. If his windows were too dark to see through, he would have taken off his sunglasses. After almost ten minutes, I got up to ask this man if he was okay. When I approached his car, he asked me if I was a homeless person.

I was polite and easygoing. "No, no, I'm not. I have a home in New York, in fact. I just landed in LA, but my friend Craig lives here, right there, in that apartment." I pointed, all casual and cool.

"Well, you look like a homeless person," he said.

"Oh, well, thank you," I said, "but I'm not. Is it my Indian sari on the grass? Because it's a beautiful scarf." I smiled back at it and looked at him again. "I'm just sitting on the grass, you know?"

"You can't sit on the grass. Who said you could sit there?" he asked.

"I dunno, the good Lord? I thought we were all allowed to sit on the grass."

"Well, you can't just sit on the grass like a homeless person," he said. "I'm calling the cops."

He didn't, but that would've been a better story. That kind of thing has never happened to me in New York. I got stopped and pulled over (in the nineties), swarmed actually, by six or seven cop cars in West Hollywood on Santa Monica Boulevard. The cops thought I'd stolen my rental car but I hadn't. I was wearing a vintage red patent leather vinyl trench coat and on the way to the theater. It was the only time I've sat in the back of a cop car. It was pretty awkward for everyone involved. I'd miss the interaction between people on the sidewalks if I lived in LA. You don't see as many people strolling: lovers throwing their heads back and with their arms around each other, or someone smiling because it's spring or the sun's come out. I tripped in my clogs on the pavement in the Village and a few people came to help me get up. When friends from the South come to visit, they're surprised how nice New Yorkers are.

If I tripped in LA . . .

I remember turning over in a hammock once with my friend Jason at some Hollywood party, I think it was Charlie Sheen's, and falling splat onto the grass. We cracked up laughing, and people looked at us mortified. Anywhere else, say, in a backyard in Louisiana, people would laugh along, thinking, "This is a fun party! You guys look like a lot of fun!" But LA is not a good place to fall. I think this was when Jason started saying "Good luck with your project" instead of "good-bye" when we left places.

After a couple of months in LA, I returned home to New York and went to some party where I was introduced to someone who said, "I'm sure you don't remember but we've met before," which I get all the time. And I feel bad that I don't remember the person's name and I usually say, "I'm sorry, I don't remember," or "Yeah, at this point I've met everyone," or "We're all connected!," or "It's a Small World isn't just a ride at Disney World!"

I don't like this feeling of being put on the spot with the "You probably don't remember me" opener, because it's assumptive and can be tinged with a condescending attitude. I like to close that up real quick with, "You're probably right, because you know why?" And then they'll say, "Why?" and I'll say, "Because every moment is new, like now, and now is the only moment that exists," which is the truth. I get all shut down and cosmically defensive and guilty.

But this time I said, "No, I don't remember if we've met before, but we can meet now. What is your name and where did we meet? I'm sorry I don't remember you—my life's had a lot of traffic and has cast a wide net."

And he said, "You asked me if I was a vegan as I was crossing the street in LA."

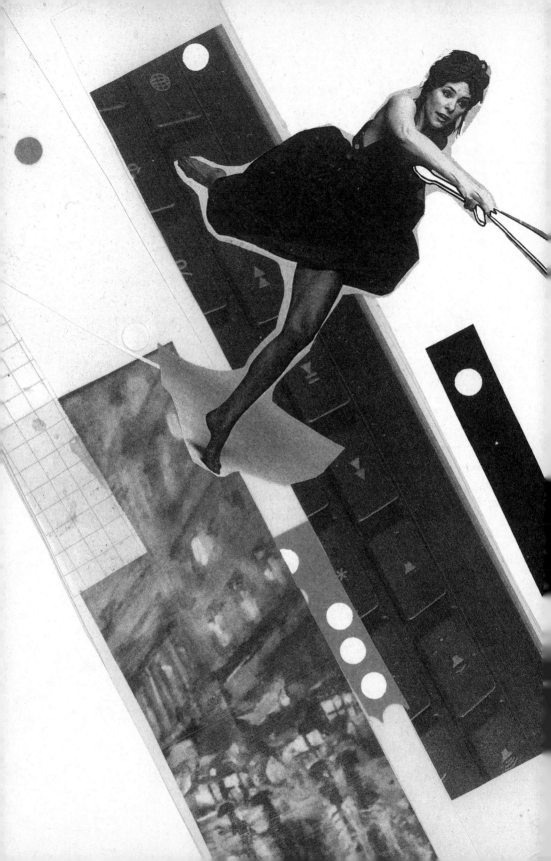

19

Moving

Moving is emotional. Did you know the root of the word "emotion" means "to move out"? The move out of my last apartment came at middle age, and introduced the Perimenopausal Puppet Troupe forming inside me. Their laughter and tears, elation and exhaustion, manifesting in a shallow puddle of sweat on my chest in the middle of the night was exciting and made me nervous. I am alive and in this body. Great job, everybody—now let's clean those sweaty costumes and you can all go home.

Nora told me to freeze my eggs at lunch at Barney's the last time I saw her, and I stood up and walked to the kitchen. She mentioned then how she got her hair blown out twice a week and that one day I would have to get work done. People in my business look at you like you don't care enough to wash your face if you don't "do" something. Truth is, people have great skin who have never washed their face; who cares? No one. So, full circle, I got this ultrasound thing on my face and neck and it's so painful and stupidly expensive but I gave birth to new collagen. I would need to keep this going for my entire career and it cost as much as my monthly maintenance and mortgage combined in my old apartment on lower Fifth Avenue, the neighborhood that's called the "Gold Coast," and not affectionately. I never heard anyone call it that until I left.

I didn't want to do a *CSI: Neverland* so I needed to sell my apartment. I used myself in the photo for the ad. "Live in the Gilded Age," it said, and I held Mary-Louise Parker's book, *Dear Mr. You*, in my lap pretending to read. This was a decision on my part that in the real estate world was considered gauche but I knew times had changed and this new gilded age was about famous people, celebrities. I ignored my celebrity as much as I could but I wasn't going to now.

The apartment felt more like a hotel suite than a home, anyway. I wasn't sad to leave, only to have to move. There were a hundred something units in the whole building so for me, it was Eloise at the Plaza—never really a home. Work was my home and I'd spent the last seven years or so living in a money drain. When I wasn't worrying, I brushed off stress with delusion, denial, and faith. I liked the gilded apartment though. Nadim (the previous owner) was into remodeling, especially the trim and molding, to get it to resemble what it was originally. I liked the apartment not filled and thinking about the history: Emily Post, who lived around the corner, as well as Edith Wharton and Mark Twain, whose apartments I'd pass every time I walked down Tenth Street. Nadim was a class act and had a vintage bicycle from the forties leaned against the wall when the apartment was staged for sale. He took me out to dinner and left the bicycle as a gift. I ended up giving the bicycle to someone who fell in love with it—I don't remember who it was but I'd been thrown in the air by a bike messenger the last time I Rollerbladed, so my time of feeling safe on wheels had ended.

My friend Rob Roth was stuck in the middle of a move, too. We'd met a decade before. He'd directed a show at Abrons Arts Center, on the Lower East Side, where the singer Theo Kogan performed with a projected image over herself as she stood still on a volcano made of TVs that were all turned to static. It had an eerie effect, as she sang songs with the spirit of herself in front of her, lip-syncing. Rob wasn't actually moving apartments but the apartments were being moved around him as he was possibly, or probably, being renovicted by his landlord, a slimeball who is now in jail and if you saw a picture of him you'd say, "Rat landlord"; he was that archetypal. The building was being renovated to up the rent for the mostly younger people whose parents foot the bill, and most everyone moved out because the re-modeling drove them crazy or they'd gotten bought out. The noise was one thing and the construction debris floating everywhere was another. It's hard to have a good day when your front door is covered in plastic, like a biological warfare zone or something out of a Tar-kovsky film, something that screams "I'm contaminated!" when you arrive at the door. It was Hispanic families and artists who stood their ground and were able to hold on to their rent-stabilized apartments—about ten out of sixty tenants remained.

The remaining tenants would watch construction workers take away the structural beams outside their windows and wonder if the work being done would cave in their entire building. The pipes that flooded Rob's bathroom had him feeling gaslit—was it done on pur-pose or were the workers simply too inept to repair the pipes above him when they'd turn on the water main downstairs? Did the rat-man landlord turn it on himself or was there just a real rat who needed a bath? Rats are smart and they're dirty. Or, if you're think-ing positive, was it all just a way to get close to his neighbors, who were all going through the same thing?

The mantel of the fake fireplace on the ground floor, which had served as a junk store and resembled Christmas all year long, had held books that had been left by neighbors, along with old costumes and a pair of buffalo horns that Rob took for his place. Now they'd demolished that and there was nothing to leave the neighbors, so say bye-bye to your found treasures and that sweet reciprocity. It's easier to throw it in the dumpster directly outside, anyway. Who cares? No one. This pissed both of us off and we called it evil. Our found pieces of furniture on the sidewalks of the city were some of our most cherished possessions because they had meaning.

Rob's dad was a policeman in the seventies in the Bronx, which makes me think of that movie *Dog Day Afternoon*. Rob's a performance artist and dresses like a wolf and sings songs by the Smiths at cabarets and theaters—and even at weddings. The wolf's name is Craig and he's pretty starved but likes to sing. Craig is Rob's protest, like Pacino's "Attica! Attica!" when he leaves that bank. The protest of the disenfranchised, of not only prisoners but gays and artists and anyone left in the margins the city had neglected—like the people without money.

It takes about an hour for Rob's transformation because he has to glue fur to his face as well as put on fake nails. We had some fun moments of inspiration where we talked about making short films in the building but it was better left as inspiration. Why give your head more apocalyptic images to fit into your dreams? We both already had dust up our noses. "And in the darkened underpass, I thought, oh God my chance has come at last . . ." "There Is a Light That Never Goes Out" by the Smiths is one of the best songs ever. Not appropriate for a plane ride but . . .

So I moved out of the Gold Coast to rent my friends Mindy and Tony's apartment in the West Village. They had two kids, Billy and Emma, who were four and six at the time, and since the town house they were in belonged to Tony's mom, Marcia, it was okay for them to put a spiral staircase in the corner and make a pop-up on the roof, as their master bedroom. They were busting out of the place and it was an obstacle course of toys and sippy cups and they could afford to move so they did. But they didn't want Marcia to be alone and couldn't think of anyone besides me that she could tolerate having around.

Marcia is a born-and-bred West Village New Yorker. She's Jewish and looks like Woody Allen's twin sister; she's just as diminutive in size and wears loose khakis and starched white shirts and glasses. She doesn't care for his movies and couldn't care less about his personal life (she's from the none-of-my-business generation), and was "a moldy fig" in her teen years—that's what a group of particular jazz enthusiasts called themselves in Manhattan at that time; they liked Dixieland jazz, pure jazz, not the Duke Ellington stuff. Marcia has distinct tastes, is sharp as a tack, and lives a full life—betting on the horses during the day, stopping at her favorite butcher (Florence Meat Market), going to "the Stupid Market" (what she calls the local grocery store), taking her private yoga class (as a cigarette burns in an ashtray). She loves a good drink, good movies, PBS, opera, and ballet and admittedly has no sense for decorating. She is an excellent cook and tells wonderful stories, even when they veer toward the medical—colonoscopies, her gynecologist, and her removed breast. I adore her.

We had a fun time on the Cape after her day of screaming at the television to cheer the horses and going outside to read or stare at the sailboats—"There's the view," she'd say in a way that made us both laugh. At night, she'd pass me the pint of coffee-flavored Häagen-Dazs, saying, "I know you want another bite, Parker Posey." We like the same treats, or "goodies," like Australian black licorice, turtles, chocolate almond bark—and anything coffee. Turtles are like Millionaires, chocolate, caramel, and pecans.

I'd move in easily as a surrogate family member and tenant, or so I thought and hoped. Mindy had moved into my rent-controlled place in Chelsea in the early 2000s, so it was an even trade in my book. There'd have to be work done so I hired an architect, as the work would have to be done by a professional—I'd heard about the mouse problem over the years. "Mouse problem" sounds so much better than "infestation," doesn't it? The kitchen was cockamamie, with the fridge door opening the wrong way toward the enormous butcher-block island that made me think of a gurney. Yes, take me away. Tony was a Deadhead and even had his own restaurant in Seattle in the nineties—his stories could fill a podcast.

I broke the wall in the kids' room to have more of an open loft and knocked out a closet in the middle of the apartment to get sunlight from both sides of the building. The man who came to repair the floors kept singing "Under the Boardwalk," and when I joined in, it got out of hand. He cornered me singing this song, as I was standing on the ledge of a window trying to pull the old blinds hardware off that had been there since the sixties. I remember one insane moment of trying to leave the apartment, pulling myself away as he was trying to grab my hands to dance, and I was instead snapping my fingers and harmonizing so loudly and off-key thinking I could stop this but enjoyed it sort of—opening the door to leave, singing "Oh Mandy. Well, you came and you gave without taking . . ." He liked the songs heard in subway stations—the songs that have a hard time leaving your head.

I'd sing these subway songs when Rob and I made many trips to Ikea and drive us both crazy. We called Ikea the purgatory of home improvement because what you'd purchased guaranteed many returns, like atonement. My entire kitchen came from there. It was around my fifth or sixth trip and an employee there who'd seen me days before said, "I never want to see you again!" when I left, and I shouted, "Me neither!" and skated my cart out of there. I saw her the next day and when she saw me coming, shouted, "I thought I said I never wanted to see you again!" and I told her I was there to make up.

The renovations seemed simple enough at the outset but were fraught with obstacles, too boring for me to go into or even to want to remember. My architect, Michael, was baffled by all the legalese stuff, permits or whatever drama or loopholes were thrown our way—it felt like I paid him mostly to handle me. I'd met another architect recently who, when I asked what his job was like, said, "It's mainly getting the wives to do what the husbands want." Ha ha ha ha, so funny.

A director I'd worked with, James, let me stay in the town house he'd bought as an investment, which was conveniently close to Marcia's. It was stark and dark in there but rich and hazy where an oil painting of a stormy mythical English countryside hung in the dark kitchen. The bathroom downstairs was tiny and painted dark teal and lacquered. The toilet flusher was a small brass button on the wall that was difficult to see from the light of the brass-flapped sconces that framed the mirror. I'd press the button thinking I was detonating a bomb or opening an escape hatch, or hoping the wall would move and get me to Narnia. It didn't, but the gray-tinted mirror granted a dark ageless glow.

The master bathroom had a seventies Hollywood Regency vibe to it and reminded me of *The Shining*, mirrors everywhere and octagonal marble tiles, and a bathtub so big I'd have to brace myself with one arm to shave my legs. I pictured myself going down the drain.

I'd make my way to Marcia's in the mornings to oversee the work once it had started and called Rob to share that I was walking in my slippers down the sidewalk. He'd tell me how a jar fell on his head as he sat on the floor putting on his face fur for Craig. The gash on his head was maybe a sign to stop performing and as he tormented himself over it, I'd encourage him by saying, "No, you were just in character. What do you expect as Craig? He's a mess but you're not."

We were both messes and we'd catch each other's heads like they were lids flying off a full-speed blender. We were in tandem, though. "Moving is one of the top three most stressful things you can do," everyone kept telling me, and when you hear that from friends who don't have time to help, it rings even more true. "Moving is one of the top three most stressful things you can do. It's up there with death and divorce," I'd hear over and over again. Moving is both death and divorce: the time you spent in that home dies and you divorce most of your belongings.

Friends would pop by to escort me and the belongings that survived the divorce and help push one of those wheeled carts through Washington Square Park to Marcia's. I wanted to keep organized and didn't want to unpack a bunch of cardboard boxes that would leave me feeling both empty and overwhelmed, so I made several trips to unload things by hand. Marcia had gone to Cape Cod and we were waiting for permits for demolition to start and I arranged my things nicely in Tony's old room—"my prince," as Marcia refers to him, always touching her hand to her heart whenever she says his name. "The renovations will be done when Marcia comes back in October," Mindy, Tony, and I were chanting like a mantra. Tony had terrible stomach problems that were more than just lactose intolerance and was getting it all checked out—moving is emotional.

I decided to leave for just ten days to do Kogonada's movie *Columbus* with John Cho and Haley Lu Richardson. Kogonada, with his mononymous name, had written about film in magazines like *Filmmaker* and I'd seen his video essays on Vimeo, which were so beautiful they took my breath away—they were edited composites of directors he admired, like Ozu and Kubrick, Soderbergh and Linklater—seen through his artful eye and understanding of cinema. He was so inspired by the mecca of modern architecture in Columbus, Indiana, that he'd based the film there. I'd never been, or at least not that I remembered, and kept calling it Illinois. The demolition (the noise) in the new place would start while I was away, and I decided that if the cost of the moving trucks matched what I'd get paid for the part, I'd consider it an equal trade; it did, so I did it. Situations had to have balance, had to be just, or I may have cracked. So when the part came, I looked at it as meaningful help.

I'd play Eleanor, an architect and writer who was assisting her mentor, Jae Yong Lee, while he was giving a lecture in Columbus. She'd spent her early twenties studying with him in Seoul and lived with his family. Kogonada said she was the bridge or in-between to two men: a daughter or creative mistress to Jae Yong Lee, and for his son Jin, his first love (who wasn't his mother) and sister figure. The different kinds of love we have for each other branch out to affect the lives of everyone around us. Trees don't compete for sunlight, like we learned at school, or fight to get taller—they collaborate and exist harmoniously naturally—that's how they grow.

In the film, within the frame, Kogonada placed architecture as if it were a character. Midcentury architecture had so much promise and optimism—the placement of buildings on the ground in relation to nature and to the space already held in the surrounding environment: the lines of symmetry drawing out vertically and horizontally into space. The harmony becomes alive when you participate, when you can stand inside the space and feel it. Haley Lu's character, Casey, would awaken Jin to those thoughts again. Casey represented Eleanor twenty years ago, before her marital responsibilities and the anguish that comes with maturity.

Within the story of the film and the characters' relationships, Kogonada wanted to explore what he called "the burden of absence that children carry in regards to their parents." The first scene takes place at the famous modernist-masterpiece home of J. Irwin Miller and Xenia Simons Miller, built by Eero Saarinen with interiors designed by Alexander Girard and Dan Kiley—known as the Miller House and Garden. The Miller family was responsible for commissioning the best architects in the world at this time and paying contractors to build their designs—it was their philanthropy as well as the Cummins Engine Company that stamped this small town of forty-five thousand people with over fifty modernist buildings.

The first shot was at the Miller House and Garden, where I run to greet my mentor Jae Yong Lee as he is taking in the view of the massive east lawn framed with weeping beech trees. It was raining that day and foreshadowed the sadness to come. The next scene, I'd be on the phone with my husband and Jae Yong Lee would collapse. I would get to drop my umbrella and run to him, admitting him into the hospital. I'd get in touch with Jin to have him fly to Columbus, where we'd sit at a bar while I tried to temper his resentments toward his father. Why be there for his dad when his dad was never there for him? We hadn't seen each other in over a decade and our relationship was still like family—I'd guide him like an all-loving mother to stay, like a sister who's "always right." "He's your father, Jin." I'd get to express my own grief and frustration with my dad's prostate cancer of over twenty years, which was getting worse now. His bones were brittle and a tumor was bumping a screw from his hip operation. His charm had pushed its edge into being erratically demanding and projections too strong for me to break through. I'd be told I wasn't listening to him and "I don't think you understand." My twin brother and I were fourteen again in his eyes and our issues with Dad would have to be resolved internally—the burden of absence active in both of us and his situation demanding lightness and humor. He'd always been a wonderful narcissist and a star patient to his doctors at Sloan Kettering. One got so worked up that she finally shouted at him, "You use your cancer to get attention!" My dad thought this was hysterical, in the way that funny things are true, and savored the exra attention. My mom, relaying the story, adorned in her Ann Taylor and gold chains, rolled her eyes and shrugged a "What're you gonna do?" How many more seats in the audience need to be filled? My brother was carrying so much of the burden down south and reaching his limit with the demands placed on him. He and his wife have three kids, and when Dad would call at seven thirty in the morning with a craving for an Egg McMuffin, it didn't bode well. I was concerned for his health, both of theirs, all of theirs—body, mind, and spirit. Making a scotch for Dad when he was on chemo was painful. I would place my father in the hospital and bring him flowers and hug my brother.

I'd get up the nerve to get on wheels again and ride a rental bike to Jill's Diner to eat breakfast, where the small-town talk of agriculture sounded like radio: "All the rain we've had is bad for the onions . . . how're your onions this summer?" I savored the talk as much as the old-timey breakfast of scrambled eggs and grits and buttered white toast, and a minister I met there even bought my breakfast, as a welcome to town. I rode my bike around Henry Moore's *Large Arch* sculpture, which stood outside the main library designed by I. M. Pei—which was across the street from the First Christian Church built by Eliel Saarinen. I'd sit in my car waiting to take Casey under my wing and away from her home to study architecture herself; the metal spire of the North Christian Church (designed by Eliel's son, Eero Saarinen) was almost two hundred feet high and stood in the frame between Casey and Jin. Haley's performance in the car as she poured out her grief was spectacular and human.

I stayed up too late on my last day of working, having drinks at a bar downtown they'd kept open for us privately—John Cho was too recognizable from *Star Trek* and fans were getting rowdy. We partied with Casey's mom in the film, Michelle Forbes—"Miksha"—and shared some war stories about being women in show business. I'd miss my flight out of Columbus, thinking it was at one o'clock instead of eleven o'clock, and would receive an email with the news that my mentor in college, Joe Stockdale, had passed that very day. A line I'd said to Jin the first day of work, how his father "meant everything to me," expressed itself again, there in the airport lounge. The Perimenopausal Puppet Troupe came back to life, speeding their emotions to my awareness—and all that pathos.

The move to Marcia's was emotional. Upheavals happened
to the building as well as to the family. Tony had been diagnosed
with diverticulitis and was in the hospital while I was shooting
Columbus. I came back to a garbage bag of food on the
kitchen floor, and saw mice scurrying out. He'd been in too much
pain to take it downstairs after he emptied the fridge. His old
room was packed to the gills with large boxes, along with my
clothes, which hung on a wardrobe rack, and the plants I'd placed
on the bookshelves. We bit our nails for two months, hoping
Marcia wouldn't mind my things stuffed in Tony's old room. She
did, though, and I had to move everything upstairs to collect dust
there.

I got *Lost in Space* and the offer to play Dr. Smith on Netflix while
I was moving some things from the country, from the house I'd
struggled to keep. I was obsessed with the show as a kid and would
wake up before six and watch the static of the TV as it turned to the
color bars and the show began. The Robinson family, stranded on
their own alien planet, and Dr. Smith, an alien family member. I'd be
moving to Vancouver in six weeks for what would be eight months,
and get paid to pay homage to a character and show that I loved.

A few days before Christmas, the last ceiling patch was spackled
and sanded. My nose had stopped dripping like a faucet and steroids
had gotten rid of an earache that had me truly unbalanced. I brought
Marcia upstairs to show her my projector screen. We both loved
TCM and an old movie was on, and she loved the renovations. I ran
out to dinner with Rob and, afterward, would finally have a quiet
night in. I started a bath when I got home and as I waited, Gracie sat
with me and we took in the new view with a sense of peace, at last.
Until I saw water gushing from under the crack of the bathroom
door.

I grabbed blankets and towels and even took off my clothes to throw on the floor. I called Rob, as I put on warm-ups, shaking, my voice small and afraid of getting into trouble. He talked me down and asked if Marcia had called. "Not yet," I said, and then she did. It would all be okay in the end, Rob assured me, and wished me luck.

"Hi, Marcia." I sounded like a child in trouble.

"*What* is happening? Outside my bedroom is dripping!"

"I'm so sorry, Marcia. The bathtub overflowed." I said it calmly and then, "I'll be right down."

I met her in her living room and she asked if I was an idiot and I assured her I wasn't. I was used to my old bathtub, which never overflowed and was louder than the one in the bathroom upstairs and had a thing in it that prevented overflowing. "That chandelier costs a fortune!" she wailed. "What about all the African art?!"

I helped her move an expensive antique table away from the wall. I moved the Chinese porcelain bowl that held her mail and photographs, which were now wet, as she shouted, "My theater tickets are in there, and *ruined*!" I moved a large African art mask as she told me it was worth a fortune and irreplaceable. "And it's Christmas!" she shouted. When she asked me again if I was an idiot I said that I was as I looked at the wall in front of us—how it was sweating as it produced tears that dripped.

I ran upstairs to get more towels, as gentle drips were falling from the flooded ceiling onto Marcia's carpet. "Marcia, I will be here in the summer to oversee repairs to whatever damage is done."

"I don't know if you will even be living here next summer!" she said as she walked into her bathroom for more towels.

I went to bed wondering about my move. Had I made a choice in hopes of a fantasy? Would the reality of it be a nightmare? Was I living in the right place? My friends had been concerned, and it *was* kind of a crazy thing to do. I'm surprised I fell asleep and slept through the night. The next day I called my dad to tell him the whole story, and we laughed hard about it. I called him on

Christmas to tell him how Marcia had offered me a hot toddy for my cold the night before, as well as Eukanuba, and how I said, "I don't think dog food will help me with this, but maybe you mean echinacea?" We laughed hard about that one, too. It sounded like Marcia was the perfect landlady for me.

20
Master of Storms

I met Woody Allen for *Shadows and Fog* and *Bullets over Broadway* back in the nineties. Juliet Taylor has been his casting director for years and he's never liked the process of meeting actors for roles, so it's up to her to choose a handful of people she thinks are right for whatever part in whatever film he's working on that year. She and I had been in Kraków, Poland, together as judges at a film festival, so that's how I landed in the right timing for *Irrational Man*. It's really like that game in Vegas with that wheel that spins and the ball lands in the right place—I don't even know the name of that thing.

It was time to reinvent and get creative. I'd met Camille Paglia when we were on *The Joy Behar Show*, and she gave me her book *Glittering Images*. A year later, her publicist proposed we make something together; we were emailing trying to figure out what that could be. Something surreal and absurd or meta—a walk-and-talk film at first, where Camille talks about art and culture and architecture and then we have dinner at a restaurant and talk some more (like *My Dinner with Andre*).

We'd reference Ingmar Bergman's film *Persona*, which Camille knew inside out (it inspired the title of her famous book *Sexual*

Personae), and maybe Anna Kendrick would play a younger actress I'm haunted by. We'd set a scene onstage where I'd perform from the Greek tragedy *Medea*, with Anna in the wings as my understudy. Camille would be sitting in the audience as a critic—critiquing both Anna and me as we took turns playing the part. The idea of doing an experimental film kept me entertained enough not to obsess about never working as an actor again. I thought about teaching acting classes at NYU and visited the acting department, assisting a class, which was fun.

My friend Jenn Ruff was an editor and teacher there and collaborating with me on the Camille project, and I took her to Poland as my guest at the festival. We'd take boat rides around Kraków with Juliet and fellow jurors and watch films during the day and hobnob with journalists and filmmakers at night. There's so much history, dating back to the Stone Age, and then all these baroque-style basilicas and cathedrals—so gothic. The sights had us looking up and down, wherever we walked, which slowed us down. The nuns from all the churches around the neighborhood had an easier time of it and I even saw a few of them walking briskly, looking at their iPhones.

I met Benedict Cumberbatch at the hotel, before he ran through a crowd of screaming fan-girls to his limo, and before he was honored for his work in independent cinema that night. I had trouble identifying his work in independent film but gushed about his work as Sherlock Holmes and racked my brain briefly to remember an actress I'd worked with twenty years earlier, a friend of his he'd mentioned. He was wearing a beautiful silver-gray suit that was perfectly tailored and dashed quickly out, leaving me bewildered and a little embarrassed and feeling on the spot.

Juliet brought me in to meet Woody the week we got back. Everyone knows you meet Woody with one foot out the door, and that meeting him could last just a few minutes—and that the amount of time was no indication of whether or not you'd get cast. I knew the part I was up for was a teacher, so I dressed appropriately and made my way to his office and screening room uptown. It's in a door-man building with a small lobby and I got there right on time so I could breeze through the casting office and into the screening room, where he was standing and waiting to the left. Juliet was next to him and introduced us.

I smiled, because I'm a fan, and shook his hand. Juliet's luggage got lost on the way home from Poland, so we made small talk about that and about Kraków—about the salt mines he wouldn't be able to visit because of his claustrophobia. He said something like "Juliet wanted us to meet because I am doing a film in Rhode Island and there's a part you could be right for." He said he wanted to meet me to make sure I wasn't crazy. I laughed and assured him that I wasn't. He went on to say that the movie was starring Joaquin Phoenix. I gushed over Joaquin, calling him soulful and poetic, to which Woody simply said, "Uh-oh." Since my foot was out the door, it was easy to get out and make my way with the rest of my day.

I got feedback later on that the meeting went well, that Woody was engaged in the four minutes we spent talking. I'd wait to see if I fit his vision.

I got a call the next day while I was in the dog run with Gracie, and my manager asked casually if I was going to be home from noon to two o'clock because that was when the "sides" (as the pages in a script are called) would be delivered. We laughed and I actually started crying because that ball on that wheel had landed in that thing in Vegas. "Roulette" is what it's called. I then dropped Gracie back at the apartment and walked to Trader Joe's for some groceries, and when I returned my sides were hand-delivered to me.

There was a cover letter describing the character of Rita: a science teacher, a flirt, in an unhappy marriage, and loose. I didn't receive a letter that flattered me in any way as an actress but maybe that was some kind of tactic. The title of the movie was *WASP*, and I smiled when I read the side pages where Rita referred to herself as "the original lapsed Catholic." How did he know that I was a lapsed Catholic?

The pages were terrific and he'd captured my voice so distinctly that I wondered if he'd written the pages the night before specifically for my cadence. I began to study the lines, to find clues to the character.

The writing was so witty and natural, but that's all I could glean when I put my detective hat on. What the tone was, I had no idea. Nor did I know what happened in the plot or if it was a darker film (like *Interiors*) or lighter (like *Bananas*). I got one clue wrong off the bat, though. It wasn't a Woody Allen film about white Anglo-Saxon Protestants. "WASP" was an acronym for "Woody Allen Summer Project." It's hard to see the forest for the trees but I'd be in the thick of Woody's island soon and game for it all.

I broke my wrist a few weeks later and it would have to be a part of Rita. There's something that's said in acting class when a mistake happens: "Use it." There are no addendums to that saying, like "even if it's your right hand that's needed for everything." So I rolled with the punches and held back tears at my costume fitting as I crept my newly splinted wrist through shirtsleeves and groaned at myself in Suzy Benzinger's wardrobe mirror about how puffy those pain pills (and the ice cream I'd eaten to go with them) had made me. Suzy could sense my downward spiral and said something about Woody's saying I had nice skin, which I didn't believe for a second.

I left two weeks later for camera tests and production and to find a place to live in Providence or Newport where we were shooting. I took my truck, a Nissan Frontier my dad had given me from his dealership, and Gracie spent five weeks with Rob. I met Emma Stone in the hair and makeup trailer and she was open, funny, warm, and bright—genuinely supportive and even respectful. Having starred in *Magic in the Moonlight*, she understood my nervousness, and if you're around the right people that energy can be close to fun—and it was with her.

Camera tests were held in a huge soundstage, and offices, like accounting and production, were off to the sides. Our wardrobes were on racks with partition sheets in a dingy room. I passed Joaquin barreling out the double doors, so we hugged our introduction and admitted to our sweating armpits and nerves and laughed as we got called impatiently to go our separate ways—him to change again and me to the camera test.

The room was huge and dark and the art department had put together a makeshift set with a lamp on a table pushed up against the wall, about fifty feet from camera. There was a line drawn on the floor for camera, to measure distance for the focus puller. They were working quietly, and Emma walked comfortably to and away from camera. In less than ten minutes, she was off and running to another change.

Danielle Rigby, Woody's first AD from Australia, greeted me warmly and invited me in as I waited for a new lighting setup. She brought me over to Woody, who was on his iPhone standing close to the wall, away from camera. He asked about my wrist, which was still puffy and stiff but would be fine for shooting. I would just have to wear my splint between takes. He said I could wear the splint if I needed to, but I assured him I'd be alright. We spoke quietly, as if talking would interfere with the world he was shaping—we spoke in church whispers.

His daughter Manzie, who was twelve at the time, came over and introduced herself. She was spirited and lovely and brought me to meet Woody's sister, Letty, where they were sitting in director chairs at the video monitor. I put my bag on the back of a chair and Danielle called me over to meet Darius Khondji, the DP, and his camera crew. Woody came over to have a look at me, alternately folding his arms and clasping his hands, as I stood in front of camera.

It really did feel like church in there, and the crew worked swiftly and in hushed tones. I made small talk and said something stupid like "Wow, we're shooting in film," and Woody said something like "Well, this is a movie," at which I laughed, alone. I turned around and walked to the mark in the back of the room feeling like there was toilet paper on the bottom of my shoe, or that my skirt was tucked into my panty hose.

Helen Robin, Woody's longtime producer, had no time to be a re-altor while overseeing production, and actors were given a fee to find their own living accommodations. Emma Stone got a house outside of Newport proper, Joaquin would live in Providence around the college campus, and I found a nice 1800s hovel with no air conditioning or bathtub, on the bottom floor of a house just a ten-minute walk from the main part of town, close to the wharf and restaurants.

I met up with Joaquin to go over our scenes and he kept quiet about the reveal of his character, Abe. It turned out Abe was a psychopath, but my character was in love with him, so why tell me about it? He had more on his plate to deal with, like carrying the whole movie. Joaquin had gained like thirty pounds for the part and we laughed about that, and about how Woody told him not to grow any facial hair or do anything weird when they talked on the phone about working together. Here's something else that's funny about Woody: his strong aversion to blue jeans. He asked Suzy what the students would be wearing and she said blue jeans. "No one wears blue jeans," he said.

"Students wear blue jeans," she responded.

"No, they don't," and that went on until everyone was in khakis.

My first day of work was on the first day of shooting and I was in the first scene up in the morning as well as the last scene of the day. It was a three-and-a-half-page scene, which is a standard, if long, scene in any movie. I drove the scene with information from the third part of the film, which I knew nothing about. It took place in a bar and there were about a hundred extras there. On Woody's sets, they call the actors in at the last minute so there's not too much distraction before we start shooting. I recognized Virginia, his script coordinator, who I'd worked with years ago. She used to be a nun, if you can believe that. I naively thought this was a sign that God was on my side that day, but this would be a day resembling more of a baptism by fire.

I was milling about briefly before sitting at the bar with Emma for our scene together. When I sat down, Darius leaned over and asked, whispering, if I could sit facing out, since that was where the light would hit my face in the way he liked. "Sure, of course," I said. Emma would be walking in and I'd notice her and motion for her to sit with me.

After the first take Woody came over and said, "Are you going to sit like that? Because it looks like you're waiting for the camera to land on you." Hilarious. There isn't much he can say that isn't funny, even if the joke's on you and it's not a joke. I was good-natured and apologized, saying I'd forgotten how to act, that I didn't know how to do this anymore. I wasn't going to say, "Darius told me to sit here and he's your DP," mostly because it didn't occur to me. I felt stupid and knew there was a chance I'd be fired and replaced but went with the flow, man.

Later I would read Eric Lax's book about the making of *Irrational Man*, which talks about this scene and how Woody wanted to cut the introduction when he heard it because he knew it was false once we were rolling. But a big part of being an actor is falling into the projection that a director wants, or being in the director's subjectivity. "Rita is a lonely woman," Woody repeated to me a few times, which wasn't emphasized in the letter. "Lonely woman" has a deeper weight to it than the "unhappy marriage" he'd mentioned in the letter.

We went into the bulk of the scene, the dialogue, and started with a two-shot. Things were going smoothly and there was good energy in the air. When Emma and I went downstairs as the lighting was being set up for her coverage, she said Woody liked me or he wouldn't have been hanging around camera. She gave me an assuring nod, like "You better believe it, kiddo." Emma is savvy and she and Woody had a great rapport, like school chums. They caught up between takes with casual witty banter, like Groucho Marx and Ethel Merman.

At one point they were talking dessert and I chimed in with "I love meringue," which is true. "How can a whipped egg white with a little bit of sugar be that delicious?" I might've added, if my initial comment hadn't stopped the conversation.

I pushed away the thought that meringue could get me fired and thought more of the lonely woman that I was supposed to be. Hitchcock was famous for saying you should treat actors like cattle, but with good directors I'd felt more like a horse, since horses are trained with subtlety and instinct and sometimes deliberate force. I would clomp to lunch like an old mare with Emma, who had the light steady gallop of a young and beautiful Thoroughbred.

Joaquin was sitting at the cafeteria table alone, like a sexy beast hovering over his script, which was laid out in front of him. He asked if I was able to sleep; he hadn't but I had. He was already sweating—it was August and hot out—and I showed him my swollen wrist, which made him wince and cower. I could barely move it up or down and the heat agitated it. We told him the morning had gone well and that we were moving on to my coverage after lunch.

During my coverage, when the cameras turned on me back at the bar, was when it all went to hell in a handbasket. I did twenty takes of the scene, which I'd never done in my life. For one line, it was important not to sound definitive, which could imply that Rita knew Abe was a psychopath. It had the words "crackpot theory" in it and I couldn't get it to sound the way Woody wanted it to, so he was giving me line readings, which is the biggest blow to an actor's ego. The hundred extras were there, though, to support my meltdown and to witness the greatest living film director's frustration at my performance.

At one point he said I was a terrific actress and a complicated woman but that he didn't want to see any of that in his movie. I don't know what I felt in that moment—caught but liberated into unknown territory? I stared into the eyes of the focus puller, who was an arm's length away, and she smiled to assure me that anything and everything was right in the world—she even gave me a thumbs-up. I guess Parker could die a little and Rita could take over. I'd forget my lines and shout to Virginia to cue me. I was flailing in the water.

I remembered how I almost drowned in a wave pool as a kid and got pulled out and coughed up water. Emma's pretty face was gobsmacked and compassionate, and she asked if I needed anything from her. I wanted a lobotomy and a tapeworm. My own thoughts sounded like pig Latin and I felt like I'd be smart to find something else to do for a living. But at the present moment, I would not forget I was being directed by Woody Allen.

By some miracle, I got the line right in the medium shot, which was met with the relief of a baby being delivered and I was happy to be moving on. I told Woody I felt like I was being chiropracted. He put his hands in a frame shot in front of my face. "Now we're going in for a close-up, so, you know, don't do too much moving around," he told me.

"I think I remember what a close-up is," I said. "We can try a few." It went more smoothly this time around, and he gave direction from the monitor, like "Do anything! Say what you want!" and came over after it was all done and told me which takes he was printing. I'd have to wait for a blue ribbon when I wrapped in five weeks.

Outside, one of the producers said I reminded him of Sandy Dennis, which was nice of him, and then I got in the van with Emma for the ride back to "holding." My makeup artist knocked on the door of my trailer and asked if I needed a hug but I said I was fine, which I was, more or less. My hairdresser referred to the ordeal as a "brain fart," but I knew it was much more than that.

Suzy breezed by like Thelma Ritter, the dresser for Bette Davis in *All About Eve* and the wisecracker in many old classic movies, saying Woody always freaks out when he starts to hear his dialogue said for the first time and usually reshoots the first day of work anyway. She said a lot of actresses have had meltdowns in their trailers on the first day of work and she really helped me brush it off further and besides, I knew what a creative process could be. But also, I couldn't afford to be anxious because I had another scene to do and had to change.

It was a little scene in which I fantasized about Joaquin taking me away to travel to Europe, "to London even," anywhere but here. Woody works fast, and I'm like that, too, so I wanted to do it right in the first take; the first take is usually the best one. So we did the first take, but the sound was bad, and then we did another take, which I felt was meh, and Woody came over and said, "That was good, the first take, that was the right temperature, but it was bad for sound so we have to go again." I told him I was good at looping, and he said he didn't like looping, so we'd go again.

He emphasized once more that Rita was "a lonely woman" and in an "unhappy marriage"; I assured him with a nod. He said, "No smiling," to which I nodded again, smiling. He moves his hands and fingers when he talks, like he's molding invisible space for you to figure out exactly what it is, to communicate some sensitivity, maybe. That's my interpretation, anyway. Before he sat back down at the monitor, he shouted out, like an afterthought, "Just make sure your voice doesn't get too soft, you don't want to sound too actressy." It took me aback, and I immediately stood up and took a deep breath like I was going to faint; and fake-stabbed myself in the stomach, letting out an "UGH"; and stuck my tongue out, like a dying possum. "That was deliberate," he said quickly, and with humor, and I took the fake knife out of my side and put it in the other side and laugh-screamed, "Do it again!" And I knew that moment said we could work together.

I went home that night and talked to my analyst on the phone. My wrist was throbbing, and I couldn't even turn a doorknob. In denial, I'd bought food for the fridge and brought my knives from home so I could cook. But it was painful just to place my hand around the strap of my purse as it hung on my shoulder, the most natural thing in real life, and I knew I'd have to carry bags and purses in the scene we were shooting on Friday. What was I going to do?

This was in 2014, when the accusation scandal wasn't as hot in the climate of the culture, but I read the articles online about the case and can relate to all the players in the story. I wonder if it will be staged as an opera in fifty years. To each his own. Social media would definitely be the chorus, or would it be an oracle? We're in choppy air—fasten your seat belt.

I called Helen the next day to see if she'd ask Woody if I could wear the splint for the rest of the five weeks I was working. Since we'd only shot Rita's final scenes it was conceivable, in the storyline. I was anxious and called Joaquin to get his experienced input. He said Woody was a maestro who I had to trust, and he was right. We talked about Charlotte Rampling in *Stardust Memories*, how open and beautiful she was, and said good night.

There's a documentary from the Criterion Collection that comes with the DVD of Ingmar Bergman's film *Persona*, where Liv Ullmann talks about working with him—specifically about a scene with a burning house where he was screaming at her to "get closer to the fire!" and she knew that he was talking to her, not the character. They fell in love when she was twenty-five and he was forty-six, and had a volatile and creative relationship. He was intensely controlling and went so far as to build a stone wall around their house, only letting her leave on Wednesdays (when she'd wash her hair and have a few drinks). But they were dear friends in the end and they kept working together, even after he married someone else.

I'd think of Claire Bloom's memoir about her relationship with Philip Roth, and how she expressed her relationship to acting as annihilating. If I hadn't had a father who was devouring, would I have had the ability to devour stories or be devoured by them? Annihilation in order to take shape all over again? I'm turning my light off.

To be kept in the dark or in the unknown is to find your way out. You have a more interesting film when you capture characters finding their way. I always loved Nancy Drew—how she tiptoed around those caves with her flashlight, moving carefully forward, listening deeply to her instincts and finding her way out.

Helen called the next day to say it was too late to wear the splint, and I almost started crying, but I played it pretty cool on the phone. It was enough that my hand hurt but being a "difficult actress" was the last thing I wanted to carry around. No, that was not the part I was going to play out.

"She feels trapped." That was another thing Woody emphasized about Rita that first day. It was there in the material in the cliff scene with Joaquin, where Rita says she feels trapped in her life as a teacher and wants to run away to Spain.

I felt trapped by what I did and wanted to run away from it. Maybe that was what Woody saw in me when he cast me: that I was over the hill and the right age for all those feelings, for that particular realization and dissolving of fantasy—that disillusionment. Like Rita, I wanted to flee so I wouldn't have to face remorse—of another life I could've lived.

One night that week, before I'd shot any more scenes, I escorted my broken wrist out to dinner on the wharf in Newport, where I met two nice ladies, one with a broken leg who rode around on a scooter, and her best friend, who was joining her. We had a nice dinner at the bar and talked about how compassionate some people were toward someone with an injury. My splint was a great conversation starter. You'd be surprised how many people want to tell you their own horror stories of falls and breaks, and the PT community is full of a bunch of angel people who are wonderful and doing real hands-on healing stuff. We had a great dinner talking about how miraculously the body heals itself and how humbling the journey of an injury can be—how people get others' attention and compassion from relating the stories of their own broken bones and recoveries.

Walking out of the place, I spotted Woody and Soon-Yi on their way to dinner, and I took off my hat and waved as if they were far out in the ocean and couldn't see me, even though they were just ten feet away. I think I even jumped up and down. It was fortuitous running into him in real life and he gave me a tiny smile, and I quickly apologized to him for Monday's work and groveled. "Dailies were good, the close-up was nice," he said. I was relieved and happy that we wouldn't have to reshoot it, and pumped my hands in the air like "Yay!"

I introduced myself to Soon-Yi, who wanted to hike the cliffs, and Woody made a gesture like "You two should go together," but then we found out that we couldn't, since I had to work and she was leaving town. I told her how bright and sweet Manzie was and mentioned the ocean, how I didn't care for the beach. "As my mother would say, 'all that sand,'" I said. I explained I felt more like Geraldine Page in *Interiors*, with moments staring out at the ocean that started with peace, but could linger into a foreboding feeling, depending on my mood.

Woody and Soon-Yi were going to the Pearl for their famous crab cakes. It's clear that they're right for each other. He shooed me away, joking, "Don't you have lines to learn for tomorrow?"

"Oh yes, I have to memorize those lines!" Then I walked away, swiftly, as directed.

The next morning, Joaquin and I were scheduled to shoot a walk-and-talk outside on the campus. Before the scene, Woody said, in his apologetic manner, "What I wrote isn't very good, um . . . If you'd like to add anything, please do. Say whatever you want. Make it better, more believable than what I wrote. And you know . . . uh . . ." What he was saying was, be in the reality of this movie he was making. So Joaquin and I did the scene, and afterward, Woody came over and spread his arms out reassuringly between us and said, joking and deliberate, "Neither of you are getting fired."

After I knew I wasn't getting fired, I felt as relaxed and cool with everything as I possibly could. Joaquin would groan loudly in agony and run to Woody to apologize for his performance or ask a question. He was playing a psychopath, and that's a challenging role. Woody reassured him over and over. "No no no, it was very very good," he'd say. Or, "Well, for me, it sounded as if people were having a conversation, but uh . . ." Joaquin would scratch his head and brood (the first week is always hard), but later in the shoot he said Woody, directing him in a scene, said he didn't have to have so much "style," which I thought was very astute. We laughed about it because he'd never thought of himself that way, and it was so obvious.

It was a relief having so many scenes with Joaquin, where I wouldn't have to be the one torturing myself. I liked that he took up that emotional space. I loved his energy and sensitivity and perfectionism. There was another walk-and-talk scene and I was feeling comfortable in my work. In the scene, I invited Joaquin's character, Abe, up to my house to "smoke some grass." When he passed on that offer, I said, "That's cool." Then Woody stopped the take and said, "That's terrible! You can't say that!"

I started groaning and apologizing and shouted back, "Okay, cool, I won't say it!" Teachers don't say "cool" anymore, Woody thought— but they don't call pot "grass" either, I could've said but didn't.

Later that day I asked Woody about the crab cakes from the night before, if they were as good as he'd heard. I mentioned being from the New Orleans area and brought up Galatoire's, a place I grew up going to that also had famous crab cakes. We were getting ready to shoot a short but sensitive scene in the rain with my husband; I'd tell him I was leaving him. I'd just met the actor playing my husband that day, and he was so tender and bright that my heart was already breaking. Woody said he liked the crab cakes, and I went to the car to film the scene.

The scene begins mid-conversation, where Rita's mentioned a break from the marriage and her desire to travel, "to see other places," she says. She tries to appease both of their feelings by saying, "Let's just talk about the details." After the first take, Woody scampered over, through the fake rain, holding on to his hat. He leaned into the car and said, "That was good. It's the right temperature. Now you have fifteen minutes to get this right and then you can have your crab cake." We were done in less than fifteen minutes and I couldn't have my crab cake because the restaurant was closed on Mondays.

I'd grown up with sardonic wit with my own father, so I was used to it. When I asked my dad what he thought of *Superman Returns*, he quipped, "At least I wasn't bored."

My favorite night of shooting was a scene with Joaquin where Rita knocks on Abe's door with two bottles of whiskey. She says she was in the neighborhood, and that she got a bottle for her husband, but she knew how much Abe liked whiskey so she picked one up for him, too. Just a sad, funny bit of dialogue between two lonely grown-ups. "Come in," he says, as she's in the room already, and Rita says, "I thought you'd never ask."

I was nervous before the scene. During rehearsal, Woody stands to watch, like all directors do, but he's Woody Allen so it's different. A few minutes earlier, Darius had asked me to come in through the awning of the door quickly, since it shadowed me. So I did. When Woody watched the scene, he was like, "Why are you in such a rush? I don't understand . . ." I wasn't going to tattle, so I went back to my "It's because I've never acted before and I don't know what I'm doing" bit, which felt true enough. Better than "Oh, Darius wanted me to find my light." How lame would that have sounded? Joaquin had run away to his rented home to rest before we shot, so I couldn't go to him for assurance or comfort, plus he couldn't give me that in the scene, either, so he didn't in real life.

When we started shooting, the first take was alive and I was "the right temperature," Woody said. Joaquin hated it so we did it again, but it was bad for sound. Woody came to apologize, and then he said, "Just the tiniest bit of irony when you say 'I thought you'd never ask.' Just the tiniest bit." His hands gesturing in that maestro way, soft and expressing the touch. We did the take, and I heard a groan again, which I didn't know how to interpret. Disdain? Relief? Boredom?

The crew started filing out, looking as if they were leaving, which they were. Woody stopped to say, "Mmm . . . It's cutting together nicely . . . We've seen some of the scenes . . . And . . . mhmm." As in, "Yes."

I nodded in a way that said, "Good good good, have a nice dinner, carry on," which he did. I went across the street to visit Tom, one of my friends from high school, who lived just a few doors down from where we were shooting. We sat on the porch belonging to his neighbors and had a beer and watched the crew wrap up location.

One time I saw Woody looking at me from about fifty feet away, and I waved my splinted wrist side to side, far away from what felt like a shore, as I stood on the porch. He didn't wave back so I took it to mean he was in his camera and so I carried on being the subject, like a character in one of his movies, which I was. But there he was, the progenitor of independent cinema, auteur and actor, around eighty years old now, in his iconic, casually chic weatherman attire, having his freedom to create whatever world he wanted. I had a good relationship with my wrist by this point and would look at it like it held all my anxieties, leaving the rest of me relaxed.

Woody listens with his headphones maybe as much as he watches. He likes to hear the subtlety of the voice. My final scene was a walk on campus with Joaquin to meet Emma, who tells him some news, a scandal about a judge who's been murdered. At this point, we had slept together but our relationship had cooled. I had a line to Joaquin before Emma came over that could express withering irony or jealousy. It was maybe seven words, off the cuff, nothing major. In the second take, I stepped back from the pain or jealousy and instead had more irony. After Woody gave notes to Emma and Joaquin, he said to me, "You lost the feeling of that line." And he was right. I'd lost the feeling, and he'd caught it.

Danielle called out, "It's a wrap for Parker," and everyone clapped. Woody came over and put his hands out in a don't-hug-me stance, smiling, saying, "I may have the Ebola virus . . ." The news had come out in the papers that very day. I mirrored him and he said, "Thank you for your performance. You delivered the lines as I'd heard them and envisioned them. And now your parents will be proud of you." I laughed *really* hard at that one.

Who in show business believes their parents are proud of them? I never did, and fight to believe it. It's an industry (an art, hopefully) full of orphans left to create their own worlds with one another. I don't feel glamorous, I feel like a possum—the animal born clinging to its mother's tail, that grows up by falling off it, and probably too soon. Acting is the possum's defense. Have you ever seen this? When threatened, they play dead—and they're very convincing at it. They scare themselves so deeply that their eyes roll back into their heads and their little tongues stick out. They'll even take it so far as to froth at the mouth. They'll go on with the act as long as they're terrified and it's truly ghoulish, because they've been known to be buried alive—they're famous for it.

Anyway, we celebrated at Cannes, where the movie premiered. Here's another serendipitous thing: on the drive to the Croisette, where the festival is held, the woman on the *Irrational Man* press team sat in front with the driver and said I lived in her sister's old apartment. I got to ask her sister if it was true that the great guitar player Jorma Kaukonen built the closet there, and he had. I hadn't been to Cannes in twenty years—I'd had some independent movies there in the nineties, back when invitations were on paper and there was dancing. I danced with Chris Isaak.

For the red carpet, I wore a dress my friend Leana designed. It was a bright coral lamé with a matching turban. She'd convinced me to go blond and I figured why not. It was Cannes and the French

Riviera and I wanted to go all out. The look or persona went viral and friends sent pictures from Instagram—in one, I was being taken away by a cop. John C. Reilly went all out too, and I ran into him in the lobby of the Hotel Martinez wearing a porkpie hat and a cane with a duck's head from Brooks Brothers. Life is too important to be taken seriously. That's an Oscar Wilde quote and it's on one of my coffee mugs so it's easy to remember.

I'd keep my hair blond for Woody's next film, *Café Society*, and it would overlap with shooting for Christopher Guest's film *Mascots* for Netflix, where I played an armadillo. I never expected a roadkill motif in the narrative of my story but I'm cool with it.

My favorite shot in *Irrational Man* is toward the end, when Emma's flashlight crosses the frame and points right into the lens, after she realizes Abe is a monster. Then she takes a solitary walk on the rocky beach, and "The 'In' Crowd" by Ramsey Lewis Trio starts up again. It scored the whole film and when it comes up at the end, it leaves us to wonder, with energy and complexity, about the big picture.

21

What We Make

My parents were madly in love during my childhood and liked being away from us. Who could blame them? We were kids! "Children are to be seen and not heard!" they'd say with humor and reprimand. They punished us but they didn't beat the shit out of us and I'm very grateful for that. When they took a break from us to go on vacation, they'd say, "We're getting away from *you guys*!" We'd stay at Nonnie and Glenn's, and sometimes my uncle Mark would give us a ride back to Monroe. A few times, I was put on a Greyhound bus, which was cool.

Mark was my father's younger brother and came into the world on a visit from Paw Paw to Granny, who had to have been at the height of her longing for him. Paw Paw delivered just on time—you could say he made his mark.

We'd roll down the windows and turn up the radio on those drives in his brown lowrider; "My Sharona" became "Rice-A-Roni" and that was the funniest thing we'd ever heard. I'd take Oblio, our miniature black poodle, and we'd both stick our heads out the window to catch the breeze. I loved Oblio. He was named after a character in my favorite album, *The Point!* by Harry Nilsson, about a little boy who

I was Oblio 100 years ago had a round head in a town where everyone else had pointed heads. It had a point about pointlessness, which is a good point.

One trip, Uncle Mark had his friends in the car when he picked us up, and I was smushed next to a lady in the backseat who was smoking a tiny cigarette with something that looked like a bobby pin, that was pretty when she put it in her hair. We were going to some backwoods place where they taught us how to shoot BB guns and we shot cans off a fence post. I stepped on the cans, crunching them down in the middle of my sneakers to make tap shoes, and danced around while the grown-ups were doing their own thing. That was a fun day.

Uncle Mark, in those days, resembled Tom Waits so much that I'd look at his albums, like *Small Change* and *Closing Time*, and ask him if it was him on the album cover. I was six. Albums were a big thing at our house and in our family. I remember showing my dad's records to a stranger at the front door once. The door was window-paned, and I could only hold, like, ten at a time, so I flipped them with my little hands. The man was laughing, because I wouldn't let him in. Even though I could tell he was to be trusted, I couldn't let strangers in the house when I was alone. Oh, the benign neglect of the seventies, I'm blessed to have been born at that time.

It was around the time the song "Wildfire" was on the radio. The song was about a woman who'd lost her horse in a fire and our narrator, the singer Michael Martin Murphey, is haunted by her ghost. She ran away, calling out "Wildfire," and that's basically the song. Those story songs of the seventies could be sentimental and intense but I loved all that. "Get these hard times right on out of our minds / Riding Wildfire . . ."

Uncle Mark would come over for dinner and afterward we all sat on the couch and watched TV or listened to albums. My mom would do what she called her "surgery," and take the shade off the lamp. She'd beg and demand him, "Come here, come here, come HERE!" and he'd go to her, like a dirty kid who's been playing outside and the sun's gone down and he's not ready for a bath.

She was ready for him to lie on her lap when she had her accoutrements (needle and rubbing alcohol) ready and then she did the surgery, which was popping the bumps on his face. I'd hear screams from both of them. "That was the BEST!" Laughing and screaming with giddy disgust. "GROSS! AHHHHH!!!!" and "I don't think that one's ready, but this one is," and, "Oh! That was a good one!" She hurt him so bad that I remember him leaping off the couch. The naked lampshade, with the bulb exposed, and Uncle Mark, holding his face—and kind of laughing? It was good times. Sometimes I perched on the back of the couch, like a gargoyle, and got my mom anything she asked for.

One afternoon, on a ride back from Shreveport, my mom broke the news about Oblio. She told us that Uncle Mark had left the fence unlocked and Oblio had run across the street and gotten hit by a car. We were all bawling in the front seat and there was nothing in the car to blow our noses with. Then my mom said, "I have some clean underwear in my bag in the back." I flipped over to the backseat and found a clean pair. "It's really okay to use your underwear, Mom?" She said that it was and started giggling through her tears. I hopped over the front to share, where we laughed as hard as we cried.

Not long after, I was wandering around the house and ended up by my mom's old sewing machine side table. I liked to sit on the two-by-two-inch pedal and rock back and forth, like I was on a sideways seesaw; I'd hold on to the outside edges of the top and go as fast as I could, rocking myself dizzy until I had to slow down.

Behind the sewing machine, a little miracle appeared. My mom, who revered a clean house and found her sense of peace in the vacuum, had overlooked something: a petrified piece of Oblio's poo-poo. It was dried and hard and mostly white and green, and it was absolutely precious to me. I considered it to be from Oblio in heaven. I took it and went upstairs to wrap it in one of Granny's handkerchiefs, which I kept in the top drawer of my chifforobe. I kept it and revisited it, like a cherished relic, with all the love in my heart.

The very first thing each of us makes in life is our poop and we don't even have to think to do it because it just happens. What a gift to the mind of a child. This, of course, wears off, and it's too bad that it smells. One of the first times I got in "big trouble" was when my brother and I were three years old and a *smell* was coming from our room. The smell was so strong that it woke up my parents. My dad came in and saw us with our shit in our hands and in the crevices of our crib and on our faces: we were happy and proud of what we'd made. My dad didn't see it that way and he swung us up by our elbows and spanked us.

That was the first time I experienced art producing punishment or shame. Oh shit, that's funny.

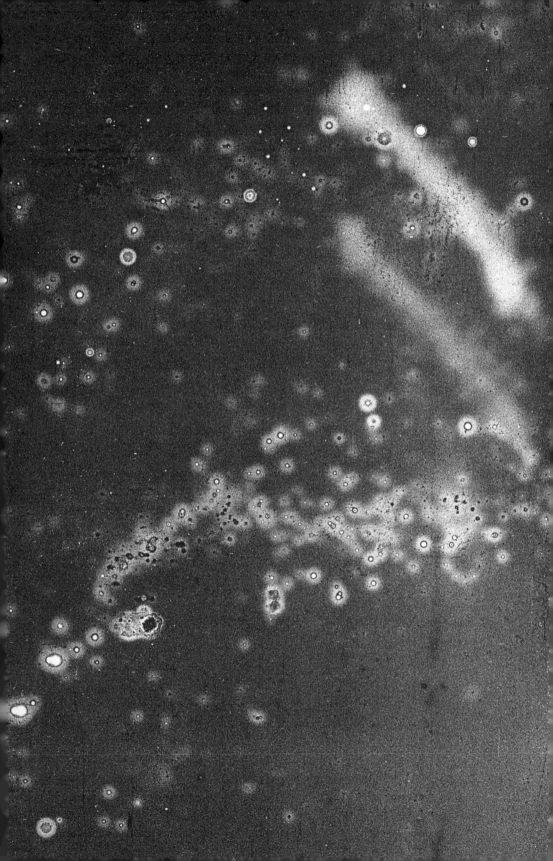

22

Rear Window/**Live Pie**

My view facing Eleventh Street from my apartment on East Tenth was like the set piece from Hitchcock's *Rear Window*. The buildings around this block shared a courtyard, so it pulled my view in even closer. There was one apartment that stood out at night because the window lit up yellow. It was on the same level as mine, to the left and easy to see into.

I could see her paintings. Her lights, the metal ones with hooded satellite cones, clamped onto her shelves, and she used bright bulbs. She didn't have curtains, which singled her out even more, making her square of window radiate like a bulb itself. If other apartments' lights were on at night, they were blue TV-screen lights, and everyone else had window coverings, and a few were just sheets.

During one stretch of time, I could see she was painting clouds—a small row of them on her wall, the size of notebook paper or smaller. It was easy to see because the painted poufs of white on the light blue sky stood out.

There was a wrought-iron love seat on the small "patio" below, in the courtyard, which got very little sun. I never saw anyone sitting on it.

In the spring, the white cherry blossom trees snowed the area, especially the sidewalks facing Tenth Street. I didn't have blinds or curtains on those windows for maybe a year when I lived there, preferring the windows to be bare and clear and easy to see out of. No one lived above me and I'd bumped out the ceiling, opening up the attic loft, and installed a skylight in the peak of the roof. I commissioned the necessary work to make my fireplace usable for years to come. I felt my body standing taller with the added space above my head. I felt my body getting smaller when I thought of how difficult the co-op board had been, nixing the central air after I'd already built the space for air-conditioning vents along the ceiling . . . after an architect on the board said it'd be cool if I just went ahead and did it. I was thinking of future tenants but the co-op board were jerks. Bob Gober, the sculptor, and his partner had central air on their two floors—it hummed so loud I could hear it, because it was right outside my window.

Anyway.

The main window, which faced Eleventh and the courtyard, spanned the width of the loft and was made of cloudy beaded glass. A painter could have lived there in the fifties. It was the kind of glass favored by the abstract expressionists during that time because it softened the direct sunlight.

I took in this *Rear Window* view more intently as I was leaving it. I'd see this woman's light on, painting not clouds this time but something I couldn't make out.

Just weeks before I moved out of there, a young man stopped me on the sidewalk while walking his dog. Our dogs introduced themselves to each other and we did, too. His name was Daryl and he was smiling, like he couldn't contain himself, and was almost laughing, "You're my neighbor!" As if I were Agnes Moorehead from *Bewitched* and had popped up out of nowhere, curled atop a refrigerator, specifically for him. He was excited, like there was something he'd always wanted to tell me. "I can see into your kitchen! It's red!" I'm sure I just mirrored his enthusiasm and smiled in a shocked way, like when a drunk person corners you as you're leaving somewhere fun.

"What else can you see?" I asked. I had seen him and his boyfriend fooling around a few times. It was fun saying, "I can see into your place too . . . You have a boyfriend . . ." I smiled knowingly, with bedroom eyes.

I told him I was moving in three weeks and would miss my *Rear Window* view, and I mentioned a woman I'd seen painting over the years who must have been a neighbor of his, with blond hair. Daryl laughed some more and said, "Oh, that's Emma, she's great! She's an amazing painter!" And then, "You should commission her to do your portrait!"

"Do you think she could do that thing where she paints my eyeballs a certain way so it seems like I'm following myself everywhere I go?" I wanted to ask. My parents had a similar picture in their house, an oil painting of me with a bobbed haircut, age fifteen, in a black vintage dress from the twenties and I'm smirking. It's what you see when you open the front door of my parents' home. I look like a character from the Rod Serling show *Night Gallery*. No, I wouldn't want a portrait of myself.

Emma left me a gallery brochure of her work called "Reflected/ Inverted Landscapes." Huge paintings of reflections in bodies of water, now surfaced onto canvas: fallen leaves, the sky and trees reflected, rippled in the water. She left her number and I called her later and we talked for at least an hour, waving to each other from our windows and drinking wine and laughing about bad boyfriends.

She invited me over to check out her view of my apartment. She had been painting flames, which was coincidental since I'd been lighting fires myself, burning papers and doubles of photographs. The flame paintings were lined up on her walls, on framed stretched canvases the size of my hand, and she gave me a painting to commemorate my move. She also gave me a large photograph, a reflection of her, framed. The photo shows her window, a vase of flowers reflected, along with her paint supplies, and small paintings that surround her bright blond hair. My kitchen window, yellow before it was painted red, is in the top left corner of this particular frame. The center is the Nikon lens of her camera, covering most of her face.

There's a pie that Emma makes, a raw-food pie adapted from a cookbook by Pure Food and Wine. Pure Food and Wine was a vegan restaurant, but it was shut down by protesters who weren't getting paid. The owner abandoned her establishment in the city and charged an Uber account more than ten grand so she could hole up with her boyfriend in Atlantic City. They were busted eating a Domino's pizza during a weekend slots bender. I'm not making this up. It sounds like a Christopher Guest plot, doesn't it? I bet the pizza was sausage or pepperoni, mushrooms for sure.

The recipe is labor intensive; some of the labor is running around trying to find all these different ingredients, especially the berries when they're out of season, and perhaps there's the labor of waiting, if you're not exercising patience. When Emma first brought the raw-food pie to my country house, I changed the name of it to "Live Pie." There was something about "raw-food pie" that made it sound like it could give you salmonella. We had dinner at Pure Food and Wine once and it was delicious and expensive and I remember shivering from the cold draft and wanting to eat more afterward.

Emma has found the time to make Live Pie between her eight-mile runs in the morning, her decorative painting job, her own artwork, going to galleries, her Buddhist practice, and the silent retreats she goes on. I've thought about going on these silent retreats but figure it would be a lot like being at work on set for me, minus the silence. Emma loves making this pie, I think, because it's a meditation for her. Her latest meditation while making this pie has been on whether or not it's a distraction from making art. There's no way that could be true because everything she does creates the beautiful edge that she needs to paint beautiful paintings. But of course it's true for her.

Live Pie Recipe

CRUST:

1¹/₂ cups almond meal

1¹/₂ cups finely ground almonds

¹/₃ cup coconut butter (blended coconut)

2 tablespoons date butter (blended dates)

¹/₂ cup maple syrup

Dash of salt

Blend ingredients together in a food processor until they reach a doughlike consistency. Press the "dough" into a glass pie plate and cover it to leave in the fridge for a couple of hours. Emma uses plastic gloves because her hands get very sticky, but I would probably forgo those.

CASHEW CREAM:

1 cup cashews, soaked for two hours

1 cup raw coconut

¹/₃ cup coconut butter (blended coconut)

¹/₂ cup distilled water

1 tablespoon plus 1 teaspoon almond extract

2 teaspoons vanilla extract

¹/₂ cup agave or maple syrup

Dash of salt

Put it all in a blender and blend until it's super creamy. Spread the cream on the crust when it's cold, then stick in the fridge again. It can get soupy when it's not cold enough but if you've gone through all this effort you probably won't care at this point and it will be so delicious that it won't matter.

FILLING:

6 cups raw fruit

¹/₄ cup agave or maple syrup

1 teaspoon vanilla extract

Pour the fruit mixture on top of the cashew cream. The leftovers of this pie could be mixed with vanilla ice cream and frozen, then saved for nighttime trips to the freezer.

My Lord

23

The Guest Films

We shot *Waiting for Guffman* in Austin, and after the first day of shooting, we all piled into a van to go back to the hotel. I lay down in the backseat and pulled my knees to my chest, telling everyone my back hurt. "That's from holding in laughter," Eugene Levy said, sounding "old hat," like a vaudevillian actor. I took a bath that night and cried from the shock of the day. It was strange improvising— like, really, this is going to work? I couldn't remember what I even said that day.

I'll explain a little more about the "improvisation" process, specific to Chris, if you'd like to know. Most films have a script, with the character's dialogue written for them. Actors learn the lines and figure out the subtext, what's "under" the line. Nowadays, though, most screenwriters don't write like that; the style has become more literal and the dialogue constructed to serve the plot. When a movie is unscripted, the character lives without the lines of the material and this allows for real things to happen in the moment and be caught on film.

Chris says, when directing, "Don't feel like you have to say anything." And, "You can take your time and have space between your thoughts." He exudes this in real life, too. He's Zen. I mean, Jesus, he's a lord. His full name, to be properly Anglo-Saxon about it, is Lord Christopher Haden-Guest.

For his movies, the actors are given an approximately thirty-page outline, describing what happens in each of the scenes—different "beats" to hit. I was young, like twenty-five, when we shot *Guffman*, and excited to work. *This Is Spinal Tap* didn't impress me since I didn't like heavy metal music, so I wasn't intimidated by Chris or the process. We were all pretty nervous about our audition scenes, though, for the musical within the film, called *Red, White, & Blaine*.

The auditions were held in the high school. Bob Balaban had just arrived to play the musical director, as well as one of the judges. I'd never met him. I knew him from *Close Encounters of the Third Kind*, and he seemed very serious and intimidating. Bob Odenkirk had come to Austin for a few days to play the priest and now he was pacing the hallways in theatrical vampire makeup, with contour makeup on his cheekbones and lipstick, prepping for his song. Fred Willard and Catherine O'Hara were in the hallway as well, sitting in folding chairs, and I remember doing some mime around them: you know, the hand wiping the smile up, showing "comedy," and then the hand swiping it down to a frown, showing "tragedy." Catherine told me she was actually nervous and I said, "Yeah, me too!" and we all told each other to break a leg.

Now, this is the genius of Catherine and Fred: in the outline for their characters, Ron and Sheila, it said, "Ron and Sheila audition for the show by reenacting their favorite coffee commercial." It was their idea to sing "Midnight at the Oasis" and incorporate the coffee commercial into the song. Chris's friend David Nichtern had written the song, so getting the rights was easy. It was Lewis Arquette's choice to wear jazz shoes with his overalls. Where and how would this man who worked as a taxidermist dig up jazz shoes? That was the best. Bob babysat the Arquette kids in Chicago, so they went way back. I think that the Arquettes had vaudeville genes and the Balabans ran theaters in Chicago. Bob's character was a beekeeper, and he had researched and prepared all this stuff. I seem to recall his entering rehearsals wearing a beekeeper's suit. It's absurd that none of this stuff was striking us as funny while we were rehearsing it. It was more like realizing that people are really interesting and more odd than we think.

Sometimes I wouldn't be able to control my laughter and Chris would just stare at me and say, "Do you think you can do this?" and I'd try to pull myself together. Catherine would help me by saying, "You just got in trouble, your dog is dying, think about something sad!" (I didn't have a dog at this point.) When Eugene couldn't control himself, he simply walked out of a scene, just left it, the cameras still rolling. We all had to take it so seriously in order not to laugh, and then afterward, we'd let loose. Like when we were shooting the dance numbers, in the high school theater, for *Red, White, & Blaine*. I remember Chris got the giggles once, over nothing in particular, just everything, that he made his way down to the floor and lay on the stage, holding his stomach.

Initially, in the film, when Corky (played by Chris) didn't get the $100,000 in funding that he needed to produce his original musical, he ended up in the ICU with a feeding drip in his arm, and we all visited him in the hospital. Catherine and I were crying, holding each other and the gifts and flowers we'd brought. Trying to get him to come around, we said, "Come back to us, Corky, please, we need you. We can't do the show without you . . . come back, come back . . ." After this first take, Chris asked for a banana, which he put at his groin, giving Corky an erection.

In editing, I guess he felt he'd taken it too far, or the whole thing went on too long (like a minute instead of twenty seconds) and so the scene ended up on the cutting room floor. In its place was a quick shot of Corky in the bathtub, with one of those funny ice packs on his head. This sort of understated subtlety runs throughout the movie. Not a lot of people notice this, but in my final interview scene, there's a quick establishing shot of a handicapped parking space—with an empty wheelchair parked in it. What person would park their

wheelchair in a handicapped parking spot and be able to leave it? I
didn't notice it, either, and I was there when we shot it.

The *Guffman* cast really felt like a family, a good comfortable family. Fred would smoke his cigar, looking out at the landscape of Lock-
hart, Texas, his mind reeling with funny things. Catherine and I came
up with a lot of the choreography for the musical and had a ball. I
didn't want to watch the dailies, but everyone else was watching them,
so I joined. And it was funny to see how funny funny people were
when they weren't trying to be funny. I was very sad the last day of the
shoot, because I'd never see Corky again. I cried in the van and Chris
held my hand. I remember seeing my first gray hairs on that film.

Soon after we wrapped, I was at the Joyce Theater in Chelsea seeing a dance piece, and I saw a man who looked just like Corky: same
wig, same style of dress, same mannerisms. I was so happy to see
Corky that I called Chris to tell him. That was the summer I sat out
on the scaffolding of my apartment as if it were a porch and talked on
my cordless phone, close to my fire escape. I'd call down to passersby
that I was running for mayor and then hide to watch them look
around. I had a tiny Weber grill up there, too, and barbecued.

Best in Show is a movie everyone loves. No one's ever said they
didn't like it, and if they did I would run away from that person. I'm
always shocked when I hear, "The person you played is my sister!" or
"She's just like my wife!" I mean, that's nuts! The woman I played
screamed at her husband at airports, was maniacally entitled and
demanding, and threw fits and yelled at hotel managers and pet store
owners. I guess we all get to that point sometimes, though? I have,
obviously.

Probably the best compliment I ever received was in the parking
lot of a Lowe's hardware store in upstate New York. This man had his
five-year-old son with him, and he said, pointing at me, "This is the
crazy dog lady from *Best in Show*," and the little kid started laughing.
I mean, done. Nothing makes me happier than a five-year-old boy

laughing at a grown woman acting like a five-year-old. It's an honor to be a part of this group and to have made so many people laugh.

In addition to moviemaking, Chris can pick up any instrument and play it. He can also throw his voice, which I saw, and heard, when we had dinner together during the shoot. His mouth didn't look like it was moving, and then the sound of his voice came from somewhere else, like a magic trick. Somewhere in his family tree he had an uncle, I think, who could throw his voice. That was his explanation. The dinner was in Vancouver, where we were filming, and Hitchcock and I shared a crème brûlée for dessert. That's Michael Hitchcock, who played my husband Hamilton in *Best in Show*. I played Meg Swan. We were lawyers who'd met at Starbucks.

The script outline described Hamilton and Meg as a "catalog couple" with nothing in their homes that was personal to them. They're both lawyers and seeing a therapist because their dog Beatrice has had anxiety since she caught Meg and Hamilton having sex. They're very nervous because they very much want Beatrice to win Best in Show. Meg and Hamilton fell in love at Starbucks. When it comes time to shoot, the characters fill in the blanks with the history and details. So much is cut, like a scene in which Beatrice had pooped in Ham's slipper to punish us. In the scene, I accosted the maid when I saw this very deliberate attempt Beatrice was making to communicate to me that she was upset—jealous, in fact. I held the slipper and showed it to my maid. "What is this? Do you see this? Why did she do this? Why aren't you answering me? Were you here when it happened? What happened—tell me! Don't I pay you? Why aren't you speaking? You're fired!" It didn't make the film, but who even dreams up a dog who takes revenge by pooping in a slipper? Chris does.

One afternoon, before we went to Vancouver, Hitchcock was in an animal training class, which I skipped, because I felt that for Meg, the dog didn't really "matter," it was her *attachment* to the dog that mattered—her projections of herself onto Beatrice. After Hitchcock's training class, we had lunch with Chris (his process is a whole other form of "laid-back"), and he said, "What if you two had braces?" Hitchcock and I were like, "Mmmhmmm, yeah, okay." So Michael got a retainer with the braces attached, which gave him a lisp, which suited his character, and I got real braces since I didn't want a lisp.

Our dog was originally supposed to be a pointer, which was very J.Crew, so we were ready to go shopping there. But then Chris heard that pointers were too difficult to train, so we switched to a Weimaraner, which seemed very Banana Republic to us. At that point, Banana Republic had ventured far away from their safari "chic traveler" gear of the eighties and landed in the gray/slate/taupe period: cashmere wool capes, pointed shoes (very Weimaraner), and cashmere key-chain balls. I could put that gray cape on and slouch and feel brittle and sad that Hamilton wasn't paying enough attention to me.

The poodle who originally played Rhapsody in White got fired. The system chewed that poodle up just to spit her out. No matter that she was a champion standard poodle; in fact, and this is the truth, it was her "star power" that got her fired. She was naturally strong-natured, as poodles can be. Their hair is puffed up and then sprayed with Aqua Net, which sometimes makes their hair break (a risk the groomers take), and if they didn't get all this attention, perhaps they'd be less bitchy. Now, that is a generalization, I know, and I love poodles, despite this. But anyway, Jane Lynch and Jennifer Coolidge's poodle got the heave-ho, and since I wasn't filming on the day of the new-poodle auditions, I got to sit in on the contenders and document them. It was a very big deal, that day in a conference room at the Sutton Place Hotel, and two days later, Rhapsody in White was recast by some bitch.

I remember having lunch with Chris one day, and he said, "That's a nice sweater," and I was in a bad mood and said quickly, "It's Banana Republic," and he said, "Okay." I caught myself being in character. Funny stuff happens around Chris. It's not just that people are trying to be funny around him, to impress him; these moments just seem to happen in normal situations, like in an elevator. He'll watch and observe and make "mmhmm" sounds to the everyday people all around him, like people who have the same hair as their dogs, or a grown man with a Little Lord Fauntleroy wig as hair. I had a neighbor who dressed like a new age version of Paddington Bear. She made me laugh with joy when I saw her. And men over sixty who wear Crocs with socks and shorts and baseball caps? They look like sweet five-year-old boys wearing baby shoes. Those shearling Ugg boots have beautiful women looking like garden gnomes with Barbie doll–top bodies.

I was at a place I like called Peacefood, and there was a cauliflower special, and I asked the waitress to tell me about it, and she said, "It's a vegetable that tastes like broccoli, but it's white." When I was getting coffee at a breakfast deli, the lady behind the counter said, "What can I help you with?" The customer ahead of me said, "I'm Oatmeal," like that was her name. People are so funny when they don't know what they're saying.

Before we enter into a scene, on any of his movies, the main direction from Chris is "This isn't too far from the truth. People are really like this." The irony is that he inspired an ironic or postmodernist position in comedies today, but he couldn't be further away from irony. The other irony is that for such funny movies there's disappointment for the actors when they see the final product, since so much of everyone's performance gets cut. After the premiere of *Best in Show* in Toronto, the actors weren't laughing as much as calculating or comparing what was shot to what was sacrificed to move the plot. The ratio of the material produced to the bit that's kept feels out of proportion. There's no clause with the Writers Guild of America for improvising being seen as writing but maybe one day there will be. As is the case on Woody Allen's films, no one gets paid anything, so you do it for the sake of the art. Chris doesn't do the awards circuits, so great performances worthy of them are left to legacy. I'm thinking of Catherine in *For Your Consideration*, who was so funny and painful, just genius. Life imitated art for her that year because like in the film, there was talk in the biz of her receiving an Oscar nomination. He gives us our very own medals, though, made especially for the production, with the title of the movie written on a round medallion that hangs by a red, white, or blue ribbon. I have four of those medals and a few Oscars of my own. They're the souvenir-sized ones from LAX, but still, it's something.

24

Shirley, the Coneheads, and Me

Shirley MacLaine told me about an affair she once had with one of her drivers. I don't remember the details—only that it was night and he was taking her home from work. Sometimes it gets plain lonely out there on the road, with no one to go home to, and no home to go home to, just some not-so-fabulous hotel in Winnipeg, Manitoba, Canada, where birds were dropping dead from the West Nile virus on the hot sidewalks. I loved it there, though.

This was in 2002, when I met Shirley on the set of a TV movie called *Hell on Heels: The Battle of Mary Kay*. She played Mary Kay Ash, the cosmetics tycoon, and I played Jinger Heath, her nemesis. Our first shot together was a fantasy scene in which Shirley was being rushed to a hospital in an ambulance while she was having a nightmare about me. I appeared over her head, staring at her, and she scream-laughed, "You look JUST LIKE Joan Collins!" And in the fake ambulance, she said her shaman told her that her soul partner would come when she was in her nineties. She also said, "It's *all* going to change, you'll see," and oh, my good Lord, it really truly has!

One morning, she camped out on the mound of grass in front

of the hotel, wearing her white Z-CoiL tennis shoes and a large straw sun hat. She swatted the mosquitos (called "birds" by the locals) and was chilling out with her friend Brie before getting picked up for work. Brie's husband was the real Indiana Jones. They'd met Steven Spielberg in the eighties through Shirley over in Santa Fe, New Mexico—new age country for the wealthy—where some members of Hollywood's elite had bought houses to hunker down for the end of the world, which was coming up in May 2003, and then again in December 2012. Now that that's all over, we can wait for the aliens.

So yes, we talked about the Mayan calendar and Atlantis, and yes, I told Shirley how much I loved *Out on a Limb*, and that she inspired the kind of woman I'd wanted to become. I have yet to climb Machu Picchu, but with the right intentions, I can eat, pray, and shove my way through any karmically riddled countryside.

One day in the makeup trailer, I was sitting in the hair chair with an entire box of hot rollers in my hair. Shirley picked up her own box and pulled out a wig. "These are just as good, if not better, than the expensive kind," she said. I gave the approving look of a woman who loves a bargain, nodding my head, and she said it was $16. Then she plopped it on her head and said, "Honestly, Parker, I don't know why you bother," and stepped out of the trailer, for effect.

I wanted to impress her, so one morning, in her trailer, I told her my UFO story, which I knew she'd dig. It begins like this: When I was little, around three, I had nightmares about cone-headed aliens, and I'd wake up pounding my head against the wall. This was in our first house, "the little house," before we moved to "the white house" in Monroe. In the dream, I'd be on a table in the garage, getting prodded in my side by a wand or something, and around five years later, when the Coneheads sketch was on *SNL*, I remembered that dream.

I did a movie about the Coneheads called *The Coneheads*. Michelle Burke (from *Dazed*) was cast as Connie Conehead, and I convinced Lorne Michaels that she needed friends, pitching my best girlfriend, Joey, and me. We both got our SAG rates up 15 percent, and celebrated by drinking Big Gulps of iced coffee from 7-Eleven that were as big as our heads. While shooting, we rode the bus with Ellen DeGeneres and chilled out with Dan Aykroyd, whose brother was a real-life ghostbuster. Dan told tripped-out stories involving multiple dimensions and time travel. I should try to track him down. He's got great stories and he'd be someone to be stranded on a desert island with.

But yeah, so a few years later, Christopher Guest called Lorne Michaels and asked him if he knew any actresses who could play eighteen and improvise, and Lorne suggested me. "Close encounters of what kind?" you ask.

When I finished my story, Shirley said, "Oh," unfazed. "Steven believes in UFOs. Lots of us do. Hollywood and the CIA and FBI. It's all a huge cover-up." She and Brie had even UFO-hunted together. Fun! I asked Shirley what she thought of my Coneheads dream, and she said, "Oh, honey, there are so many species, too many to count," and she stepped out of the trailer, for effect.

My friend Craig was with me on that trip and we had an interesting dinner with Shirley and Brie. We were talking karma, showbiz, past lives, love, sex, therapy, and gurus—astrology, Atlantis. Shirley knew a lot about things like reincarnation, and explained it further: that anything in this life could be dated back to something in a past life, so that if we figured out what that connection was, we'd figure out why we had to go through whatever we had to go through, and if we did it right in this lifetime, we probably wouldn't have to do it again in the next one.

Craig had a story that needed karmic riddling and took center stage. He had a condition called "long face syndrome," where his jaw grew faster than the rest of his face. When he was sixteen he had to have his mouth wired shut and his chin reconstructed. It was a whole ordeal, to say the least. He couldn't speak for three months, and on his birthday, his mother blended up brisket and birthday cake, which she fed him through a straw. A great story, which Craig would turn into a book aptly called *Why the Long Face?*

The next day, Shirley went up to him and said, "I've been think-ing of your story all night, and what it means. You have so much karma in this lifetime for that to have happened to you, and I just want to know . . ." Pause. "Did all that surgery interfere with your cock-sucking abilities?" And then Craig quipped, "No, because I suck cock like a vegan." Like he's not good at "eating meat." It was an utterly tasteless joke and I stepped out of the trailer, for effect.

Speaking of fruits and vegetables, Shirley had a giant raspberry on the roof of her mouth, some kind of a birthmark. I'll never forget seeing it when she opened her mouth wide to show us, there on a tiny hump of grass in front of one of the only hotels in Winnipeg. She said that a shaman told her that this raspberry on the roof of her mouth was an indication that she was also a shaman. Then she said it was also great for blow jobs. Ha! Come on! She is one funny lady!

She tooled around with Craig thrift shopping while I was work-ing, and she told him which Frank Sinatra records to get. She spoke about her Rat Pack days, and how Dean Martin—"Dino"—was into her, and how she wasn't really into him. She was *that* cool. The one that really pulled at her heart, though, was Robert Mitchum. She said he had the soul of a poet and was into astrology. Hey, when you've hung out with the Rat Pack, you can go out on a limb and be as far out as you want.

The last night of work, Craig and I were in my room packing and watching TV when a show about UFOs came on. It was around two in the morning, and there on the screen appeared Brie talking about UFOs. We started screaming, "Oh my God! This is crazy! What are the odds?!" And then, I'm not kidding or making this up: the TV went out—it went to black.

They're here, everybody. They're here on this flight.

25

Mom and the TV

My mom loves making things beautiful. I think it's because she's very beautiful but was never told so by her own mother. Nonnie was jealous of her daughter's looks and her youth, but my mom developed a great sense of humor out of it. Her sense of self comes into play when she's making things aesthetically beautiful, whether it's herself, in her own style, or in the continuity of beauty and harmony in the rooms of our house. There are always things to mend and make whole again, things to organize and put in their right place.

I loved going to fabric stores with my mom. There was a buzz she'd get when she was in the zone of seeing possibility in something, and I dug that. And of course I loved shopping with her. My brother and I favored the department stores that had circular racks, where we'd use the hanging clothes for a game of "blind man's bluff"—closing our eyes, with our arms out like little zombies, going clockwise, then counterclockwise. And yes, hide-and-seek, where a few times I hid too long and had to go to the front to page my mom over the intercom. Kmart was prime for this number.

Both my parents were great-looking, but compliments were foreign to their natures and upbringing. Compliments were withheld or "not believed in," as my father would say, for my brother and me. This was mainly in regards to "appearances," despite the both of them looking like movies stars and kind of acting like them, too. They said things like "Looks don't matter, it's what's inside that counts." Years later, when I was in my teens, my dad realized how weird this was and said, "Ya know what: Looks do matter. They're the first thing you notice about a person." By that point I didn't like brushing my hair or looking in the mirror much. In high school I'd leave the house and my mom would ask, "Are you going to a funeral?" And I'd say, "Yeah." And the screen door would slam for effect. But wearing black clothing helped pull that look together.

It's how the limbs are cut that makes a tree blossom in a particular direction. Both my parents had some harsh pruning that trained their growth, making them very colorful people. Maybe that's why my mom started a gardening program at the elementary school in Laurel a few years ago now—we'd had a garden in the early seventies that she loved tending to. She taught cooking classes at Viking, in Oxford. This was in Mississippi, in Greenwood, which is in the Delta, but also simply referred to as "Oxford." When she'd say, "I'm going to Viking in Oxford," it sounded like a trip to Camelot or some other mythical kingdom.

When my family got a microwave, my mom invented "Cheese Crisps." She sprayed Pam on a plate and grated cheddar cheese onto it and put it in the microwave for three minutes. When it came out, she'd pat the oil off with a paper towel, and because the cheese had hardened, she'd lift it off the plate in one piece, like a giant communion wafer. Sometimes she put jalapeños, from a jar, on them. I remember my mom and her friend Susan putting Worcestershire sauce in their palms and licking it off like dainty cats.

Cheese Crisps
by Lynda Posey

Spray a dinner plate with cooking spray.

Grate cheddar cheese and sprinkle evenly on the plate.

Put it in the microwave for three minutes.

Watch it bubble and turn into a darkened orange crisp.

Remove it from the microwave when you hear the "ding," and let it cool for about a minute.

Pat it dry with a paper towel and then lift it off the plate with your fingers.

If you like it spicy, add however many jalapeños from a jar to the plate beforehand.

Other toppings include cracked pepper, Parmesan cheese, and, I suppose, anything. But I don't believe in microwaves.

While I'm at it, my mom's friend Claudia makes the best "Trash" at Christmas. Before you could buy Chex Mix in the store I had it homemade at Claudia Woods's house. We'd pop by and visit when she was making it, which took all day, but she'd start late so it would take all night. She simply calls it "Trash," but you may know it as "party mix." Claudia's a brazen beauty and I loved when she'd belch loudly and say "excuse me." It was hilarious because she was so glamorous, with her add-a-bead gold necklace and other gold chains and gold bangles and bracelets heavy with charms from the days of yore.

Claudia Woods's Trash

1 box Wheat Chex cereal

1 box Crispix cereal

2 boxes Honey Nut Chex cereal

6 5-ounce bags of sesame sticks (or a 30-ounce bag)

2 pounds honey-roasted peanuts

5 sticks butter, divided

$\frac{1}{3}$ cup of cayenne pepper (less if you don't like spicy)

$\frac{1}{2}$ cup of Lea & Perrins Worcestershire sauce

1 tablespoon lemon juice

2 cups raw pecans

Preheat oven to 250 degrees. Pour out all the cereals, sesame sticks, and peanuts into a tall kitchen trash bag and gently shake it around (you don't want to break up the mix). Melt 4 of the sticks of butter with cayenne pepper, Lea & Perrins, and lemon juice in a saucepan. You'll want to strategize how to fit as many pans in your oven as you can because you'll have a lot of trash to slowly roast (I used six 15 × 10-inch pans to fit snug in the oven). Make sure the pans have a lip, and don't use flat cookie sheets, or you'll have a mess. You'll also need to get space ready for when the pans come out of the oven. There's lots of tending-to with this recipe. Get your spatula and spoon ready, and a little cup for the butter mixture. Get an apron, too, because you'll be using your hands a lot. For the ratio of butter to trash mixture, I'd say it's 2–3 tablespoons of butter per pan. Drizzle it onto the pans, slide it around evenly and then add the trash mix.

Slow-bake it all at 250° for 3 hours, taking it out to toss around every half hour. When all that's done, take it out and let it cool. This will go into the trash bag and get mixed up again but not now. Now it's time for the pecans—break them up in halves and quarters. Turn the oven up to 275°, put the pecans in a roasting pan, and cook them for 45 minutes. This will give the pecans enough time to cook the oils off of them so they can hold the butter and salt. Then melt the last butter stick, drizzle enough butter onto the pecans to coat them, and salt it all. Put it in the oven and take it out every 15 minutes, moving the pecans around and salting them again each time. You want the pecans almost burnt, and that takes a little over an hour. When all this is done and cools to room temperature, put it in a trash bag and shake it all up. How much does all of this make? Enough to fill around seven tins. Or five large Ziploc bags. You can store it in Ziploc freezer bags as well, and it'll keep forever. Marcia's review of the recipe was "This is disgusting." Which means it's delicious. "I can't stop eating it. What's it called again? I keep saying 'mush.' Is it 'garbage'? 'Shit'?"

My mom had a groovy and crafty friend in Shreveport who I stayed with for a weekend. We made God's eyes out of sticks and yarn, and she made one so big she put it above her couch. The color palette of the seventies was great and so much better than black, with the earth tones of burnt oranges and browns, true greens and bright yellows. She had a shag carpet so everyone could just relax for a minute and chill out on the floor—that was a real take-your-shoes-off time, the seventies. Years later, some reporter asked where I got my style from, and I said, "I dress like the woman I want to save me, a version of my mother from the seventies when she was happiest, making things."

When *The Mary Tyler Moore Show* would come on, we'd run up to
it and say "Mommy!" and kiss the TV. We'd tell my mom she was
more beautiful than Mary Tyler Moore, because she was, or just as.
"Well it's you, girl, and you should know it. With each glance and
every little movement you show it . . ." That theme song inspired so
many girls. When *Family Affair*'s theme song came on and the boy/
girl twins, Buffy and Jody, ran and hugged each other, so did my
brother and me. TV was an extended family for all families back
then. *All in the Family* was the ultimate, though. That show had true
genius in it, and pushed the whole country forward—it got small
towns thinking bigger. And then *Roots* was a much-needed phe-
nomenon that inspired everyone to look at racism. I remember
teachers talking about these shows in the classroom. Can you imagine teachers talking about television shows in classrooms today?

I loved the Zen of Mister Rogers—and very much wanted to be
on that Neighborhood Trolley to the Land of Make-Believe. My
mother was so affected by the powers of entertainment and cinema
that she actually became a Catholic after she saw *The Exorcist*. You
could say I hail from Fantasist's Island, but you could also say we all
do. "Mr. Roarke! The plane, the plane!"

I think, also, that the thing I loved about *Lost in Space* as a kid
was that it starred a kid my age—Bill Mumy, as Will Robinson, and
I was already a fan of his work from *The Twilight Zone*. In *Lost in
Space*, his most trusted friend was the robot. It was the first close
relationship on television between a kid and technology and brought
into our collective reality this new intimacy between ourselves and
the television—this box, this frame. That the robot only said "Dan-
ger, Will Robinson" was so prescient—the dangers we've seen from
technology and the weird brainwashing of mass media, how sad it is
no one talks to people on airplanes anymore.

Is that Werner Herzog?

Is he on this flight? I thought it was but it's not.

Our mothers show up in so many ways, in powerful images we never forget that play like stopped images in films. I see my mom all the time in other people, passing by, and tell her I love her. But one of the images that comes to mind from my childhood is of my mother sitting in the passenger seat of the car on one of our trips to Shreveport to see the family.

She had a Styrofoam cup stained with dark red lipstick in her hand. My brother and I sat in the backseat with a Playmate cooler between us. I remember this moment clearly, how she turned around and said, with such earnestness and praise and beauty, "Chris, you make the *best* Bloody Marys," and how my brother beamed. She looked like a movie star then, while Chicago's "Does Anybody Really Know What Time It Is?" played on the radio.

26
At the Wheel

In the early aughts, or as some say, "the early ought-nots," I learned something that ought not to have been so difficult: pottery. There was a studio around the corner from me, called La Mano, and when I wasn't working I didn't want to spend all day in my apartment. So I was at La Mano (Spanish for "the hand"), and that's where I learned to "throw."

"Throwing" is what they call the action part of pottery. When you're sitting "at the wheel," you're "throwing." In woodwork, at the lathe, they call it "turning." I would lose fingers if I wood-turned.

Clay is safer and distinctly malleable, as well as having different "clay bodies." The amount of grain within the clay determines how difficult it is to hold on to when it comes time to center. Brown clay has thick grains, so that's the easiest; gray clay is much smoother, with its finer grains. Porcelain is for the advanced and has no grain at all. When I tried to throw with it, after a year or so of being a student, I'd think of the clay as a difficult but

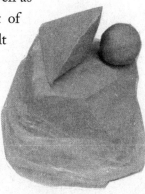

beautiful actress—someone you had to work hard at getting to know, who was unreliable and impossible to hold on to.

Different clay bodies have different personalities, so it's good to know what you're getting into when deciding to take your clay to the wheel.

The first thing the clay must be is the right size and shape, which, at first, is a ball. As a beginner, the ball should fit into the whole of both your hands when they're cupped and closed together. It needs the right firmness for stability. When the clay is fresh from the manufacturer, it comes in about a four-pound block, about a foot in diameter and a few feet high, and the firmness is perfect.

Then you can unwrap the plastic around it and, taking your string of wire, section off the amount you'll need.

After you do this, you'll have to wedge the clay. Think of it as exercise: you have to do it. If you have a fresh bag of clay, you won't have to work it out so much, but if the clay has been recycled from the re-con bucket, it's bound to have specks of dried clay, the odd piece of hair, or some kind of grit in it—or air bubbles.

Bubbles in your clay can cause your piece to collapse, so if they're not popped with a pin tool before your clay goes into the kiln (before it's "fired"), your piece might explode and ruin other people's work.

Check for air bubbles and wedge further if you find some. If your clay is too soft it will also need to be strengthened by wedging.

Wedging is like kneading dough:
Have a strong stance, with your pre-
ferred leg in front. Now rock your body
back and forth, like a runner at the
gate, or like you're holding a baby and
about to rock it, but with force and intent.
Bend forward a bit and stand in front of the wedging table, contracting your stomach muscles, both physically and mentally.

Before you do anything, focus yourself to the center, in that
great in-between place in yourself, the slightly unfocused (or relaxed)
place that's actually focused.

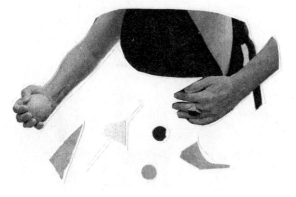

Imagine a softball
has been thrown at you
from underneath—it
has the energy of being
caught—and roll the
clay ball, into and onto
itself, tightening and
strengthening it, get-
ting those air bubbles
out and the odd specks
of hard clay dust, or tiny piece of paper or strand of hair—all that
garbage on the beach.

You're in that strong stance, that lunge, so the strength of
the rocking motion will roll the clay to wedge it. Your
back won't like you if you try to use it to do this, so
don't. Use your legs, slow and steady, like a
bull—strong as an ox.

It can take a while, but once you've
wedged your clay, you finally bring it to
your wheel.

Here's the fun part: Sit down, focus on the
bull's-eye of the wheel, and get ready to throw

the clay hard, like a fastball. Throw it, BAM, onto the wheel, right into the center, where it lands, *thwack*!

I got excited and wanted to get to the fun part first. I forgot to mention the necessities: a bucket of water to keep your hands and clay wet. It will be a container for the "slip" (the wet excess clay that will splatter around your wheel and onto your hands), towels to keep clean, and of course, your tools.

thwack!

Wet the clay just enough and get ready to push the pedal, full speed ahead—you're going to be like a race-car driver, so prepare yourself. At the same time, you're going to tackle that ball of clay like it's that alien in *Aliens*. The stomach force you have at this point is like someone punched you in the gut and is refusing to take their fist away. Don't ask why or you will lose, so keep your eyes on the road—pedal to the metal.

Before I turn the wheel on, I straddle it and squeeze, like I'm on a horse's saddle.

Get ready to pounce on that clay with every aspect of your hands and body/mind force—not grabbing it like it's going to leave you but like it was yours to begin with. Your mind's eye is an archer, connecting to the center of the wheel and the center of you, like a fast-flying arrow. You are now in its energy, and that energy knows itself to *be* centered.

You know your clay is centered when it's not wobbling or shaking. There's also a perfect little circle at the top of the mound, like the tip of a spinning top.

If your clay gets dry, wet it, and if it hasn't flown off the wheel by this point, you're safe.

Trust your hands as they begin to learn how to listen to the clay— where and how to move it and when—and here, you'll begin to find your centering *zone*.

Now, the technique of centering: You start at the base, and it looks like squeezing from the outside, but what's really going on is that every muscle in your hand is like a chiropractor's hands and body on a patient, positioning the body into alignment. What appears by this force is a phallus.

Your hand is listening now, keeping your mind's eye centered as you push it down with the heel of your palm, still using your strength.

You're raising the phallus at the base and then pushing it down to the center of the wheel. It goes up, then it goes down; it goes up, then it goes down. It feels so amazing in your hands that you could do it for hours. It's an erotic thing, what can I say?

Now, the *speed* of the wheel is very important. If you're scared and too slow (it happens a lot in the beginning), your ball of clay won't have the force to sustain itself and it will become a hardened, twisted blob. Defeated, you'll need to take it off the wheel, throw it in the recycling bucket, and go back to the wedging table. I usually wedge three or four balls before I sit down at the wheel so I don't have to get up so much.

So now you make the walls. You slow the wheel ever so slightly. Your hands must be wet, especially your fingers. Put your strongest finger (usually the middle), at the center of the clay mound. Your other hand is protecting it with strength and sensitivity. With the wheel spinning at its fastest centrifugal force, *press* the center and let the clay take your finger to what your mind's eye sees to be an inch above the base.

The clay is spinning fast and your finger will go directly to the center if you're not scared. Once you know the feel of the clay at its center on the wheel, you'll trust it and have confidence.

Now, to make the "walls" of the vessel, you slow the wheel down slightly. Your finger in the mound is about to draw a line, pulling the center back toward you. This happens quickly and naturally, if you trust it.

The next step is to "pull up the walls." Slow the wheel considerably. If you're right-handed, you will use your left hand's fingers to go into the vessel and the fingers of your right hand for the outside.

Starting at the base, your fingers press equally on either side of the wall, bringing up your walls. Beginners make the mistake of thinking that they are the ones bringing up the walls, but it's clay at the base that forms the walls naturally—you will tap the lip of the wall gently to strengthen it as it comes up— pulling up the walls just three or four times so you don't exhaust the clay, otherwise it'll get tired and collapse.

Now you've made your vessel. The cosmic forces have taken shape to form in the material realm.

Is that Carl Sagan?

My teacher's name was Manousha, like "minutia," which was funny because Manousha loved to go little; her pots were tiny worlds, teapots, mainly, with little spouts and lids, like Balinese rooftops the size of a pencil point. She was in her mid-

forties, from England but of Russian descent, and she had distinct character. She piled her curly red hair high on her head, like a pioneer woman, and always dressed nicely—careful that clay would only chalk her apron. I respected her immediately. A few times, as

I straddled my wheel, she told me I had an erotic lower back, to which I smiled and batted my eyelashes. Manousha was the epitome of femininity for me, at that time. Having produced exquisitely feminine teapots, which exhibited in galleries, she was in the process of trying to get pregnant to produce a baby, which she did in the years that she was my teacher.

She was a terrific teacher and we all adored her. She instructed us in the classic way to throw and the traditional teachings. Her own teacher had been from Japan and was a meticulous expert. She told us a story about how, before he even turned on the wheel, he'd spent several months practicing throwing the ball to the center over and

over again. Throw, throw, throw, bam bam bam. He already knew
how to throw, but his teacher made him go back to the very beginning. Before this, he'd wedged clay to the perfect size for his teacher
for a year or something.

Another potter Manousha talked about
was a man who made *huge* vessels and would
slash a giant X into each of them, with a pin
tool, like a fencer. That was his signature. If
the vessel collapsed, he tossed it; if it stayed, it
was sold. How intense is that? The *risk*! We all
paused for that one and I fell in love for a minute. We were just stu-
dents, challenged in simply making what would be small dishes for
earrings or containers for salt.

In the beginning, throwing was the best—getting into the
sensuality of the clay and centering for hours. My mind would go
right to the stars and into the dirt and think about how we're so disconnected from where things actually come from—that there's so
much more energy in things and objects than we give them credit
for. I'd think of cavemen, and the first cavewoman who threw a pot
from a kick-wheel. I'd think of how excited and pleased she must've
been, how hairy her eyebrows were, or if one of her caveman friends
ever threw a pot at her, how quick she was to duck out of the way and
how fun that was for everybody. There was a time when vessels held
offerings to the gods, and we know this because we've seen those
pictures painted in the pyramids. We see now, in museums, how
clumsy and childish those relics were.

Manousha reminded me of Glenn Close in *Dangerous Liaisons*,
corseted in her upright posture. There's a scene where John Malko-
vich asks her how she managed to invent herself and she says,
"Women are obliged to be far more skillful than men." How she
stabbed a fork in her hand under the table because it drove her

bonkers to be pleasant in the face of some disgusting troll-man. If I had directed that movie, I would've had bugs coming out of the wigs every now and then—allowing the scenes to have even more passion.

I made composite pieces that Manousha described as "chaos/control." I had improved some and would throw "off the hump," where I'd center a bigger amount of clay (around four balls' worth) to make vessels from the top of the mound. I'd catch the clay "fabric" that would spin off the mound, by accident and some-times with intention by pinching my fingers, to catch the collapse. The torn pieces would then dry to "leather hard" along with the ves-sels, and I put them on a wood tray to cook under a heat lamp. They'd be assembled to form something that looked like a strange flower or wreckage from a spacecraft.

I was invited to fire some of my pieces at a fellow student's house upstate, where she did raku firings in her kiln, which take place out-side. Raku is a type of Japanese pottery dating back to the sixteenth century. This process is fired by the atmosphere within the kiln, at the most molten state, a few thousand degrees Fahrenheit. A normal firing isn't as hot. Your piece is *glowing* red-hot when it's taken out of the raku kiln. With tongs, it's placed into containers filled with your favorite combustible materials—sawdust, horsehair, leaves, paper, or copper wire. It will react, creating its own atmosphere. The result is left to the forces of smoke, forming an imprint designed by this new atmosphere. Filmmaker Rich Sibert has a beautiful video on Vimeo of the ceramics master William Shearrow called *Raku*. One of the things Shearrow says is "Every piece is unique and one of a kind and it's that way intentionally. And it evokes an emotion inside you."

The studio became a co-op while I was there, so I joined. I got my own set of keys, and a group of us would go in at night to drink wine and whine about guys and throw. We tended to our pieces as if they were little babies, placing them carefully on a wooden board and wrapping them in cellophane to keep them moist. It wasn't uncommon for someone to say, "Look! It's a family!" and show you their board.

As a member of the board, I had to perform certain duties, like clean the place, recycle the old clay into the new clay (hard work), wedge the clay (which hurt my back), sweep the studio (which was boring and dried out my nose). If you couldn't or didn't want to do the chores, you paid $15 a week. Well, I could spare the fifteen bucks and paid the money a few times to do away with the dirty work.

I thought it was cool until one of the members came over to my wheel while I was in my zone and tapped me on the shoulder. A tap on the shoulder never feels good, does it?

I jumped a little and took out my earbuds, interrupting my Brian Eno music.

She squatted next to me. "You haven't been doing your duties," she said.

"I know," I said. "I've been focusing, and, you know, meditating. I paid the fee, so . . ."

She breathed in deeply, through her nose, and nodding to herself, said, "Well, I just don't think that you want other people to think that you think you're special."

I sighed and said, "But I am."

She looked at me, blank-faced.

"I'm famous."

She blinked a few times.

"Okay," I said, trying to explain. "Say I'm standing looking at vegetables at the grocery store, holding a bag of carrots, and someone taps me on the shoulder and scares the crap out of me, and then says he's a fan. That's not an average day at the grocery store . . ."

She took in what I had to say and went about her duties and left me to my centering.

Every person is unique and one of a kind and it's that way intentionally. Every person evokes an emotion inside you.

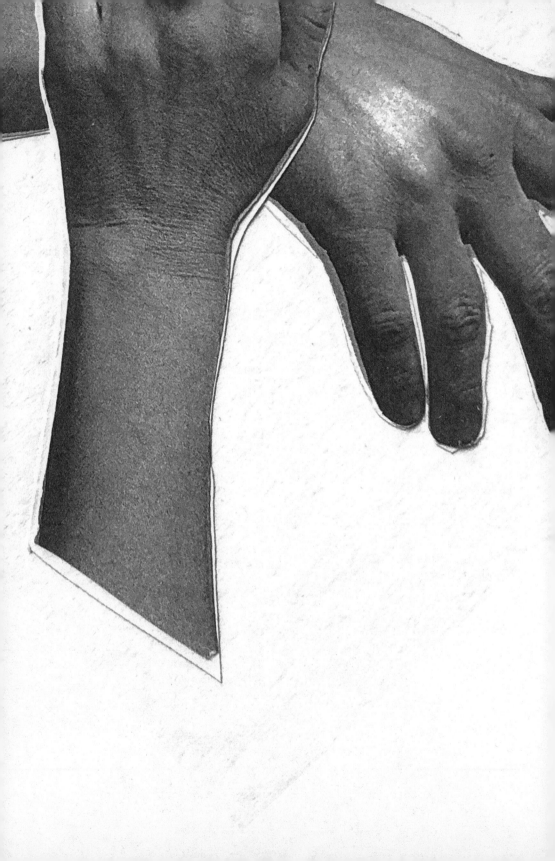

27

It's Mine

Nora Ephron loved butter. Almost everyone at her memorial service spoke about her love of butter. Their speeches were savored, like butter. Mike Nichols, Tom Hanks and Rita Wilson, Meryl Streep, and other entertainers and artists I'd looked up to spoke so brightly and lightly, with such wit and intelligence, that it seemed Nora had written their material. She planned her service while she was in the hospital—what music would play and who would speak and in what order. I thought maybe she'd given everyone direction, something like: *Be* butter. "Don't be better, just *be* butter." My favorite note I ever got from Nora was "Just *be* funny," which is why I was thinking that. The butter-talk spread its richness naturally into a creamy love and appreciation of the ingredient that savors everything it puts itself in and onto. It's too rich for words, for words like mine.

The memorial was at Alice Tully Hall at Lincoln Center. To the right and left of the stage were two enormous planters filled with white-bloomed flowers—the structures towered well over ten feet high. Her name appeared in an elegant font written on the screen as the song "As Time Goes By" played.

Earlier that week, I'd had a dream that Nora and I were

backstage before a show, hanging out in front of the dressing room makeup mirror. I reached into her makeup bag and found some blue eyeliner and put it on. We were standing up and we smiled at each other. I thought of taking the makeup pencil at a moment when she wasn't looking. If I took it, I wouldn't be able to come backstage to see her after the show so I could borrow it.

The dream made me think of Mildred, because I wanted to share it with her. Nora had seen Mildred during her *Heartburn* years—the scandalous book about her former husband Carl Bernstein and the affair he had while she was seven months pregnant. The book was her revenge, and I'll never forget her smile when I asked if the revenge had been sweet. It was a smile that said it had been. Mildred and her husband, Bernie Berkowitz, led a therapy group in their offices on West Ninth Street, off of Fifth Avenue, where Lynn Grossman was also "in group" with Nora. In fact, it was Lynn's husband, Bob Balaban, who connected me with Mildred.

We'd wrapped *Waiting for Guffman* and were doing Bill Maher's show (at the time it was called *Politically Incorrect*) and it was there, backstage, that he'd asked how I was. It wasn't a casual question but one to consider truthfully. Bob is someone I'd describe as "directly human." I hadn't been doing well and had found myself zoning out in my apartment, holding a pile of dirty laundry and not moving. I told him I was doing alright, but it wasn't the truth and he knew it. And then he asked, "How are you handling your success?" I was taken aback and answered, "Is that what this is? Not very well." He gave me Mildred's number and I went to see her.

Mildred Newman was an archetypal "great mother." She was playfully nurturing and imaginatively simple. She'd say, "Your world is not so big as to make yourself so small, nor is your world so small as to make yourself so big," and I'd think of Alice in Wonderland, who made herself both big and small, and the rabbit holes she got herself into. When I was in a state with a boyfriend, Mildred would say: "You must remember this / A kiss is just a kiss / A sigh is just a sigh / The fundamental things apply / As time goes by." She'd also say, "There are two parts to feelings: having them, and acting on them." I would still sink in my feelings then, afraid to navigate in order to get out of them. The battery low, my flashlight flickering. She'd say, "Do what you approve of." And like Jiminy Cricket says to Pinocchio, "Always let your conscience be your guide."

I met Nora before *Dazed and Confused* and she cast me in a little part in *Sleepless in Seattle* that got cut from the film. Afterward she wrote me a letter on her stationery, explaining that it had nothing to do with me, but the scene just didn't move the story along. In the scene, I knocked on Tom Hanks's door after hearing him on the radio, let loose a gush of fandom, and made a quick exit. In the letter, she said I was a gifted comedienne and that she would work with me again, which I felt was genuine, and her support meant everything. And besides, it's not like *Sleepless in Seattle* did any big business, so I wasn't that upset about it.

The next year, she hired me for a movie she was working on called *Mixed Nuts*. I was cast as Rollerblader #2 and Jon Stewart was cast as Rollerblader #1. So Jon and I learned how to Rollerblade at the Roxy, which was a nightclub in the Meatpacking District. On Sunday afternoons it turned into a roller rink, where we Rollerbladed to disco—looking like dorks in our helmets, wrist guards, and kneepads.

We shot *Mixed Nuts* in Santa Monica, in the newly opened Shutters on the Beach, a gorgeous hotel right on the water where we had to stay for three weeks. We couldn't believe that we had it so good, and we didn't share more than fifteen lines in the film between us. We pretty much just had to Rollerblade past Steve Martin holding a Christmas tree. Now that I think of it, we didn't even do that, because our stunt doubles did it for us.

I gave Shutters my credit card to check into the place and Jon and I went out for burgers close by. When I went to the ATM to get some cash, all I had was $1.75 left in my bank account. My credit card was also my cash card and I shuddered. Nora happened to be walking by, and I showed her the receipt, like it belonged to someone else. She got her wallet out and gave me a hundred dollars.

A dollar seventy-five in my bank account, isn't that too much? It doesn't make sense, right? But all those independent movies I did in the nineties were done on the cheap. I was counting coins, which I'd put in those paper roll-ups to take to the deli so I could buy pasta to make for dinner. I didn't know anyone else who was famous and broke.

Jon Stewart was *so* funny. I wonder if people know just how funny he is. On the record, I'm saying that he's not only funny, but he's fun. The layout of the rooms at Shutters made the beds super entertaining for us—but not how you're thinking. You could take a bath and open the shutters to see the bed, just a few feet away, or you could close the shutters for privacy. No, Jon wasn't there when I took a bath. After housekeeping cleaned the rooms and tightened the beds to the utmost, we'd team up. We'd start at the toilet, then run, stepping on the bath's ledges, and fly, like Superman, through the open shutters— plummeting across the bed and sliding off the edge. We were like daredevils all of a sudden, since now we knew how to Rollerblade and it's clear to anyone we were Method actors.

You know who else is funny and fun? Jimmy Fallon. He has his own TV show now. He was a rising star when I met him, just starting on *SNL* and all of twenty-six years old. I was about to hit thirty and had completed *Best in Show* in November. I still had braces but was waiting to take them off until after the new millennium. I don't remember the reason why exactly, except that time was speeding up and I didn't want it to. I wanted to shake off the character of Meg as well as time-travel back to the eighth grade, which was the last time I had braces. I wanted things to be new and blushing.

For New Year's Eve, Jimmy and I went to his parents' house to bang pots and pans while walking up and down the street, which was Fallon tradition. The house was full of guests, friends of Jimmy and his sister, Gloria. It was like *Animal House*, but instead of frat brothers, the house was full of people resembling elves, much like the Keebler cookie family. There was so much laughing that it seemed like everyone was on mushrooms. I remember we visited someone's home whose bathroom was chock-full of Santa Claus decorations: a Santa cozy on the toilet paper, Santa towels and hand towels, Mrs. Claus by the toothbrush holder, Santa shower curtain, Santa bath mat. I'd meet Jimmy late, after his *SNL* stuff, to go out dancing. He's probably the best dancer that has ever lived.

I was still anxious about my fame and success, and was only really happy when I had a fiction to carry around. Back then, there was no media in being social, so long phone calls were fun—as was going out. I remember seeing Nora around this time, and she said to me, "You know, Parker, you will always feel the same. You will just keep getting older." That was stunning news to me, since I'd had this fantasy that after I turned thirty, I'd become Mariska Hargitay, or another womanly-type woman, instead of the impish woman-child I'll remain forever. I'd always *feel* the same, and I'd never exactly fit in. Now that I'm older, I accept myself and realize it's okay to be different—and also okay that a ball gown makes me feel like I got lost in a swath of someone else's curtains that got twisted around my body unsuccessfully. I never wanted to feel like a trophy of myself because if I did, I supposed I'd feel as if I won something. And if I won something, I might lose my desire to do what I do. I may just knock myself off the pedestal. Winning is lonely. It means more people will talk behind your back. And if they're talking behind your back, then they're more likely to have knives to throw at your back.

I would love some coffee, how wonderful.

Mildred told me this story over and over again: "When Bernie and I, when our book came out . . ." Mildred and her husband, Bernie, wrote *How to Be Your Own Best Friend*, which came out in the early seventies and was the first self-help book ever written, or one of them. "When Bernie and I, when our book came out," she'd say again, "we had lots of success with it. We were famous for it." She'd smile, beaming, and I'd eat some of her tuna fish salad from the 2nd Ave Deli that she'd serve me on stone-ground crackers. She enjoyed this story every time she told it, like a grandmother telling a bedtime story—she took her time, taking you *in*to it. "There was a party for the book, and lots of people came, my patients over the years . . ." Like Neil Simon, Erica Jong, Richard Benjamin . . . "I was in the kitchen and this woman, a friend, came up to me and said, 'You know, you and Bernie have everything. A great marriage and famous patients and now this book . . .'" Mildred would huff with frustration, imitating her. "'And I can't stand it!'" Shaking off her portrayal of this woman, Mildred would shift in her chair, aggravated, shaking her head. She'd pause for the aggravation to leave her. "And then this woman said, 'I want what you have.'" At which point Mildred would take a deep breath of astonishment and collect herself, as if she were still in the moment. "And I looked her right in the eyes"— and then she'd hold my gaze, lowering her voice for her punch line—"and I said, 'You can't *have* it. It's MINE.'" She'd penetrate her gaze at me and through me. She'd then lean back and slowly smile—and we'd sit there.

Once, after a breakup I couldn't get over (the guy married a girl-friend of mine soon after), Mildred said, "I want you to put him in front of you, and I want you to chop his head off with an ax."

28

Being a Twin

It's funny, the response I get when I tell people I have a twin brother is almost always "Are you identical?"

"No, he has something I don't have," I say. Then I watch their face register what that something is. I explain that identical twins share the same egg, whereas fraternal twins each have their own egg.

They usually say, "Oh, I knew that." Then they ask if we have "that twin thing" where I know what he's thinking or can sense when he's in trouble. We're more "opposite sides of the same coin" is my rote response.

But there was one time, on a trip to Monroe, where we were silent for a good while and then I brought up the name of a girl we were in second grade with and he said he was just thinking of her. That happened once. There's a mole between my pinky finger and ring finger that he shares, but it's on his opposite foot. He got most of the potent DNA, like skin pigment, thicker hair, and eyes that are a deeper green. He's also taller than I am, which shouldn't surprise you.

When I told Mildred all this, she directed me to Freud's theory of penis envy, but I never liked the sound of it. I suppose the thought that a man came up with this idea made me jealous. She'd explain that Freud's idea says that boys view their penises as gifts, like a birthday present for boys only, which lasts for the rest of their lives. And girls wait for their gifts to appear when they hit puberty, in the form of breasts. I didn't buy into this because I never looked at my breasts as presents. I wonder if Mildred or Freud would say my penis envy castrated my breasts, in order to have my own figurative penis. My mother summed it up nicely when I'd ask her if she wanted one: "I never wanted any of that stuff between my legs."

This conversation's ridiculous.

My analyst Mark would say to just "drop it," and so I will. No, that wasn't a castration joke. Or was it?

Let's take a break and look at the SkyMall catalog; it's fun to look at all the weird home stuff you never really see in people's homes. There should be a word for the fear of opening one's own mail. There should also be a phrase besides "excuse me" for when someone is standing in front of the very thing you want—it should be something funny that would make you both laugh. These solar-panel footprints that light up at night in your backyard are funny. I'll order these for my funeral. If you want me again, look for me above my solar-panel footprints.

I wonder if there will ever be an "off the grid" airline? Maybe I'll finally get to Burning Man and pitch that idea to some Silicon Valley types.

If they're going to make body pillows, they should make them look more like bodies—give the pillow a face.

Being a twin is confusing. When you're a baby, you're not aware of being in your own body yet, so you identify and think of yourself as the other person: the me, myself, and I comes later. That's why a mother's nurturing gaze into her child is so important, so when the child grows up, the nurturing mother will live inside. If not, it's up to the individual to create her. But if you have a twin, you have this melding of the other person from the get-go. My mom said she'd watch us "speaking" in mumbles and gestures while we played for hours, passing toys to each other. "Goo gahgahgah," Chris would say.

"Mlah mlah," I'd reply. It was mostly pleasant and reciprocal.

Who knows what fantasies and promises were agreed upon then—what was promised and wished for and was then granted in my imagination. And then the disappointment or confusion with what wasn't granted. I recognize a particular loneliness and confusion when I meet other female twins—a puzzled disillusionment. We talk about the desire to have another person's eyes see like yours, their mind think like yours, their heart beat like yours—how easily the other comes alive inside.

It's nice that we've kept these maps on the screen.

I made a twin friend in Vancouver named Anna. She had a vintage clothing store in Gastown, just blocks from me in Chinatown, called Duchesse. Anna was down the street getting her hair cut when we met at Nicole's one-chair hair salon. Nicole is pop-art chic, with a bobbed haircut, Liza Minnelli eyes, and red lipstick that never smears. She wears art smocks, loose mom-pants, and jazz flats. She's cool but nice and ready to laugh. She also carries a Narcan pack, in case she sees an addict dying on the sidewalk, which she's used a few times.

I liked her immediately and we became fast friends. I respected how she manifested becoming her own boss at a one-chair hair salon and asked how she tore herself away from the drama of the many-chair-hair-salon world, which can be fraught with personalities and unnecessary "hairarchy." She told me at my first haircut for Dr. Smith that I had something to do with it.

Her first and only boss suggested she change her name to attract more clients, and so she went by Parker for a while. She was laughing and freaking out a little that she was about to give her double a haircut. Then she said she knew I liked her haircuts because years ago, when I was doing *Best in Show*, I'd complimented one of her clients' haircuts on the street. We riffed on the idea of *The Sisterhood of the Traveling Haircuts*, connecting stories through strands of hair . . .

braids of hair, hair in drains, hairballs in cats. I liked watching her hands as she cut my hair—the scissors an extension of her fingers, more like an artist and less like a haircutter. The scissors were Japanese, gold and small, and she'd flip them easily into her palm and then out, like a card flying out of its deck.

Being a twin is a predicament you're born into. Wrapping your head around being a twin, the idea that you can't be one without the *other*, is confusing enough. The answer is simple, though: I don't know anything different. I was shooting a short film in Watford, England, and I don't remember much about it. The director wore cow-print pants the first day, I remember that much. One of the locations was in a mental hospital that was still functioning. I think they shot some of *Harry Potter* there—it's a ghoulish and beautiful old building, a historic landmark. A bunch of us actors were hanging out under a tree when a schizophrenic patient, shirtless and carrying a wooden branch as a staff, walked toward us, smiling like a figure come to life from a tarot card.

He was gorgeous and happy—blond, blue eyed, and tan, barefoot and in cutoffs. I was lying down as he approached. "Look at ya . . . you're a Porsche car," he said. He had a thick Scottish accent. I had never been called that but liked the sound of it.

"My dad has a car dealership," I said.

He liked this connection very much. "You're my sister," he said. I told him that I have a twin brother. "I have a sister. You are my twin." Then, the strangest thing, he started counting. "One and one is two. You are my twin!" He was excited, saying all of this in singsong. "Two threes are six and two threes put together make an eight and eight is DNA and it connects us all."

"Whoa, you just said the numbers of my birthday," I said. "Eleven eight sixty-eight."

"You are my twin, you are my sister, we are connected . . ."

I was taken with him at this point, we all were, but there was a woman behind us, waiting for him. He pointed upward. "There's a string connecting, that goes up to the sky and into my head and through to the center of the Earrrthhh . . ." He's gesturing this. "I listen to Tina Turner music and I shake." His knees were pumping to a song. He also had a yellow Walkman clipped to his pants, and headphones around his neck, remember those? "You're a car . . ." he said, his *r*'s rolling in that Scottish accent, "you're a Porsche car . . . two threes make eight, eight is DNA and it connects us all! It connects us all!" He threw his arms up in a grand gesture, as if on his way to the king's court, and walked to his therapist—his lady-in-waiting.

I covered my face when he left and cried into my hands. We all just looked at each other, with our mouths open, like, "What was *that*?"

One of the extras that day, who was with us under that tree, had known someone who went to college with me. His friend was the girlfriend of a film student who had drowned, and I had dated that film student's friend, who committed suicide a few years later. I'd learned of his death from a friend of his, who told me in a Chinese restaurant in Chelsea. I had been away, filming, when it happened, and he dropped the news in passing, which was cruel. I was famous, so what could hurt me? I covered my face with my hands and cried in the same way I did after talking to that schizophrenic patient.

Simon was the name of the man in Watford. I'm just remembering this because I remember thinking of the game Simon Says. I asked about him later, to his lady-in-waiting. Against protocol, I'm sure, the lady told me that he had murdered his sister.

In *The House of Yes*, I played a young woman, a twin, so obsessed with Jackie O and the JFK assassination that she's made a game of it with her twin brother. It was writer Wendy MacLeod's Yale thesis and was a filmed play, really; it's all contained in one house over Thanksgiving. I played Jackie, a young woman who isn't taking her meds and freaks out when her brother, Marty, the love of her life, brings home a date. The sublime Josh Hamilton played my brother and Tori Spelling played his fiancée—she was terrific.

Geneviève Bujold, the French-Canadian actress, played my

mother, and she presided over all of us. Her vibe had the intensity that only comes from being French (or half French). Did you see *Dead Ringers*? It's the movie where Jeremy Irons plays twins and Geneviève plays his love interest. Jeremy Irons—do they make men like that anymore? Anyway, I was twenty-five and she was around the age I am now and after saying I was talented she said to wait until after my forties, when I'd be more grounded, because that was when it would get "really interesting." I've never forgotten that and she was right, of course.

In the movie, I kill my brother, shoot him, while reenacting the Zapruder film one last time. The night before filming began I took one of those razor callus removers and dug too deep, gashing my foot to the point that it hurt to walk in Jackie's pumps. After filming, I was pretty freaked out, so I called Mildred and she talked me down. When I talked to my real brother about all this, Chris said something like "Don't worry about it. Jesus, that's crazy."

We couldn't be more different. He practices law down south and, with my sister-in-law, does my accounting and contract stuff; they manage my business. They swept in after I'd gotten screwed by Kenneth Starr, accountant to the stars, who ran a Ponzi scheme and went to jail. *You've Got Mail* was more like "you've got my money," so they flew in to help.

Ha, this is funny: a mai tai–scented men's T-shirt. I should get that for Chris. A John Lemon T-shirt? Are you serious? They should make a bananas T-shirt that smells like bananas. I'd wear that. Or one with an airplane that smells like this. Ew, gross.

Speaking of smells. Anna, the vintage clothing store owner, took me rag-picking at one of the rag yards about thirty miles from Vancouver; it's where she gets clothes for her store. It's in a warehouse space run by an Indian family where these oversized post office bins, the size of a dining room table, were full of other people's discarded clothes. The stuff came from America, as far away as Utah, as well as from Canada. There was some kind of system or arrangement with all the other "pickers," but Anna asked if it was okay for me to come and they said yes.

You climb into the bins wearing a surgical mask and you rummage. It smells, but you get used to it—it's a colorful place. The workers use forklifts to pick up packs of smushed clothing in plastic wrap, as big as a refrigerator, and then load it into bins, where they separate it into categories: dresses, shirts, T-shirts, kids' clothes . . .

I took my shoes off and sat in the dresses and chatted with Anna's friend, a fellow scavenger named Megan. She was wearing a toque knit cap—the standard wear for damp rainy days in Vancouver. We had loose and laid-back chatter, not as much of the ambitious "nonversation" work stuff you can get in the city.

I know that jumping into a giant bin of smelly hand-me-downs is not for everyone, but when people ask what it's like being a twin, my trip to the rag yard is a good analogy. How fun and satisfying it was to sink into the mass of clothing and think about the lives people led in those garments. All the different sizes, fabrics, and trends: this person size, that person size, this age, that age, that decade, this decade. The special-occasion dress, worn maybe just a few times; the housecoats of the sixties and seventies; the muumuus. Millions of people's lives were lived in those clothes.

I like being on the hunt and hope that even a conversation comes to life and there's a sense, even just a thread, of feeling connected. Those threads shoot out and tangle tightly or loosely and take form inside as a whole—it's also fabricated. I make a twin for myself whenever I play a part.

29
Wait Till Spring

It had been at least a year since I'd been on the mat, but I got back to my yoga practice in Vancouver, before my shooting began for *Lost in Space*. I had six weeks off before Dr. Smith entered the series full-on, so I would live there until I started shooting and stay all the way through July. The Robinson family would be on a glacier built on a soundstage, with fake snow particles blown from industrial fans the size of a breakfast table—"snow" the size of oatmeal going up their noses. They would be moving in space suits made of car upholstery material, which inhibited normal movement of any kind, especially the lifting of arms. I would be taking in Vancouver, and the rain, wearing everyday clothing.

I'd love a hot cookie and you can refer to me as one, too, if you'd like. My dad has a picture that he keeps in his wallet that he likes to pull out, of his "pride and joy" on one side and his "kids" on the other. It's the old pun of the laundry detergent and the dish soap on one side and the "kids" which are two goats on the other. I gave him a card that says "stop talking" that's typeset lowercase on a sturdy white business card. I'll give you one, once we land.

It was record-breaking rain in January 2017, the most they'd seen in sixty years. The locals talk about the rain and the weather like it's their culture. I loved that. They apologized about the rain whenever I introduced myself as being from out of town. I'd say, "I love it." When the snow came, they apologized about that, too—when it wasn't even cold enough to stick. I'd mentioned the winter in New York when it got so cold that I'd wrap my scarf around my neck, including my face, so I looked like a Muppet.

"Wait till spring," they said. It made me smile because it felt so small-town, like you're sitting on the front porch with Granny. I'm in a rocking chair, shelling peas, shucking corn, talking about the weather and how handsome that Justin Trudeau is. I ate it all up. Justin Trudeau had *his* coffee at the same place I had mine; it was a place called the Brixton. It felt like *The Commitments*, the high-spirited movie from the nineties that took place in an Irish pub where they'd sing out of nowhere. There was a competition where they could win a trip somewhere? It was directed by Alan Parker, who did *Fame* and *Bugsy Malone*—both classics.

Anyway, I could see the Brixton from my room on the eighteenth floor of BlueSky Properties Chinatown. There was an assisted-living facility for drug addicts smack in the middle of the Brixton's sister bar, called the London Pub, which was right on the corner.

The first yoga class I took was on Hastings Street, which reminded me of Chelsea in the early nineties, during the crack epidemic. There was a homeless man in the Chelsea days who liked my corner who I'd give change to and chat with. He was good-natured despite living on the edge. He told me he recognized me from *As the World Turns* and I didn't know how that was possible. He was homeless. Did he watch it on a television set in a storefront window? I asked him, but he wouldn't give me a straight answer. It positively mystified me.

When I didn't see him anymore, I thought of him as Clarence Odbody, the in-between-worlds angel who appeared when Jimmy Stewart wanted to commit suicide in *It's a Wonderful Life*. "Strange, isn't it? Each man's life touches so many other lives, and when he isn't around he leaves an awful hole, doesn't he?" That movie couldn't be made today, because Clarence would've just told Jimmy Stewart, "There's medication for what you're going through, George Bailey."

On Hastings, there were even more addicts living on the sidewalks, because drugs aren't really illegal in Canada. There are the dispensaries where they can get methadone to wean themselves off the hard stuff with the light stuff. Now there is Fentanyl, which can get you off all of the stuff and into nowhere. There are the marijuana places to get pot that doesn't get you high but takes the pain away. It isn't unusual to see needles strewn on the streets or to look down alleyways and think of *Night of the Living Dead* as people drift-walk to make their deals, their bodies jumping out of their skin, causing them to shake what they were kicking with a spurt of energy like an overcome fan at a rock show where the bass solo has become overbearing and painful and you have to dance like Billy Squier to get comfortable.

I thought of the strange music one man must've been hearing in his brain when I saw him humping a garbage can and playing drums on it at the same time. And I saw many skinny bodies looking close to death itself. There was a blond woman in pigtails, with the particular style of a talisman, fringing on the edge, and receiving the guidance of the gods. She was probably around my age, and dressed in rainbow colors that were mismatched. She pointed at me, laughing like she knew me, and I smiled back at her as we were both crossing the street. When she passed me she said, "Hey, crazy lady! It's good to see you came out!" Right on, me too! The way the community existed in harmony made me think of bees returning to a strange and self-destructive honeycomb— their system was working and they didn't have to confuse it further with prison. They didn't have to be locked up. It just felt more humane over there, like they give people a chance even if everyone else is paying for it. One life to live, you know? We're really not here that long.

In the same neighborhood, there was a brand-new yoga studio called Stretch. It was a huge industrial space that had been remodeled in the same modern and recycled style that I'd seen in Berlin. The front room was huge, with lots of light, and I was greeted by a nervous greyhound when I entered. It belonged to the owner, a Frenchwoman named Emmanuelle who had her hair wrapped in a scarf, in "gleaner" fashion. She was sitting on a bench and warming her back by the fireplace. It wasn't a real fireplace but an assemble-yourself modern design, made of cardboard logs with self-contained battery-powered lightbulbs placed underneath for a glow. She was breastfeeding her baby as I sat down and introduced myself and then signed up for class.

I'd taken another class at a donation-only place where you pay however much you want. It's called Yoga to the People and they have a studio in New York—you can go when we land. It's great because it's so varied experience-wise, and it's crowded to the point of becoming private. The teacher asked the students to share something they were grateful for and several said that spring was coming soon. This was *January*. When the long-haired blond fellow in front of me said that he, too, was grateful for the upcoming spring, I scooted up my mat and asked him why I kept hearing this, that it was January and it was supposed to be cold. He shook his long blond mane. "Well, I live on a boat off one of the islands and this weather's not good for sleeping," he said. "When spring comes, you'll see. This place is different in the spring."

Stretch had a teacher named Risto, who became my favorite. He teaches a "rocket" class, which is a "self-made series" that he'd learned from one of his teachers. It speeds you through some key poses of the Ashtanga practice to get you stronger for, say, handstands in the middle of the room, straight up, like a rocket. He describes the series as a shortcut but it's cool, it's copacetic. Risto is short for Christopher, someone pointed out.

He smiled big when I saw him at first, recognizing me from my work, which I mistook for flirting. He's very handsome and over six feet tall and covered in tattoos. He'd been in showbiz, as a creature actor and stunt worker, but he left all that to do something more meaningful and less of a grind. He got tired of the fifteen-hour days dressed as a predator or snake-man character, and ripping all that stuff off his face and body once the day was done.

It was easy to go to his class; he was inspiring. He took the "Vancouver people are outdoorsy" vibe to a whole other level—he skied and snowboarded, and when I noticed he was limping, he mentioned an impending hip surgery that wasn't his first. When I asked what happened, he laughed and shrugged. "You know . . . flying into trees . . ."

I liked the difference of these men, a type I imagined to be specific to the Pacific Northwest—active in the manly way I'd mostly only seen on TV: Keanu Reeves, Evel Knievel, Michael Phelps, Liam Neeson, Björn Borg. I like thinking about what creates that force, that speed, that grace, and that authenticity. In a good man, it's just fantastic.

I'm thinking now of Manly from *Little House on the Prairie*. He was twice the size of Laura, or "Half Pint." Manly's full name was Almanzo, which was a strange name for a prairie man in the middle of nowhere, so everyone called him Manny. Laura mistook his name for "Manly" and he said she was the only one who could call him that. Manly wore mainly khakis and linen button-downs and donned a dusty beige pioneer hat, which was the fashion then in prairie times. He'd enter scenes mopping his brow with a hand towel, from the sweat of chopping wood, or he'd be yodeling, having finished his carpentry work.

In *Lost in Space,* we had our very own creature actor, Brian Steele, who played our robot. I had met him during *Blade: Trinity* when he played the Beast. I'd conversed and snacked with the devil, you could say, and he was really a nice guy underneath all that rubber and plastic and horns and glue. I'd found myself drawn to him and listening to his stories, which involved so much physical prowess that I was humbled. I think he's ridden his bicycle around the world.

He still had that same force and energy now. At his first reading as the robot, he showed up in costume looking all fierce and I held my iPhone to his body, asking to check my email. He took it almost as a slight to his character but he was good humored about it. Brian smiles most of the time, with the satisfaction of endurance that makes athletes high. He sported a short Mohawk that swooped on the top of his head, like the top of a soft-serve ice-cream cone. His voice naturally boomed without being overbearing.

In the Stretch studio, I cried in Risto's class, and not because he didn't ask me out or I'd never gotten a tattoo. I had started breathing again—that ujjayi/*Star Wars* breath. I started to let go of all that had been overwhelming. The past few years had been a meltdown of my Porsche. And then of everything that I couldn't control, like the strangeness of the culture, and to quote Dave Chappelle, "When has America ever given a fuck about how anyone feels inside?" The disastrous happenings everywhere, all over the world—the weather, for instance, easily causing turmoil and taking over the peace of mind of absolutely everybody—and the guns.

What's the Lou Reed song where he says that people just don't act rational, they think they're just on TV?

I have a Lou Reed story, but we're landing soon.

Many yoga classes end with a prayer: "May all beings be free from suffering." Risto ended his class with that, as well as with "Be kind to everyone out there." All my teachers and mothers and fathers out there (especially my actual parents) and my brothers and sisters (especially my twin)—bless them, everyone, everything. "It takes courage to live a life," as Mildred said, and "hold on to yourself," everybody. We never expected life to look like this and it will never look like this again. Grace is hard earned. "There aren't enough books about loneliness," was another thing Mildred said.

After class, I stopped in the front room and sat by the makeshift fireplace. There were colorful pieces of stretch fabric hanging from the ceiling—maybe ten of them. I asked Emmanuelle about them—"Is this for acroyoga or Iyengar yoga?"—and she said they weren't for either. They were for the "hammock classes," an idea that she'd come up with, saying, "People come to lie in the hammocks and listen to live cello music." I wondered if hammock classes were a *thing* in Canada. She said no, not that she knew of, so she had figured, "Why not?" How French of her, how Canadian. I went to lie down in the yellow one. The fabric was as big as a tablecloth and I stretched my body out in it and swung, sinking my weight into the yellow, which enveloped me like the sun, and I started to get excited for spring.

How do I land? Something, come here.

Acknowledgments

Thank you, formerly Blue Rider Press, and its publisher, David Rosenthal, for his enthusiasm over a book by an actress that included a chapter about pottery. Sarah Hochman, my first editor, for her early and essential work and her push toward a seriousness in the writing, before she left. And to Jill J. Schwartzman, who took over as editor, for her perspective in structuring the book and support of this new foray. David Kuhn and his team at Aevitas, especially Becky Sweren, for her early editing, and Kate Mack in the art department. Jason L. Booher, the art director, for not only helping me cut cardboard but assisting with the photographer, Craig McDean, whose talent in capturing the images was a real coup. Seema Mahanian, for additional editing support, flying in for freelance editing, and Shubhani Sarkar, for freelance interior design—two smart and gifted beauties. Leana Zuniga of Electric Feathers for her brilliant clothing designs and styling and her cousin Jean-Paul Miller, for his assistance. Jess Rotter, for her illustration work, as well as being a new friend. Diego Montoya, for building the mirror-mask with me! Jeffrey Loura, whose giant sphere was handed graciously over for the Carl Sagan moment. To La Mano Pottery, especially Julie Hadley, for squeezing me into their studio to shoot. Jane Berliner, my manager at Authentic, whose support and intelligence has given me strength and confidence. Josan Giletti, for her spiritual guidance, as well as Alexander Tolken for his. Michael Marsman, my Jungian analyst friend, for his archetypal awareness and insight. Jack Ferver, who for years has inspired and supported me to produce something that is mine. And Tonya Hurley, who mothered me through the process, and Mary-Louise Parker, as sister wife. Mark Stafford, my psychoanalyst, who taught me to listen more deeply to language and instinct, and helped open the door to writing. My parents, my greatest teachers, in the most profound sense, and my twin brother, Chris, for telling me I was an artist when I didn't know what it was. To my extended family, especially Aunt Peggy, for her amazing memory and Samantha Constant, my-cousin-as-sister, for her wisdom. Keagan Funk, for his love and support and design of the Fireball Cocktail. For my other friends, who have been a part of my stories, and to the quick acquaintances, in passing, like the ones on airplanes. The kindness of these strangers I've always depended on, as well as my companion on the journey, my Jiminy Cricket, Gracie, whose wig work in this book was done by paw. And last but not least, my new *Lost in Space* family. And, finally, Marcia Brill.

About the Author

Parker Posey is well known for her work with many independent filmmakers of her generation, including Richard Linklater, Hal Hartley, Zoe Cassavetes, and Rebecca Miller. Following her break-out role in the cult hit *Dazed and Confused*, she starred in Christopher Guest's classic mockumentaries and appeared in such Hollywood films as *You've Got Mail, Superman Returns, Josie and the Pussycats, Scream 3*, and *Blade: Trinity*. Posey currently plays Dr. Smith in the Netflix remake of *Lost in Space*.